San Antonio College
In the Beginning...
1925 - 1956

Jerome F. Weynand

Adrome House
San Antonio, Texas

Cover design: Alex Díaz
Cover credits: San Antonio College promotional brochure ca. 1956;
old campus rendering by Benny Grijalva; The
University of Texas Institute of Texan Cultures
No. Z-2158 (Zintgraff Collection).
Photo credits: *El Alamo* and *La Retama* yearbooks; The University of
Texas Institute of Texan Cultures at San Antonio (*San
Antonio Light* Collection);
Personal photo files.

Anniversary Edition

Printed in the United States of America
LEBCO Graphics, Inc.
Boerne, Texas 78006

Adrome House
159 East Sunshine Drive
San Antonio, Texas 78228
(210) 736-0156
Adrome159@Earthlink.net

*Dedicated to the unlimited
fraternity of all San Antonio College
students past, present and future...*

"...preserve a copy for the future years when retrospection becomes such a pleasant diversion."

--J.O. Loftin, 1948 El Alamo

CONTENTS

ACKNOWLEDGEMENTS

More than 65 persons made individual contributions to the preparation of this work and deserve singular recognition at the opening of the book. They know what they did to help and will see the materials in the pages to follow. My personal appreciation extends to everyone named from A to Z in the listing. By seeing your name in print may each of you know that I will always remember your cooperative input into the collective efforts relating to the early history of San Antonio College. You are a part of that history.

Nicole Alvarado, Noel M. Alford, Vanessa Taylor Antwine, Diane P. Benson, Lanne E. Brehmer, Dr. Paul R. Culwell, Dr. Margaret C. Berry, Bill and Barbara Ezzell Candler, Maria Linda Casas, Mary Clarkson, R. Bruce Cole, Dr. Alice Cook, Jimmy and Shirley Fletcher Elrod, Frank Faulkner, Shirley Newman Felcam, Charles W. Ford, Rose Lynn French, Cynthia Dean Guyon, Carolyn Haisler, Dr. John Hammond, Charles Hanus, Dr. Thomas M. Hatfield, Robert Hein, Lady Jane Hickey, and Gloria Garland Homburg.

Also, thanks to Rosemarie Hoopes, John Igo, E. Howard Jones, Dr. Jan Kilby, Chance Kinnison, Trudy Chance Kinnison, Sandy Kirchner, Kay Lewis, Florence Lieb, Jim and Martha Loftin, Dr. Vern Loland, Edith S. McAllister, Phyllis Anderson McCarley, Thomas E. Moseley, Clyde Gerald (Jerry) Nail, Georgia Cottingham Needham, Rodney Nelson, Dolores Olivares, Linda O'Nave, Candace Peterson, Carmen Ramirez, Carla Reyes, Gerry Rickhoff, Juan Rodriguez, Magdalena Garces Saldana, Stanley H. Schmidt, Tom Shelton, William R. Sinkin, Mattie Smith, Bryan Snow, J. O. Wallace, Edmund Weynand, John A. Weynand, Robert S. Weynand, Zula Vizard, and Cynde Moody Zietlow.

"Honored" best describes my feeling when Dr. Truett L. Chance graciously accepted the invitation by his former student to write the Foreword. His words lend credence and his name prestige to the total effort. I am very grateful for his long and unfailing friendship over more than 55 years.

My utmost gratitude is extended to my wife Adrienne Brown Weynand, who served unflinchingly as chief research assistant, copy-reader, and consistent supporter; to Glendora Brown Stanush, research assistant, especially for her diligence in spending many hours screening microfilm files.

Kudos are showered upon Delores Ragsdale who so willingly accepted the tedious and laborious task of converting the manuscript into computerized formats for printing the text and screening the photographs. Her expertise is laudable.

Summarily, I believe that I speak for all of us when I say that this exercise truly was a "labor of love" for San Antonio College.

First Official Seal -- 1940
By James A. Hurry, head of physics/engineering
Five-point star for Texas -- Alamo for San Antonio
Wreath motif stands for achievement
Latin phrase: "Nothing is gained without labor."

FOREWORD

"In the beginning"--the early history of San Antonio College and the foundation on which the giant educational institution rests today--is a story worth telling in such detail that has not been evident in previous short versions in print, video, speeches or oral history. This book pieces many little known facts with the more important facets of that development based on research and interviews against the background and social context covering a 30-year period.

When Jerome Weynand approached me to write the Foreword for his book--allowing free rein--it gave me pause to reminisce about those early days spent on the South Alamo Street campus as one of about 23 instructors and four administrators; the quaint but inadequate old buildings which had creaky steps with time-worn treads where generations of students had walked; the old coal-fired stoves with apertures that allowed emission of enough smoke to fill a classroom. Men instructors were obliged to wear white shirts and this caused my wife Opal some concern and a little bit of complaint when she laundered soot and cinders from my shirts.

My own role and collegial association at San Antonio Junior College began in January 1947, when I was employed on a handshake agreement by President J. O. Loftin to teach economics, history, and government to the overflow of students registered for the spring semester. The assignment was for five classes in three disciplines for this full-time teaching load. The pay was $250 a month. Could I handle it? Yes.

Little did I realize at the time, by answering a newspaper ad seeking a junior college instructor, that my application would be considered and, eventually, lead to an interview and job offer. I was working at Fort Sam Houston when this timely opportunity gave me the chance to continue my professional teaching career--which had been interrupted by military service--and enjoy the next 42 years at one institution working with students and faculty at San Antonio College. And, what a ride it has been from the ranks of an instructor, to professor, to department chairman and, in the twilight of my active career, to serve as president under the Alamo Community College District's reorganization. In what was referred to internally as "a new management technique," deans became presidents and the former title of president of the colleges became chancellor on the chart. Thus, I served for a short time as President of San

Antonio College until voluntary retirement in June 1982.

I was not alone in a relatively good rise in mobility of occupation. The cessation of hostilities in World War II made possible for many the resumption of normal activities. In many cases, this meant continuing educational activities at the junior college because it was convenient and inexpensive for those purposes. It was rewarding to be a part of that period of renewal for many students. Being a teacher, rather than an administrator, was my true calling. I was of the same generation of many of the students I taught in the 1940s, and readily identified with their reasons for going to college.

In the 1940s, the College still had a student council, held all-school assemblies, dances, picnics, honored beauty queens and selected the "most popular boys and girls" on campus. The move to the San Pedro campus saw a gradual decline in the esprit de corps, the general togetherness known on the old campus. This change was reflective of a changing society, the enlargement of the physical campus, and the rapid enrollment increases. Many students were older, often employed and had diverse career interests.

In the 1960s, there was a general feeling of unrest among college and university students--probably not as much on the two-year college campuses--that led to discord and distraction not conducive to study. Later, there were a few problems involving faculty members, administrators, maintenance personnel and trustees on our college campus that were not unique in higher education, perhaps. As a dean, I truthfully feel that students in class did not suffer when San Antonio College went through some periods of upheaval. The faculty, to their credit, made sure that nothing affected the primary mission of the College. We were there to do our job--to educate. It is my strong belief--even to this day--that trustees, presidents, and deans have no reason to be in a college unless they can facilitate the work in the classrooms.

Education has been my life and I wouldn't have it any other way. I have no complaints about teaching. I have been well treated and well compensated along the way from that initial pay check amounting to $250 a month. I had good relationships with Mr. Loftin and his successor, Dr. Wayland P. Moody, with whom I worked on the old campus. There was disappointment to many of us in not getting sooner a new location for the college. About the only time I saw President Loftin really mad was when he returned from a conference only to learn a "deal" he thought he had with the mayor for a site in San Pedro Park was "off." Loftin thought he had a firm commitment from the mayor to donate the northeast corner of the Park for a campus site, only to be denied by a vote of the mayor and three of the four commissioners in 1948. Loftin was redheaded--had a hot temper to go with the red hair--and had some prize remarks to say about the mayor, particularly, but to no avail. The search ended with the purchase of the current site which allowed for expansion of buildings and grounds that were not possible had Loftin been able to develop a few acres across San Pedro Avenue.

I have traced the development of the College from my contemporaneous timeline in speeches and interviews, but I hope that I never left the impression with an audience or readers that I equate buildings with a great school. Nothing could be further from the truth: San Antonio Junior College and San Antonio College had excellent reputations when they owned no physical property to speak of--certainly, no real estate. Reputations were based on the quality of faculty and the excellence of the instruction provided. There are two essential elements of an institution such as San Antonio College: students and faculty, in that order. The other things are amenities we all enjoy.

If I have digressed, somewhat--as professors sometimes are wont to do--I return to my original thought that the tale of the origin and adolescent development of San Antonio College needs to be told before the trail of history grows colder. Many of the principal players have been lost in the passage of time. Certain recognition is due the prominent figures in the narrative which begins in the "golden age" period of 1925 and extends through the 1950s.

I remember Jerome Weynand as a student--a former Marine identifiable by the clothes he wore--among the many ex-GIs I had in my classes in 1947-1948. He had but little choice than to register in my classes. From that "chance" meeting, a solid teacher-student relationship grew into a personal friendship that embraced our families, as well. I watched his stint as a newspaper reporter and his ultimate return to the campus in September 1954, when Mr. Loftin employed him as registrar.

Weynand's vantage points as a participant and observer of San Antonio life stem from 1932 when he began in local schools; to his student days at San Antonio Junior College; as a reporter who covered beats on education, health, federal, courthouse, and city hall, he well knew the area. Finally, he uses the knowledge gained from the 27 years he served as an administrator at the College and the District. All of these experiences contributed to his understanding of the subject and where to look in research for the detailed writing involved in the presentation of this book.

I feel confident--from my own perspective--that *San Antonio College, In the Beginning*...can be relied upon as a foundation set in concrete for reference by other writers and publications in the still unfolding history of the College.

The statute of limitations has run out, but if I could re-grade Jerome now--after 55 years and knowing how things turned out in our lives--I would feel compelled to raise a course grade or two by one letter grade.

I commend the reading of the entire book as a source of information and understanding about an outstanding two-year college, once called "Junior."

May 2002

Truett L. Chance, Ph.D.
Professor and President Emeritus
San Antonio College

PREFATORY REMARKS

It was my original, good intention to research and write the sweeping history of San Antonio College prompted by the euphoria of the 75th anniversary of my favorite alma mater. Three months into the project, I found the scope too broad; I revised the outline and decided to concentrate on the first 31 years of the development of San Antonio College. The approach was designed to be informal in writing and chronological in content. I took license to intersperse profiles of meaningful short subjects between chapters. I interjected [within brackets] personal comments and observations about issues and times. These departures are signaled detours for the reader and can be avoided. Parenthetical remarks, however, may clarify the topic and are recommended reading. This book never was intended to be biographical.

San Antonio Junior College and the compassionate people on the staff gave me the opportunity to begin college and encouraged me to remain. The College and I are contemporaries in that we both were born in 1926. Our destinies were bound to converge--which they did 20 years later in September 1946.

I brought to the preparation of this work a certain "institutional memory" as a student and administrator for a total of 30 years during the adolescent period of the College. I had the compelling desire to record the early period of investigation within the context of local, state, and national progress in educational and social institutions. There was a period of economic depression, war, integration...to name a few. I write from a unique position as follows: impressionable student days 1946-1948 under the GI Bill; newspaper reporter covering the education beat and specifically the District Board of Trustees and events on campus, 1950-1952; 27 plus years as an administrator with the College and the District, 1954-1981; and continuous interest in the welfare of the College since 1982.

One has to begin a book at some point. "In the Beginning..." is the first unit which describes the unique American junior college movement in the history of education. This chapter is the most "bookish" of all the essays and contains the most attributable sources. I relied on some of the material as déjà-vu in my dissertation entitled "The Role of Public Junior Colleges in Texas as Viewed by Their Presidents and Board Members," The University of Texas, June 1963.

Some observers of the junior college history in San Antonio attribute Walter W. McAllister, Sr. as a or even *the* founding father of the San Antonio Union Junior College District in 1945. Others, including McAllister, credit J. O. Loftin as the instigator and person who guided the concept to fruition. When Texas Governor John Connally spoke at the dedication of the Nail Technical Center on the campus in 1966, he extolled the virtues of San Antonio College as "the largest and finest college of its kind in Texas." Next to speak was then Mayor W. W. McAllister who referred to "Loftin's dream as the little acorn from which the great oak that is today's San Antonio College grew."

Jesse N. Fletcher--long-time friend of both Loftin and McAllister and one of the "original seven" trustees who succeeded McAllister as chairman--also referred to Loftin's dream of a college district, his role in selecting the present campus site, and Loftin's foresight to expand the District someday to include all of Bexar County.

Or, should Dr. Walter M. W. Splawn, President of The University of Texas, who put in motion the junior college concept with the help of the local school superintendent; or should the first Director Joseph E. Nelson share in the limelight of "fatherhood" of the College district? Let the reader decide.

The "University Junior College," as it was known colloquially in the community that first year 1925-1926, was founded because of the motivation and work of Dr. Splawn and Mr. Joseph Nelson to bring public higher education to San Antonio on a permanent basis. Perusal of many pages of the old bound volumes of the Minutes of the San Antonio Board of Education helped to set the tone of the story of an infant school everybody wanted as a child, but nobody wanted to change the diapers!

Perhaps, the hardest research task was to nail down the often quoted but elusive ruling in 1925 by the Texas Attorney General that a local branch of The University of Texas violated the Constitution of Texas 1876, Article 7, Section 14 (Sections 10-15 pertained to The University), and that no tuition could be charged. I became very familiar with Range 251 in the St. Mary's University Law Library.

The profile of the historic German-English School campus on South Alamo Street and the other numerous citations of its role throughout the text may reveal a romantic fixation on the place bonded by memories shared with all students and their instructors there. Edmund Weynand, Class of 1940, in 2002 still refers to the old JC campus as the "Sixth Mission," after the Alamo, Concepcion, San Jose, San Juan, and Espada.

The election of 1941 to create a junior college district stands as a time capsule of San Antonio politics, of people who worked together for what they believed was a good cause only to have it sidetracked by enough dissenters who showed up at the polls bent on defeating the proposition.

Actual creation of the District on the second-go-round attempt in 1945 still featured a wisened J. O. Loftin as the dreamer and the doer-- a man of action. Through his perseverance, the students were the real winners for generations to follow. Less ink and advertising were used on the election won in October 1945 than in the election lost in November 1941.

The move "uptown" to the San Pedro Campus--only about a mile from the "Uptown Theater" in the Beacon Hill neighborhood--was almost anti-climactic after the College had gone through many tribulations in a search for a suitable central location with bus service accessibility. The site ultimately selected was just across the avenue from a small parcel in San Pedro Park that Loftin really had his eye on in 1948.

The "Old Doctrine" of separate but equal was overcome, finally, and San Antonio College was a player in the drama. Segregation/integration was an era of limited participation by this writer, but one of the most memorable experiences as a newspaper reporter, registrar, and as a person.

The Loftin to Wayland Moody administrative transition went smoothly, almost as if fully planned, in the light of the tragedy in losing President Loftin's leadership at the height of his career. The veteran educator was on a "roll" of successes at the time he was killed in the automobile accident December 31, 1955. Dr. Moody's experience and as an understudy to Loftin served to sustain the mission of further development of the "College on the Grow" both academically and physically. That slogan was depicted on the first promotional brochure of the College and has been revived to grace the cover of this book.

The choices of subjects to "profile" and the use of these short pieces to add human dimension between the topical chapters are attributable to me.

The Appendices are a repository of names of persons and activities that played important roles in the early days of the College. The exhibits are intended to supplement the text.

The lengthy "Student Organizations" treatment resulted from the writer's perspective of years spent working with students in activities as their dean in good times and other times.

Emphasis on the military and former servicemen aspects was necessary to portray the impact that World War II had on the character of the College and its students.

In each case, I have tried to relate a true story of the founding and development of the institution. Unintentional omissions of names or events are regretted.

On one of my last official appearances as president of San Antonio College I met with members of the Faculty Wives Club. At the meeting I made a statement that was duly recorded in *The Ranger*, February 1981--so I can't say that I was "misquoted"--under a headline which read: "Weynand Reminisces About Career." The article captured the essence of the farewell moment by reporting that "Weynand, a former journalist, says that he would like to write 'something meaningful' someday, but it probably will not be a history of the College District."

I have attempted to document the early history of San Antonio College, to fill in the space between 1925------1956, but had to take the route through the San Antonio Independent School District, then follow the road to observe the creation of the San Antonio Union Junior College District, finally settling on San Antonio College. I respectfully leave to others the immense and important job of completing the rest of the story. This is only the beginning...

June 2002   *Jerome F. Weynand*

1.
IN THE BEGINNING...

The most significant development in public education in this century is the public junior college--the people's college--where one does not need a pedigree to get in, but must prove oneself to stay!(1)* This folksy asseveration by San Antonio businessman Dr. W. W. Jackson, chairman of the Texas Board of Education--in an address to the faculty of San Antonio College in 1961--is typical of the effusion of role concepts prevailing at the time characterizing the genesis of this relatively new institutional type in American education (2).

A national junior college spokesman appears to sum the farrago of junior college roles being voiced at meetings and penned by both professional and lay sources in periodicals when he wrote in 1960: "Junior colleges now find themselves at the right place at the right time in history" (3:488).

The "movement" was 60 years old, by then, without a truly defined national image which was thought improbable by some leaders (4;5;6). There was a mounting pressure in many states for the whole inchoate junior college to define its role: chief features, operational specialties and its raison d'être. For years, proponents had been mouthing things about junior college "advantages" and "functions" and doing it for so long that words had become platitudes--without ever thinking whether or not the sayings were true or false (7:307).

Graham, in his book, *Instant College*, opined in the 1970s that the colleges still seemed to defy accurate classification because it is both higher education and less than that. It was both community oriented and totally unplanned. "Now that the development of the public community college extends over three quarters of a century, many people are still trying to describe this product of American inventiveness" (18:11).

Harbeson chimed in with his essay in a compendium on the American college by calling the junior college "a twin sister of the junior high school--the two institutions respectively an upper and lower extension of the secondary school program." He outlined the first junior high school was organized in the City of Berkeley, California in

---

*Denotes bibliographical reference listed under "Endnotes" at the end of the book.

1

1909; the first public junior college was established in the City of Joliet, Illinois in 1902. He traces the idea of the junior college to a much earlier period believing it originated as a practical answer to a conceived problem in education (19:199):

> Standard college covered too long a period in a student's career; students were graduating at too advanced age; overlapping and duplication between high school and college; much work of freshman and sophomore college years was purely secondary in character; sought to end duplication and shorten the college course.

Harbeson cites President Henry R. Tappan of the University of Michigan as early as 1852, and President W. W. Folwell at the University of Minnesota in 1869, as advocates of a "junior" or two-year college idea. Later, more than 16 other distinguished proponents of the junior college concept from coast to coast were ahead of their times in even thinking about the two-year college.

Perhaps, at this point, it would be well to look at the birth of this phenomenon: the two-year, public junior college. As the youngest member of the higher education family--compared to Harvard College founded in 1636, opened in 1638--the junior college had humble beginnings, a difficult adolescence and was facing a mid-life crisis before age 50. It is a history not unlike the recorded birth and development of San Antonio College as we shall see when this story unfolds...

A Brief History of "Junior Colleges"--Interested academics agree that the junior college is a uniquely American product of the 20th Century, but its latent seed was planted ca. 1869 by the aforementioned Tappan and Folwell and reiterated by the name to remember: William Rainey Harper of Chicago. These three men strongly pushed for a "bifurcated university"--a model not widely accepted--that would place college freshman and sophomore courses at the secondary school level. Thus, the "university" would begin its work with the traditional third or junior year (10:11).

But it was Dr. Harper, first president of the University of Chicago, who is credited historically with making the most progress in setting up a system of affiliated colleges in connection with private academy or public high school units for conducting lower-division course work. Harper, also, is given credit for coining the term "junior college" (11). [As any Kellogg Fellow in Junior College Administration can recite the history...] Harper helped establish the Lewis Institute of Chicago after

2

designating the freshman and sophomore years as "Junior College" at his University. Likewise, he referred to the junior and senior years of study as the "Senior" College or Division at the University of Chicago.

The first, public "junior college" was established at Joliet, Illinois in 1902, again through Harper's influence. The foundation was now set. Turn-of-the-century figures indicate one public and eight private two-year colleges, all with very limited enrollments. By 1916, the total had swelled to 74: 19 public and 55 private two-year colleges. By 1922, there were 207 total colleges of this type in the country: 70 were public and 137 private, a remarkable growth in less than 30 years (12:17).

Jump to 1926--when there was an "awakening" in San Antonio to think "junior"--the number nationwide had reached 325, of which 136 were public and 189 private schools. San Antonio would be on the cutting edge of the movement as the count continued with 258 public and 217 private two-year institutions by 1939; the number reached in 1952 was some 327 public and 267 private schools, many of this class being thought of as "finishing" schools with good names and equally rich prices!

Enrollment had jumped from some 100 students in 1900 to 75,000 attending two-year colleges by 1930; 136,000 students in 1937; climbed to 325,000 in 1943; 562,000 in 1950; dipped slightly to 560,000 in 1953 (possible effect of the Korean War); but bounding upwards to 863,000 students in 637 such colleges by 1959. That latest figure denotes 90 per cent of the enrollment was in public-supported (community or state) institutions as the private academy sector declined for various reasons (13:77).

[It is noteworthy that in Texas at this writing only two independent two-year colleges remain in operation: Jacksonville College (Baptist, ca. 1899) and Lon Morris College (Methodist, ca. 1854); both are in Jacksonville, Texas, and have small enrollments.]

In 1956, Decatur Baptist College was still being hailed as the oldest junior college then in continuous existence in Texas by Dr. C. C. Colvert, noted junior college professor at The University of Texas (14). Additional sources credit Decatur College, established in 1891, and organized as a private junior college in 1898, with not just being the first junior college in Texas, but arguably the first (oldest) in the nation! In 1958, Decatur went so far as claiming the distinction of being the "oldest junior college in the world," with all that history now absorbed by Dallas Baptist University (ca. 1968) in the Oak Cliff section of Dallas (24:25).

The Texas Historical Commission recognized Lon Morris College as the oldest junior college in Texas in 1972 and approved a marker for the campus. The College is credited as the first junior college in Texas accredited by the Southern Association of Colleges and Schools, and the first approved for a chapter of Phi Theta Kappa, national junior college honor society (22;23).

The early two-year schools, usually church related, offered standard freshman and sophomore courses; they had many name changes and sponsorships or ownerships; they provide an historical marker in the birth and development of "junior colleges" as institutions of higher learning in Texas, whichever school wins out on being "First."

Add to these early claims the Diamond Jubilee 75th Anniversary celebration of San Antonio's own St. Philip's College founded in 1898. The historical panoply of events of St. Philip's College presents an interesting case study arising from its original, single-purpose and oft-obscure mission to the very comprehensive role and scope spanning parts of three centuries. It enjoys today respect as one of the fastest growing community colleges in Texas and as a full educational partner with San Antonio College since 1942.

The humble beginnings trace St. Philip's Saturday Evening Sewing Class, comprised of just six Black girls, that was founded in 1898 by the Rt. Rev. James Steptoe Johnston, Episcopal Bishop of the Diocese of West Texas. The original site has an historical marker in the LaVillita district of San Antonio. In September 1902, Miss Artemisia Bowden took charge of the work developing St. Philip's from a parochial day school into a grammar and industrial school with boarding facilities to cope with its expanded high school role. It was moved to the present site--now greatly expanded from the original--on Nevada Street on the City's East Side.

In 1926, when the demand rose for a junior college in that sector, St. Philip's grasped the opportunity to become a "junior college" by 1927 on a parallel--but segregated--track with San Antonio Junior College. In the 1930s, there were eight junior colleges for Negroes, including St. Philip's College (30:8). Survival was imperiled by the Depression of the 1930s, but the indefatigable Miss Bowden approached the trustees of the San Antonio Independent School District to transfer and assume operations in the same manner that San Antonio Junior College was accorded a few years earlier (15).

Enter the Texas Public Junior Colleges--Notable is the fact that many of the State's public junior colleges were established in the late

1920s as units of public school systems and were housed mostly in high school buildings with classes meeting in the late afternoons and evenings. The chief administrator of junior college units attached to the public schools were known as "deans," with the superintendent acting as the ex-officio president (26:22). San Antonio was not unique, except that in its initial year instructors were under supervision of The University of Texas Extension Division and the on-site head was called "director" for many years. Rural areas, small towns and cities took the lead in the formation of two-year public colleges in Texas.

One group must be singled out--among the many due mention and recognition--as giving the primary impetus to the development of the schools: The Texas Public Junior College Association, operating as a "sort of loosely organized confederation of presidents and deans," was functioning as an advocate group as early as 1924 (26). J. E. Nelson, director of the University Junior College and its successor the San Antonio Junior College, served as President of the Texas Association of Junior Colleges in 1929. Ten years later (January 24, 1939) Nelson requested payment of a subscription required by the Association to further the cause of influencing funding legislation, but the local trustees refused (27:244).

The first junior college statute, Article 2815-H, was passed by the Texas Legislature in 1929, while Nelson led the "lobbying" group of colleagues. Tribute is due him for leadership in this landmark bill. The Texas Public Junior College Association was formerly organized in 1947 and dues were assessed at $1.00 per full-time student. Legislation affecting the public junior colleges in Texas has been the continuing interest to Association members--with professional fellowship as a by-product--as they work with the college trustees and state legislators even to this day. [Jerome F. Weynand, third "president" in the San Antonio College District, took a turn during 1979-80 serving as president of the Texas Public Community/Junior College Association, still a viable force in Austin.]

Writing the Foreward in a 93-page, definitive and highly statistical study of Texas junior colleges in 1929, State Superintendent of Public Instruction S. M. N. Marrs likened the transition of grammar school students entering high school to the junior college using methods of teaching adapted to helping students in the college field.

> Owing to the large number of students being graduated from accredited high schools at a comparatively early age and the dangers confronting such students in the first year of

the senior institution--socially, morally and intellectually--the junior college idea has become more popular (30:3).

The top school superintendent continued: that owing to the wide demand for instruction of college rank, the State School System was confronted with the danger of over-promotion in cities and towns that were persuaded by ambitious school administrators and enterprising civic clubs and commercial organizations to enter the junior college field when they had not demonstrated their ability or willingness to support a first-class elementary and secondary school system by employing a sufficient number of teachers or paying adequate salaries. This, he wrote, caused the 41st Legislature to enact the "junior college law" in 1929 (30:4). [Good thing: Marrs had a son who taught mathematics at Lanier High School. A granddaughter and two grandsons of the superintendent later were destined to enroll in San Antonio Junior College. One of the men attended under the G.I. Bill and later earned a degree in engineering.]

In 1949, the 51st Legislature created the Legislative Council and directed that it study and report on the "junior college problem." Prior to this time, public junior colleges had operated with no real supervision at the State level. As a result of the Legislative Council study, public junior colleges were placed under the administration of the State Board of Education (26). During the administration of Governor John Connally (1963) the Coordinating Board, Texas College and University System, was created by the Legislative enactment. But, statewide coordination and administration of technical programs continued to be a responsibility of the State Board of Education and the Texas Education Agency in Austin. [One of the Governor's brothers was teaching at SAC at the time.]

The next milestone came in the 64th Legislature which passed in 1975 enabling legislation authorizing the State Board of Education to contract with the Coordinating Board for the administration and supervision of post-secondary vocational and technical educational programs in public institutions of higher education. In July 1976, the Texas Public Community/Junior College Association voted unanimously and strongly recommended to state officials that these functions be kept under the Texas Education Agency and that no effort be made to transfer them to the Coordinating Board. Done.

All of the flurry and fuss to legitimize and finance the public junior colleges in Texas was an attempt to fix the problems inherent from the sweeping junior college interest that Superintendent Marrs had experienced in the early 1920s, mentioned earlier.

The establishment of these contemporary colleges with San Antonio College (the first one started in an urban area) were in the smaller communities from the Texas Panhandle to the Rio Grande and west to east from El Paso to Beaumont. Eby (29:58) a pioneer educator, cites El Paso as the first public junior college in Texas and lists others in order of their opening session after establishment:

El Paso, 1920; Wichita Falls, 1922; Hillsboro, 1923; South Park, 1923; Gainesville, 1924; Paris, 1924; San Antonio, 1925; Temple, 1925; Victoria, 1925; Brownsville, 1926; Ranger, 1926; Tyler, 1926; Clarendon, 1927; Edinburg, 1927; Houston, 1927; Texarkana, 1927; and San Angelo, 1928. Add to Professor Eby's early list, Lee College (Baytown) in 1934; Kilgore in the piney woods and coastal Del Mar Colleges (Corpus Christi), both with 1935 birthdates (17).

Wichita Falls Junior College, perhaps, is the first municipal-supported junior college in Texas (23;24), which evolved in 1937 to become Hardin Junior College; became a senior Hardin College, in 1946; in 1950 it was known as Midwestern University, and in 1975 settled on the name Midwestern State University.

Edinburg Junior College operated under a junior college district for 25 years, but became Pan American College in December 1951, then Pan American University in February 1971.

San Angelo Junior College remained a municipal college until 1945, when it became known as Tom Green County Junior College, but in 1965, the Legislature made it Angelo State University. There were other junior to senior mutations in Texas.

Hillsboro Junior College--which also lays claim to being the first municipal JC because in 1920 public school leaders became interested in providing post-secondary education for local students--opened in 1923. It was closed in the Summer of 1950 due to lack of community support. However, a latent charter was re-activated as Hill Junior College in 1962 (23). [Lamar Fly, a Kellogg Fellow, was named president. He asked this writer to assist in preparing the new catalog for Hill.]

These are just examples of "success" stories. Blinn College in Brenham often cites its origin in 1883--that's the same year that The University of Texas opened with classes for 218 students--as a Methodist missionary school; then operated as a private academy owned by Brenham residents from 1934-37 as Blinn College. It claims to be the first county-wide junior college in Texas, dating to 1937. Another example of pride among junior college folk.

Emergence in the metroplexes, by contrast to the smaller communities, would come much later for the public two-year institutions: Tarrant County (Fort Worth and environs) built four campuses from 1965 to 1975; Dallas Junior College District (now Dallas Community College District) began small with El Centro College located downtown--as the name implies--the initial of seven satellite colleges in the master plan. Eastfield and Mountain view opened in 1970; Richland in 1972; Cedar Valley and North Lake in 1977; then Brookhaven in 1978. Houston Community College District dates to 1971; others followed in Harris County population centers.

In the post-World War II years--especially in 1945 and 1946--voters in nearly all corners and crossroads of Texas petitioned their local governments to reorganize existing support or to establish through elections in school districts, multiple (union) school districts, county-wide, multiple-county tax units all authorized under State law. Governing boards ran the gamut of lay trustees elected to terms of two to six years to serve a given independent college or the shared dual-control role of serving as trustees for the school district and the college unit. Chief executives were called "President," in most instances.

Texas public junior colleges were slow to gain recognition as institutions of higher learning for the stated reasons that (1) early development and nurture by independent school districts, and (2) the evolving movement remaining for many years under the same or similar type of administration as to the Texas public elementary and secondary schools. Junior colleges actually were in a dual roll of higher education identified as the 13th and 14th years of school, educational roles not unlike the dichotomy that existed for so long in California (16:66-71).

Texas and the entire country, for that matter, would soon experience in the mid-1940s and continuing for years another phenomenon: higher education moving from the elite class to the masses--not education *en masse*--and take on new and greater proportions in the mid-1950s (8:29). Much of that stimulus can be attributed to Public Law 16, with amendments, the so-called G.I. Bill to provide education and training for all military personnel discharged without dishonor and who had served a minimum of 90 days on active duty. San Antonio College would get its fair share of returning GIs.

Yet, as late at 1961, the two-year institutions--which had assumed variable roles and "opening the door" to so many students--were being called individually the "stepchild" of higher education, its baby and even its *enfant terrible* (9:193). The junior college was controversial, but it was here to stay!

Detractors remain, however, to this day albeit subtle. Sports columnist Dan Cook wrote a sympathetic piece published in the February 17, 2001 edition of the *San Antonio Express-News* about the head football coach at Texas A&M University "taking a rap he doesn't deserve." The veteran writer said that after 16 years as an Aggie assistant coach, R. C. Slocum was elevated to the top job, and he's now preparing for his 13th season as head coach at College Station. He is the winningest football coach, by far in Texas A&M, Cook goes on to say, but not without his critics who want Slocum replaced because his team can't seem to win the big ones! Buried deep in the story on the jump page that is at once noticeable and offensive to any junior college *aficionado* [especially to one who was graduated from San Antonio College and transferred full credit to The University of Texas; a wife who earned her A.A. degree at SAC, but more so for the son who transferred 58 semester hours from SAC to Aggieland and received a B.B.A. degree in accounting before earning a Doctor of Laws degree from arch-rival UT. Diluted degrees, indeed!]

Returning to Cook's article: more country boys prefer the smaller College Station and A&M, while city boys like Austin and UT. Nearly every major football power in the nation welcomes star athletes who graduate from junior colleges. Not so at Texas A&M which does not actively pursue them. Aggies only had three junior college transfers on the 2000 season's 90-man roster, according to Cook's analysis.

"School President Dr. Ray Bowen is firm on his stand that taking junior college grads would dilute the value of every other A&M student's diploma," Cook wrote (21).

Leave it to Richard Richardson [a fellow Kellogg Fellow at The University of Texas in the early 1960s] who lends a sweeter taste in the mouths of two-year college students who read his guide published shortly after completing his doctorate in junior college administration and becoming a university professor. He puts it succinctly:

> The two-year college is an institution dedicated to a belief in the worth of an individual and to the belief that all individuals can benefit from the college experience...the two-year college accepts those who come with pride and with the desire for their success...(20:136).

Summary--This ends the abbreviated historical sketch--an exercise not intended to serve as a complete academic review of the vastly expanding literature in the junior and community college field--prepared as an on-the-record, background-briefing laying a foundation for the reader to understand better the climate in which the public two-year institutions were built in the United States and Texas.

Now is the time--within that broad context particularly in the mid-1920s--to examine the historical setting in San Antonio and the establishment of The University (of Texas) Junior College, San Antonio Junior College and San Antonio College, as the name evolved. Many may think the College is a senior institution because of its breadth of curricula and the large enrollment; others had wished it had become a four-year institution pre-empting the formation of the University of Texas at San Antonio, possibly, but holding no grudges...This is the saga of San Antonio College--and what an adventurous and glorious tale it will turn out to be--as it emerges from technical "illegitimacy" of birthright through throes of adoption by a foster parent; survival of an unsteady adolescence; subject of charitable offers during the Depression; the needed transfusion of an abundant crop of students who could pay tuition plus the aid from the State to help cope with a mid-life crisis needing buildings and more faculty; and, finally, into mature adulthood of an institution worthy of higher education standing and leadership. It can brag about generations of successful offspring and take measured pride in what it has to show the broader community after some sacrifices, stickability, and its adaptability of staying slightly ahead of demands in changing roles and mission.

San Antonio College in its 75th Anniversary Year has reached an honorable--don't refer to it as venerable (old), yet--and a viable senior citizenship status recognizing its thousands upon thousands of former students, dedicated faculty and dependable staff; not to forget the support of the District and its elected officials who guide and direct the College.

All of the above, and then some--when you add the members of the Texas Legislature, the Coordinating Board and the Texas Education Agency, City and County officials, school districts, etc.--have contributed in some measure to San Antonio College's greatness as will be revealed in the pages following...

"A REAL PARAGON OF VIRTUE."

Profile: *JOSEPH EDWARD NELSON*

Early recognition in this treatise should be given to the educator who provided great leadership in the formation and nurture of San Antonio Junior College: Joseph Edward Nelson. He was born February 9, 1882, number eight of 12 children born to John Edward and Mary Elizabeth (Wimbley) Nelson in Parker County, Texas. His father and grandfather served as school trustees in the 1870s and 1880s and shared profound interest in education which was instilled to inspire their progeny to enter the profession.

Of Joseph's eight siblings who lived until adulthood, three became certified teachers, one became an actuary, and the others were farmers/ranchers. Brother Hugh A. Nelson chaired the Department of Agriculture at Southwest texas State Teachers College in San Marcos; sister Myrtle Agnes was head of the Home Economics Department at Middle Tennessee State University at Murfreesboro; brother I. I. Nelson received a B.A., M.A., and Ph.D. degree from The University of Texas at Austin, was Phi Beta Kappa, and was a teacher and author of mathematics textbooks; and brother Ralph, another Phi Beta Kappan, received his undergraduate degree in mathematics and worked with figures in the insurance field.

Joseph also had a leaning toward mathematics and earned both bachelor and master's degrees in mathematics at The University of Texas. In his undergraduate days he was a pitcher on the Longhorn's baseball team, ca. 1903. Also, he liked to play golf and football.

Before coming to San Antonio, J. E. Nelson was superintendent of schools in Clarendon; served as principal of Midland High School; director of physics at the summer normal school at The University of Texas.

He began employment with the San Antonio School District in 1918 as a mathematics teacher and remained in that position until he accepted appointment as "Director" of the University Junior College at the outset in 1925. His title and leadership were transitioned smoothly to the successor San Antonio Junior College under the full auspices of the San Antonio Board of Education in September 1926. He and his wife, Lillian Lee (Martin) Nelson, bought a home on Fresno Drive in an undeveloped section of northeast San Antonio in 1929--apparently putting down roots when they paid $9,000 cash because of his penchant for paying upfront under his slogan: "if you can't pay cash, you can't afford it." He maintained a cow (until 1950) on the lot ensuring fresh milk for their son.

He prevailed over many financial and facilities hardships while serving as the "Director" with added teaching duties on the organizational chart of the SAISD until his abrupt resignation into retirement in August 1941. Weeks later, J. O. Loftin took up the position and was given the new title of "President" of SAJC by the Board of Education. During Nelson's tenure, enrollment at the College grew from 130 to 400 students.

J. E. Nelson was a real paragon of virtue as described by his students in the first yearbook, *The Alamo 1928*: self-effacing, unassuming man; rare sense of humor; deep convictions; refused to play political games; a good golfer; rejects all pompous distinctions; has a genuine respect of all faculty and students. He returned the compliments with praise for the mature students he knew from his vantage points of teacher and chief administrator.

In the 1931 yearbook, Nelson cited the characteristic contributions of each student of the College who had entered a period of thoughtful and responsible living with identified personal ideals, abiding friendships, and a love for developing scientific and abstract truths. He only asked that his students forever hold in grateful remembrance where they had gained such maturity: San Antonio Junior College.

J. E. Nelson died August 30, 1952 in a local hospital at age 70 years. Funeral services were held at the Beacon Hill Baptist Church with burial in New Braunfels, Texas. Survivors included his wife, Lillian [she had taught at Edison High School and for many years was an English instructor at SAJC; the writer was in her freshman English class in 1946], and son Gale H. Nelson, born in 1917 in Clarendon, Texas; four brothers and two sisters. Gale taught in the New Braunfels High School for 16 years, later teaching in the Alamo Heights District for 17 years before retirement.

Gale's son, Rodney (Rod) Gerald Nelson (grandson of J. E. Nelson), received his B.S. Degree in Industrial Arts from North Texas State University, but followed a career in business. Rod's wife obtained her teaching degree from Southwest State University and is still involved in the classroom; their daughter is a graduate of The University of Texas in Austin and teaches in Laredo; son completed his degree at SWTSU and works in a school in San Marcos. [Rod contributed biographical information based on memory and family records to better humanize Mr. Nelson above the official records.]

A small bronze tablet may still be seen in the foyer of the McCreless Building which houses the Mathematics Department, among others. Once the building served as an administration-classroom-library-auditorium, the original centerpiece of the new campus fronting the 1300 block of San Pedro Avenue in 1951. Today, there is not much foot traffic by students or faculty in the building, and the obscure plaque is the only physical reminder of his contributions and the legacy left by the pioneer junior college educator. The plaque was provided by faculty, students, and friends and dedicated in February 1953 with his widow, Lillian; her long-time faculty colleague and English teacher Miss Mamie McLean who served as chairman of arrangements; and W. W. McAllister, president of the SAUJCD board, participating. A photo ran in the *San Antonio Evening News*.

The humble man would never have sought such recognition, but there is no building named for him, yet, at San Antonio College. He followed the family plan and became a teacher *extraordinaire*, nurtured the baby College with care, was instrumental in its survival--without J. E. Nelson the institution might not have reached adulthood and still be on the grow. His many monuments, therefore, are his students. Take for good example: Robert G. Cole, Medal of Honor, whose profile appears later in the pages of this book. Nelson taught Cole analytics and probably a lot more...

2.
THE UNIVERSITY
JUNIOR COLLEGE

What was the impetus...who or what...that prompted President Walter Splawn of the University of Texas at Austin to do some "missionary" work through the extension division and personally coordinate operational details to set up a "junior college" with the San Antonio Board of Education in 1925? Perhaps, it was his background.

Walter Marshall William Splawn (1883-1963); native of Arlington, Texas; graduate of Baylor University (B.A. 1908, honorary LL.D. 1925); Yale University (M.A. 1914); and a graduate of the University of Chicago (Ph.D. 1921, dissertation entitled "A Review of the Minimum Wage Theory and Practice, with Special Reference to Texas"). Did Dr. Splawn know personally of the work of President William Rainey Harper at the University of Chicago? Was Splawn somehow influenced by Harper regarding university-run junior colleges? Did leaders in San Antonio invite The University of Texas to bring public higher education to the Alamo City?

Dr. Splawn taught social science at Baylor (1910-12 and 1916-19); he was admitted to the bar (ca. 1909); practiced law in Fort Worth (1912-15); taught economics at The University of Texas (1919-28), including the term of his presidency. He was appointed president about the same time that abundant oil reserves were discovered on University lands in West Texas. His relatively short tenure as president was from 1924-27, when he was credited with development of the Graduate School. Shortly after leaving the post, Dr. Splawn wrote a treatise, "The University of Texas: Its Origins and Growth to 1928," which remained unpublished. In it there is no reference made to the role he played in the establishment of the junior college in San Antonio. A biography of this public servant in *The New Handbook of Texas* (1:31) also makes no mention or credit of his persistent pursuit to establish the two-year college in San Antonio or elsewhere.

His career was varied: served as a Texas Railroad Commissioner (1923-24); he worked for the War Claims Commission (1927); moved on to become Dean of the Graduate School of the American University in Washington, D.C. (1929-34); held more federal bureaucratic positions in interstate commerce and as special counsel to Sam Rayburn on a U.S. House committee before serving for 19 years on the Interstate Commerce Commission using his experience in areas of securities, railroading and communications, the biography notes.

Insofar as known by this researcher, Dr. Splawn never has been referred to as the "Father of the Junior College in San Antonio," or given any other recognition that might well be afforded the one who planted the seed for the start of a junior college in San Antonio, save mention in the press and in the Minutes of the University Regents and local Board of Education Trustees.

Extension Teaching Center As Forerunner--Dr. Splawn may have had an experience teaching off-campus in 1920 that influenced him to continue extension work later when he assumed the presidency at The University. Professor Charles Aubrey Smith, author of a book telling stories about 50 years of business education at The University, regales the reader (4:41):

> One of the most interesting experiments in this era (ca. early 1920s) and one which might have changed the entire complexion of The University of Texas in its academic program outside Austin had to do with its Extension Teaching Centers. The first of these centers was established in Houston in the fall of 1920, and was built around courses in business. Later, other courses such as education, economics, psychology, and the like were added.

Accounting Professor Smith served as Director of the Houston Extension Teaching Center which held classes evenings in Central High School that attracted more than 100 students. Dr. Splawn was one of the six UT profs that commuted by train from Austin to Houston once or twice weekly to teach classes. Professor Smith continues:

> The initial success of the Houston Center spurred the Extension Division of The University of Texas at Austin, headed by Dr. D. A. Penick, to establish comparable centers in San Antonio and Fort Worth. The San Antonio Center, under Clyde E. Barnes, was an immediate success, registering as many as 200 students in one year.

All three centers--Houston, San Antonio and Fort Worth--ended operations before the Great Depression Years. To which Smith opined: "What might have developed into branches of The University of Texas at these other locations did not come to pass. The University was having considerable difficulty securing funds from the Legislature to operate even the Main University in Austin...all teaching activities should be concentrated on the Forty Acres" (4:42).

He continued in his retrospection years after he returned to the main campus as a self-proclaimed "permanent fixture," that the centers would have provided the nuclei for expansion that was attested to by later development of Houston University, San Antonio College and other colleges in South and West Texas. No mention was made by Smith about the "University Junior College," other than his reference to the teaching "Center in San Antonio."

That particular "Center" in San Antonio obviously is a reference to the extension courses for teachers offered beginning with the 1920-21 session of The University of Texas under Dr. Penick's promotion of similar centers in 27 other localities. Extension classes were undertaken in any community in Texas which could muster enough students to pay travel and a small honorarium for the instructor. Classes were generally in the field of education and were offered for graduate credit, according to the man who should know, Thomas H. Shelby, dean of the division of extension at The University of Texas from 1921 to 1951 (5).

San Antonio public school leaders had requested approval of the faculty by the Graduate School in 1925 to offer graduate credit for the classroom teachers because of the equality of instructors and library support considered to be on a par with the main campus in Austin, Dean Shelby added in his history. While neither Smith nor Shelby implied that the teaching centers as explored above were the true genesis, the Center in San Antonio may well have been the forerunner of The University Junior College experiment because of the successful outcome and generally-good working relations with the public school authorities.

The University Junior College is Born--After the review in Chapter 1 of the history of public junior colleges in the United States and the tangential look at Splawn's contributions and the extension teaching centers in Texas, attention turns now to the first inkling of an impending birth of The University Junior College. First recorded official action locally begins with Item Number 1 of Superintendent Marshall Johnston's report on the Agenda of the San Antonio Independent School District Board of Education Minutes of the meeting on June 16, 1925 (2:159):

REGULAR MEETING of the San Antonio Board of Education held this day (June 16, 1925) at 4 p.m. with

17

President Hal Browne, presiding, and the following additional members present, Mrs. Byron S. Eastburn, secretary; Mrs. Wheeler Pettus, Mrs. C. W. Satterfield, Mr. Frank Haines, Mr. William L. Hoefgen and Mr. Charles Wynne, Jr. None absent. Minutes not read. Superintendent Marshall Johnston's report: (1) President Walter Splawn's proposition--Mr. Johnston submitted a communication from President Walter Splawn of the Texas University, outlining a proposition by which the University and the city school system of San Antonio may cooperate in making the freshman and a sophomore work that is now given at the University available in San Antonio to graduates of the San Antonio high schools and to other citizens of San Antonio who may satisfy college entrance requirements. Motion of Mrs. Eastburn that Supt. Johnston's recommendation be accepted and he be authorized to establish this Junior College. Seconded and carried.

Dr. Splawn's proposal was backed up by an authorization--just a week before presentation in San Antonio--as noted in The University of Texas Regents' Minutes of June 9, 1925:

Junior College -- Division of Extension

Following discussion, the Board on motion, authorized the establishment of junior college work in one Extension Teaching Center (to be selected by the President) under the following conditions:

1. The High School Board in the city selected should agree to financial use of their building, including heat, light, and janitor service, from 5 p.m. to 10 p.m. without cost to the University.

2. The University shall provide a teaching staff of necessary instructors and guarantee a total amount to be paid as salaries, not to exceed $15,000.

3. Students taking work in the junior college, so established, shall pay instructors at the rate of $35 a term, or $105 for a nine months' session, in addition to the fees ordinarily paid at the Main University.

4. It is recognized that this plan is largely an experiment and that the fees for the first year will likely be less than the salaries to be paid for the instructors and staff.

In a caveat, "It is provided that the Board of Regents in January, request the opinion of the Attorney General as to the power to use University funds in the establishment of Junior College work outside of Austin."

At the same meeting on June 9th, this entry:

Upon motion of Judge Boyston, seconded by Mrs. O'Hair, the Board voted to ratify the appointment of the following faculty of the Junior College authorized by the Regents and to be established under the direction of the Division of Extension.

J. E. Nelson, Director in charge of the San Antonio Teaching Center, at $3200 for nine months, beginning September 15, 1925.

Miss Janie Baskin, adjunct professor of English, at $2800 for nine months, beginning September 15, 1925.

Miss Rebecca Switzer, adjunct professor of Spanish, at $2800 for nine months, beginning September 15, 1925.

W. P. Udinski, associate professor of Chemistry and Physics, at $3,000 for nine months, beginning September 15, 1925.

Nisson Szapu, instructor in Latin and Ancient History, at $1800 for nine months, beginning September 15, 1925.

W. J. Carnathan, associate professor of History, at $3,000 for nine months, beginning September 15, 1925.

C. E. Barnes, instructor in Business Administration, at $2,000 for nine months, beginning September 15, 1925.

It was that first entry in official Minutes of the local school system, which began in 1899, and heralded the advent of the "Junior College" in San Antonio. Dr. Splawn's historical "proposition" is the first of the 138 entries under the subject "Junior College," reference number 52, of a huge (14x18x3-inches) and heavy Index, Volume 2, part of the codification of San Antonio Independent School Board Minutes completed ca. 1939-40 by diligent workers in the Work Project Administration Project No. 265-1-66-60, and designated as the Texas Work Project No. 18450. [If it had not been for this reference guide, this researcher might well still be in the school district archives searching...]

No further "Junior College" citations appear in Volume 5 of the original book of Minutes from June 16th until August 11, 1925, when a proposal to advertise in the daily newspapers--at a cost of $87--the advent and opening of the Fall Term 1925 at the fledgling University Junior College was brought up at the meeting by Trustee Mrs. Eastburn. Action was postponed. Perhaps, trustees were too caught-up in the bond election held July 16th, in which local taxpayers voted approval of a $300,000 bond package to purchase sites, erect and equip schools. The bond issue passed by 2,499 For and 267 Against floating bonds; the program was not related to any junior college issue.

While the official Minutes didn't record any items of discussion or action on behalf of the junior college, the school trustees had a full plate of other concerns during the Summer of 1925, including the six-months' old nagging issue and lawsuit over the legality of paying 429 teachers a total of $94,000 out of a certain fund. Here's a chronology of some activities vying for attention with the junior college planning and probably prevented some excursion to the Gulf Coast for those educators who could afford it.

On June 8th--a week before he would lay a proposition on the table before the school board to start a junior college here--President Splawn was the speaker at the 42nd annual commencement exercises in Memorial Stadium at The University of Texas under the theme that "the truth will make us free..." only if citizens are willing to financially support higher education and the faculty must be highly trained, give to their best teaching with high standards. He pledged an "economical administration."

The night's activities also marked the inauguration of Dr. Splawn. One of the investiture platform speakers was the noted Professor of History E. C. Barker, whose responsive remarks took issue with some of the president's statements and inferred that conditions mentioned might infringe on academic freedom of the professor. The San Antonio newspapers, especially the *Express*, took notice of the controversy. It blazoned an 8-columns-wide, page-one headline: **TEXAS U. FACULTY ASKS ACADEMIC FREEDOM**, with a sub-head, "Victim of Smug Insularity..." a week after the speech by Splawn, then ran Barker's entire address which took another 20 column-inches of space. San Antonio press fully ventilated the controversy raised by Dr. Barker who was, of course, championed by his colleagues. All Austin was astir; San Antonians read that "The University commencement exercises are over but the echoes of Professor Barker's speech are by no means stilled" (10).

June 10th news accounts told of School Board President Hal Browne's indecision to resign over charges that he had relatives employed in the district and he could not legally sign payroll checks under the state nepotism law, although the issue had not been raised earlier during his trusteeship and teachers had been employed between 10 to 15 years. Another trustee, William L. Hoefgen, faced a similar problem of having kin working for the district. [Perhaps, just a hint--or smell--of politics soured here!]

June 17th dawned with a news report and accompanying photograph that an old home on Newton Alley and North Flores Street had been purchased for $12,250 cash and will become the new administrative offices of the San Antonio Board of Education. The property is adjacent to Main Avenue High School on the North Flores Street side of the campus.

No mention, however, was made in the papers about Dr. Splawn's "proposition" proffered at the board meeting on June 16th; even though it was an item of business on the agenda, reporters did not pick it up. Detailed mention and enumeration of teachers elected and the hiring of buildings and grounds maintenance personnel and clerks received notice, but nothing about the new concept of a junior college in San Antonio.

The *Evening News* on August 5th carried a story about early enrollment in the University Junior College, expecting to have six teachers for every 100 students enrolled. Over 150 reportedly had been signed up by this date for first- and second-year classes. If students successfully complete their work here for the first two years, they may enter the third-year University courses without examination and credits acquired locally will be listed as straight University credits under plans outlined to the Board of Education by Dr. Splawn. So, something WAS going on behind the scene...

The very next day, the *News* reported that more than 180 students had enrolled with officials predicting upwards of 800 before opening day set for September 21--far exceeding the 100-minimum student enrollment set by The University before it would come in and hold classes. Working people of the city accounted for about half of the total registrants to date. Supt. Johnston said a tuition fee of $35 per three months' term, or $105 for the nine-months' session, will be charged (in accordance with University policy).

On August 11th, the *Evening News* bannered this headline on Page One: **Former S.M.U. Professor to Direct Junior College Here.** Dean Shelby of the UT Extension Division, following a conference with Supt. Johnston, announced the appointment of J. U. Yarbrough, 38, former professor of psychology at Southern Methodist University in Dallas as Director of the new Junior College scheduled to open on September 21. Sources said that it was learned Yarbrough also will head all extension centers in the State. The University hopes to establish more centers within two years, but Yarbrough will be stationed in San Antonio. Applications from other cities in Texas for schools similar to the one in San Antonio have been received since the announcement of San Antonio as the first link of these small branches. Shelby also said that he would announce names of the faculty selected for the junior college here by next week.

Yarbrough had joined S.M.U. faculty in 1919, and taught there until 1922; went abroad for a year before teaching at the Carnegie Technical Institute in Pittsburgh; he then returned to S.M.U. in 1924. He had B.A. and M.A. degrees from The University of Texas and a Ph.D. degree from Chicago University!

On August 12, Yarbrough got publicity for his plans to create a student loan fund from contributions made by local citizenry. The last time his name appears in print--so far as this research could determine-- was on August 18th. Soon another director would be named with just a month to go before opening day of school [although one wonders about the June 9th naming of J. E. Nelson as director of the center by University Regents].

Also at a Special Meeting on August 11th, school officials pondered plans for a new junior high school promised to build on the Southside to cost about $260,000 out of bond money.

The *Evening News* of August 11 also featured a large group photo of a "Trio of Leaders in Texas Education," and identified in the cutlines as Walter Splawn, Nasson Dupre and Marshall Johnston. The three had been "snapped a few days ago while Dr. Splawn was in the city arranging for the opening of the new junior college of The University of Texas which takes place next month. More than 200 are enrolled already," the cutlines explained.

Dean of Students Dupre revealed in a news story appearing on August 18 that he had mailed letters to business heads asking them to allow their employees to attend classes by giving them part-time off and to offer part-time jobs to help students work their way through college. Also, Dupre called upon women's associations to support the college in his letters mailed to presidents. The same article in the *Evening News* reported that 230 students had registered, still a month away from opening of the term. Dr. J. U. Yarbrough (last mention of his name in the local press) and Dupre were in charge of the branch of The University of Texas.

As the chronicling of events continued during the countdown to opening day, another article in the *Evening News* dated August 27 urged potential students to submit high school or college transcripts to the junior college office in the Russell Building. In addition to meeting scholastic requirements, students must show evidence of vaccination against smallpox in conformity to requirements of The University of Texas. Matriculation also was possible by examination if students lacked credits or didn't graduate from high school and were under age 21 years.

In somewhat contradictory or confusing news coverage of the requirement for vaccination for entering college students, there were statements from the school superintendent, the City health officials, and even Mayor Tobin was quoted as saying the health department would urge the anti-smallpox shots for college-age students, but he didn't know if the ordinance would be enforced. The mayor left it up to The University officials to decide the issue; vaccination was required on the Main campus, and would be required at the junior college, too. Free shots were made available to enrolling college students.

Finally--after leaving the long, hot summer behind and phasing into fall--clarification was given to several issues: (1) enrollment was in the final days, with new estimates climbing to more than 300 expected for the initial term; (2) students were to sign up at Main Avenue High School for the undergraduate courses and also could register for advanced (graduate) level courses through the University teachers' extension center headed by Clyde E. Barnes (a man who would later have a long association with San Antonio Junior College) with classes meeting one night a week for two hours. Students were allowed to cross-enroll at both levels concurrently; (3) the junior college, per se, will be directed by J. E. Nelson. No mention having been made publicly of the departure of the erstwhile Director Yarbrough who had served for a matter of days in August; (4) two representatives from the University Co-Operative Society (the "Co-Op") from Austin had arrived in San Antonio to sell books and necessary supplies during three or four days (8).

September's initial meeting records the approval by the board to lease staff quarters (office space, not living) at 203 Romana Street on the northwest side of Main Avenue High School near Romana Plaza. With an office in place came the announcement of faculty. On Wednesday morning, September 23, 1925, readers of the *San Antonio*

23

Express woke up to read over coffee a story with an accompanying photograph showing a group of people assembled on some steps with their names listed in the cutlines and identifying them as the first faculty members of the Junior College from The University of Texas. Pictured were Dr. W. P. Udinsky, professor of chemistry and physics; W. J. Carnathan, history; Nisson Szapu, Latin and German; Director J. E. Nelson, mathematics; Miss Janie Baskin, English; Miss Rebecca Switzer, Spanish; Mrs. Evelyn Kerns Taylor, botany and chemistry; and N. K. Dupre, dean of students, appointed by the Board of Education.

The article described the office at 203 Romana as where Nelson and associates were putting in full-time to get a brand new educational institution underway. It is some little task to start a college "from the ground up," the story continued, but members of the faculty are throwing heart and soul into the task, turning night into day for the work of registering the students from 5 p.m. to 10 p.m. using facilities of Main Avenue Senior High School.

While much of the groundwork had been laid in open board meetings, "The University Junior College" had arrived in the eyes of San Antonians! There was something tangible about seeing articles and photographs in the newspapers. However, there was more work to be done in the board room later in the same day that the faculty photo had appeared in the paper.

A Special Meeting of the school board was convened at 4 o'clock, September 23, 1925, to receive in person President Splawn of The University of Texas in Austin. He came fully prepared by presenting a resolution worked out in conjunction with the Attorney General of Texas, the purpose of which was in substance: (1) to have the San Antonio Board of Education collect tuition and fees from the college students, and (2), to pay the instructors selected by the State University for teaching in the Junior College of San Antonio.

After hearing out Dr. Splawn and discussing the matter of operation, the Board adjourned with assurance from the new Board President Frank Haines (who had succeeded Hal Browne during the summer, but stayed on as a trustee) that the matter would be acted on by the Board at the next meeting in October.

September 23rd would continue as an historic day, but a long day for Dr. Splawn. After his late afternoon appearance before the Board of Education, President Splawn was the principal speaker at the first convocation of the 175 students, six new faculty members, the dean of students and the director of the University Junior College held at 8 p.m. at the Main Avenue High School. Classes had formally opened at 5 o'clock, with a recess granted allowing assembly for the inaugural convocation. After this night, it was announced that classes would meet five nights a week. Registration figures released showed 110 full-time students, 30 part-time in the junior college proper; 35 more were enrolled in extension courses for teachers that were also conducted on site by The University. Late registration was to continue.

Press coverage ran 30-column inches in the *San Antonio Express* the next morning; the *San Antonio Evening News* on September 24th carried a page one story of 10 inches, both newspapers giving full and favorable coverage of the event. Answers to earlier questions about the impetus of starting the institution came to light in the remarks of several guest speakers.

The invocation was given by the Rev. Hugh McLellan, pastor of Central Christian Church across Romana Plaza from the high school. Director J. E. Nelson introduced Mayor John W. Tobin who voiced his appreciation of the united efforts of The University and the Board of Education in establishing the college. He offered the City's "every assistance in making the college a success."

Marshall Johnston, the new superintendent of schools--who was elected at a special board meeting April 20, 1925 by a 6 to 2 vote of trustees, replacing Dr. Jeremiah Rhodes--said:

"I never had expected to see so many San Antonio high school students enrolled in a university unless I went away from home, but the sight makes me very happy indeed" (6:9). He also lauded the scholarship of the faculty.

Frank Haines, age 25, the dynamic new board president--elevated July 10th when former board president Hal Browne stepped down amid questions about nepotism, but remained as a trustee--spoke briefly, assuring students of the "hearty approval" of the board in all that had been done. On behalf of the board, he said that "we stand ready to render every financial aid and moral support you may need in making the college a success," as quoted in the *Express* story. Haines--born in San Antonio, a graduate of the Main Avenue High School where he was speaking, having served as secretary of the Junior Chamber of Commerce, a member of the Kiwanis Club of San Antonio--was the leading vote-getter in the February 10, 1925 heated school board election featuring two opposing tickets of trustee candidates who exchanged unpleasant words among themselves and city officials. He led the winning Citizens School Ticket.

Dean T. H. Shelby of The University of Texas Extension Division--referred to earlier in conjunction with teachers' centers--was next to speak. Just 10 days earlier he had released to the Texas press the names of the faculty that had been assembled for the college. The *San Antonio Express* picked up the Associated Press story with an Austin dateline of September 13, and ran the release on Page One of the morning edition of September 14th. (The photograph of the faculty would appear in the local paper on September 23rd.)

"My heart is in the work of this junior college. I am not concerned about the success of the college--there is no doubt of it right now. Success rests with you students," the dean said.

But it was Splawn's evocative message that drew most of the attention as he likened the faculty preparation and abilities in their academic fields as being equal to the instruction available at the State University, asking only in his plea that students here concentrate on their courses. Speaking of the application which students should make to their studies, Dr. Splawn was quoted about grades:

> We have the same system of grading here as the State University: "A" means to master and give back, to appropriate, to assimilate. Determine to be "A-1" in one thing at least; "B" in everything else, and "C" in nothing except the very hardest subject of all. If you make "D" you are just "dumb," and "G" means get (6:9).

[The grading system used in the 1925-26 session as noted on the Instructor's Class Report for the Fall-Winter-Spring Terms was the following: A (excellent), B (good), C (fair), D (pass), E (failure), F (bad failure, G (failure too bad to continue the course). That explains President Splawn's remark at the first student assembly " 'G' means get."]

Finally, President Splawn told the audience of the origin of the University Junior College--sometimes referred to as "Junior Branch of The University of Texas" or "Junior U" in the vernacular of reporters--the idea having sprung from the recognized need for a junior college that would offer a course of study acceptable at universities for two years' work, at the same time giving the student the benefit of being able to live at home and save a considerable sum in board and lodging, the *Express* quoted him as saying.

He continued in his address to unravel the story of the origin by citing that it was just at the time The University board of regents gave their consent to a try-out idea in some city in the State, the superintendent of San Antonio schools asked to have the experiment tried in San Antonio. [Research did not reveal whether Dr. Splawn was referring to former Superintendent Rhodes or current Superintendent Johnston as the one who had asked for UT to set up the junior college in San Antonio since their services overlapped in the Spring of 1925.]

The convocation program ended with students, faculty and guests joining in the singing of "The Eyes of Texas" (6).

Adding to the revelation by Dr. Splawn that the University Junior College was "experimental," were remarks made 10 days earlier by Dr. P. W. Horn, president of Texas Technological University in Lubbock. Establishment of a junior college in San Antonio is one of the biggest things that has happened in an educational way in the city, he was quoted as saying in an article in the *San Antonio Express*, September 12, 1925. He had been in San Antonio for a week as a lecturer at the Southwest Texas Institute, when he said:

> I believe the establishment of a junior college of The University (of Texas) in San Antonio is a good thing because, in the first place, it means a big saving in dollars and cents to the parents of college students. Of course, any boy or girl can stay at home and attend this junior college much cheaper than go off somewhere else to school. Again, it means an opportunity for many young people who otherwise could not attend college.

Dr. Horn also pointed out in the interview that another good feature of the junior college is that it relieves congestion in the freshman year at the universities, something that is a serious problem in many institutions. He said his institution was set to open on September 29th, expecting 500 to 1,000 students and 40 faculty.

It was his opinion that the San Antonio Junior College is only the beginning of similar institutions over the State, bringing the same opportunities in other communities. If the junior college here proves successful, Dr. Horn predicted that it will doubtless be followed by others.

Within a week after the opening of the University Junior College, it was announced that affairs of the student body will be administered by a students' council. Dean of Students N. K. Dupre listed the elected officers of the freshman and sophomore classes: Hal Long, president of the sophomores; John Kirby, vice-president; Thea Goldschmidt, secretary-treasurer. Philip Montalbo was chosen president of the freshman class; other officers would be elected soon. Organization of a student band was in the offing, according to the dean (7).

Nasson Kelley Dupre, for two years prior to his assignment as dean of students, had served as principal of Harris Elementary School. Both Splawn and Johnston had agreed that Dupre was an able man for the job under a director to be named. Dupre's position was the only one which was filled by local school officials. Dupre was graduate from The University of Texas with B.A. and M.A. degrees. From The University he came to San Antonio and the Harris School. Before working on his master's he had been head of schools in Crosbyton, his hometown. Dupre was said to be working toward a Ph.D. degree.

Returning to the main story after that detour on Splawn, Haines' word was good: "The University Junior college Resolution" was, indeed, presented somewhat after the fact on October 6, 1925. It was three weeks after the college opening when Board President Haines explained the substance of the agreement. Mrs. Byron Eastburn moved, seconded by Mrs. C. W. Satterfield, the motion was adopted by all members present for this meeting. The Resolution is basic to the history of San Antonio College and is presented in full here (3:327):

RESOLUTION
By the Board of Education of the San Antonio Independent
School District

WHEREAS, it appears that numbers of citizens residing in San Antonio Independent School District desire an opportunity to pursue a course of study in the sciences, history, literature, and other subjects usually included in the curriculum of the freshman and sophomore years in a college of liberal arts and sciences; and

WHEREAS, the Board of Education of the San Antonio Independent School District desires to afford such residents of this district an opportunity to pursue such studies; and

WHEREAS, the Board of Education of the San Antonio Independent School District has submitted to the authorities of the University of Texas a proposition whereby the Board of Education of the San Antonio Independent School District will furnish the necessary class rooms and equipment, and will pay the cost of instruction, conditioned that the University of Texas will supply the necessary instructors and generally supervise the courses of instruction; and the University has agreed, through its Division of Extension to select and furnish the necessary instructors and fix their salaries, and generally to direct the courses of instruction and select the subjects in which instruction is to be given, and direct and control the internal management of the school so conducted, provided all the costs of said instruction is paid by the Board of Education of the San Antonio Independent School District.

NOW, THEREFORE, be it resolved by the Board of Education of the San Antonio Independent School District that the Superintendent of Public Schools of San Antonio is authorized to register students upon the payment of a matriculation fee to be decided upon by the Board of Education; that suitable quarters be allowed in the public school buildings of this district for the teaching of said courses, and that the necessary equipment be furnished by the Board of Education of the San Antonio Independent School District; conditioned that The University of Texas will direct the courses of instruction and the subjects upon which instruction is to be given; and that from the matriculation fees so paid by the students registered, the cost of said instruction shall be paid to the instructors selected by The University of Texas, and The University of Texas is given complete authority in the selection of courses of instruction and control over the management of the internal affairs of the school contemplated by this resolution.

[San Antonio Ind. School Dist. Board MINUTES, Oct. 6, 1925, V5, p127]

Time was of the essence since students commenced fall term classes on September 23rd in the new college setting. The Board authorized a study after adoption of the working agreement to enlarge the chemistry rooms at Main Avenue High School to meet University requirements. Trustee J. F. Fentiman said a partition will be removed between two rooms making one large science and chemistry area needed for the larger-than-expected enrollment.

At the same meeting, the Business Manager reported that $10,050, collected in tuition from students had already been sent to Austin for payment of junior college instructors as agreed. In still further action at the Board meeting on October 6th, was setting Mr. Naason Dupre's salary as the Dean of Students at the junior college at $2,500 per year, plus a month's pay for services in August 1925 in preparation for the opening of classes.

A little squib did not go overlooked in the newspaper when it reported that students attending the junior college were to receive care in the gastronomic department by having a cafeteria fare each evening at the high school with the same prices offered to regular district students during noon meals, according to Mrs. Mable Noble, director of cafeterias (9).

Barely a month into the fall term of 1925, Dean Dupre issued public notice that the mid-term graduates of Main Avenue and Brackenridge high schools--the only two in the district--could enroll for freshman courses to begin February 8th at the junior college. Students will be allowed to register in the same week that they will be graduated in January 1926.

Fourteen of the original class of college students succeeded in making the honor roll upon completion of the historic first session which ended January 26, 1926. Honored for their A's and B's while taking three courses were Helen Upschulte, Lucian LaCoste, Fernando Uribe, Dorothy Rooke, Mrs. W. L. Evans, Martha A. Hodgin, Mary Newton, Dorothy Owens and Hal Long. Taking two courses with honors were H. T. Mueller, L. E. Marshall, J. O. Hamilton, Ophie Moore and Harry Wise.

The University Extension Division Dean T. H. Shelby made another visit to San Antonio and was quoted in *The San Antonio Express* on February 13: "I find that the students are taking their work seriously and that the teachers are on the job...presenting the courses in their proper form." He lauded those students who attend classes after their regular work day.

> I know of no work being done anywhere more sat-
> isfactory than that in San Antonio. In fact, San Antonio's
> accomplishments along this line are unique and are attract-
> ing the attention of other Texas cities and of educators in
> other states...some are coming here to observe the workings
> of the Junior College.

Dean Shelby arranged courses and helped to select faculty last September. He revealed that the teachers in the junior college here went to Austin after their appointments and worked with department heads in their respective fields on the main campus before starting instruction. The local school board drew praise in the article for the "strictest cooperation" and equipment provided. He appeared pleased that the second semester picked up 27 new, full-time students.

An assembly of the students on March 15th heard Dr. Frederick Eby, professor of education at The University, expound on the "modern" generation, comparing it to the bobbed-haired girls with their permanent waves to their mothers--who were accustomed to spending two hours curling their hair. He posed a rhetorical question to the students:

> If you have gone mountain climbing with two
> friends, the three of you being tied together, and the two
> friends fall over the cliff, what would you do--would you

cut the rope; or be pulled in after them? (*San Antonio Express*, March 19, 1926.)

A notice in the *Evening News* on Saturday, March 20, 1926, announced that the second term of The University Junior College was set to open Monday, following the completion of the final exams for the first term on Friday the 19th. The second session of the school corresponds to the winter term of The University; the first term just completed parallels the fall term in Austin, the report outlined.

[It appears the terms "semester" and "term" are used interchangeably. The 1925-26 school year under The University's supervision was divided into terms: Fall-Winter-Spring. Students could carry one, two or three courses per term. Freshman English course, e.g., was numbered 1a, 1b and 1c, and if completed satisfactorily had a value of six semester hours September through May. Recall earlier that the first semester ended January 26, 1926; the next term began Feb. 8. Instructors' grade reports examined clearly show three terms Fall-Winter-Spring with three letter grades.]

Year-old Orphan Seeks Foster Parent--Near the end of the first academic year--whatever the instructional units one uses--there was a shocker for most people when Superintendent Johnston read a letter in the open meeting of the Board of Education held on May 18, 1926, from President Splawn. The letter (which was not attached to the Minutes) was in reference to ways and means of operating the college for the ensuring academic year beginning in September 1926. The plan as summarized proposed that the Board assume the financing of the junior college, henceforth...Whether or not this letter caught trustees off guard is not reflected in official papers, but after the reading a motion was made and prevailed to defer action until the next board meeting when the superintendent could make a report.

Returning to the flow of events in the chronology of this history, school board Minutes were silent and clean--truly a tabula rasa or blank pages void of any junior college mention in action entries--from the agenda item about the dean's appointment in October 1925, for nearly seven months later on May 18, 1926 mentioned above. Here, then, was the first question raised or the hint of possible financial or legal problems arising in the operation of the local junior college. Was it to become orphaned if nobody wanted to support it? Still no mention of a conflict or illegality of state support had been publicized in the press or official records.

Looking back to December 1925--for a better understanding of the root of references that had been made concerning the legality or "unconstitutionality" of the operation of the junior college by The University of Texas--the statement that..."the Junior College was taken over the next year (1926) when the Attorney General of Texas ruled it cannot charge tuition," (*San Antonio Express*, June 5, 1929) may have helped fuel the legal uncertainty. Other references to the state university's support of the college appeared in local newspapers and annually printed in the historical sketch of the college in its official *Bulletin*. Writers and speakers within the College often cited December 30, 1925 as the date of the Attorney General's opinion that the operation of junior college in San Antonio by The University of Texas was in violation of Article 7, Section 14, of the Constitution of Texas of 1876. [This researcher has been unable to verify that statement of "fact" in the 1924-1926 *Biennial Report of the Attorney General of the State of Texas* (11).]

What occurred on December 30, 1925--quite possibly the attributable cause of legal concern--was a letter signed by Assistant Attorney General George E. Christian and sent to Dr. Splawn advising the president that the Attorney General (Dan Moody) had placed on Christian's desk a copy of a resolution passed by the San Antonio Board of Education of the SAISD providing for the establishment of a special school by that District. As Christian understood the cooperative agreement, courses of instruction would be given under the direction of The University of Texas, including securing qualified instructors and without cost or expense to The University which will not charge tuition or matriculation fees.

To the extent the cooperation was outlined, Christian "respectfully advised that, in my opinion, the Board of Regents is authorized to perform the acts contemplated by the resolution".

Ralson, in his 1933 thesis on the history of San Antonio Junior College (12:126), exhibits a copy of the Christian to Splawn letter. At the bottom of the page is the notation "(Based on summaries of Numbers 2730 and 2731 which follow.)" [However, those opinions were not rendered until April 18, 1928 by Assistant Attorney General D.A. Simmons (13) and could not have been "attached to the letter" because they appeared 30 months after December 1925. They are offered as information.]

"Attached to the letter" was a summary of two opinions: (1) Number 2730 - Branch School of Dentistry - wherein the Attorney General opinion held that the Texas Legislature is without authority to establish additional branches of The University of Texas. If a School of Dentistry is organized as part of the Medical Department of The University of Texas, it must be located at Galveston; (2) Number 2731 - University of Texas - Branches - School of Mines and Metallurgy - clarified in the opinion that the School of Mines and Metallurgy in El Paso is not a branch of The University of Texas within the Constitution, but is a properly constituted college of the State and entitled to support and funds of the General Revenue.

(3) "Article 7, Section 14, of the Constitution of Texas of 1876 construed" (12:127). [The "lost" Article now found: but, is it applicable and pertinent?]

Dr. Splawn wrote to Superintendent Johnston May 13, 1926 in an exchange of business concerning the director's salary, a personnel matter, leaving the chemistry laboratory in place and other matters. He lauded the junior college program and said faculty salaries were guaranteed for the scholastic year just ending "believing that the College would be self-supporting." His letter continued as follows:

> Having demonstrated that fact, we feel that we are no longer justified in assuming the financial responsibility particularly as such a policy would be setting a precedent in dealing with other communities. Obviously, The University cannot go into the business of establishing branches in all the towns that would like to have Junior Colleges. We were interested in cooperating with your School Board in order to demonstrate to the state what could be done. Through this cooperation we have proven that a Junior College can be self-supporting in a community that has over one hundred high school graduates a year.
>
> Permit me to express my deep appreciation to you for the most cordial relations existing between the San Antonio School Board and The University authorities (12:119-120).

In another letter, this time to Director Nelson dated June 3, 1926, President Splawn began as follows:

> You have been informed that it is necessary for The University to avoid the appearance of financial responsibility for the junior college program in San Antonio. As I am informed, the San Antonio Board of Education will care for the Junior College organization...and that certain citizens of San Antonio will guarantee...any possible deficit...since the

school has been financially successful during its initial year, there is of course no risk during the years to follow (12:121).

From the lay standpoint, it appeared that The University of Texas helped to establish the junior college in San Antonio; that the intention was good; guided by tangential opinions (San Antonio Junior College was not styled in any opinion, per se) in December 1925 that the State could not fund "branches" of The University of Texas unless specified by law; that The University could not charge tuition at the school in San Antonio, but could cooperate in ways of helping to guide the courses and in the selection of instructors. The ruling came in the form of a letter from an assistant attorney general, not a numbered opinion.

President Splawn and the local public school officials had cooperated and fulfilled their contractual agreements. They parted company as friends, on a professional basis, gentlemanly to the end in breaking new ground that lasted less than a year, historically, but held strong promise for the future.

Sure enough, as requested, Superintendent Johnston appeared before his board at its May 26th meeting with two items of business pertaining to the junior college:

(a) he reported that the local organization of the American Branch of University Women (San Antonio Branch of the American Association of University Women, it turns out) has offered to help the work of the junior college for the ensuing year and to underwrite any difference (deficit). Trustee Wynne moved, Trustee Fentiman seconded, and the motion prevailed to instruct Supt. Johnston to write a letter of appreciation to the local AAUW members. [No amount was given, nor the answer to accept or not; nowhere, to date, has the letter or amount been found in research and interviews with long-time AAUW members who are searching their memories. No doubt, the offer was genuine.]

It is well known that Dr. Jane Feild (cq) Baskin, head of the English department at the college since its inception--and with 20 years prior teaching at Main Avenue High School--was a member of the AAUW, serving on its executive board. Miss Emma Gutzeit, another veteran teacher and principal in the San Antonio Independent School District, was president of the local chapter of AAUW in 1926. Either or both of these educators--and others--could have been responsible for the financial offer to continue operation of the college.

(b) an item on the agenda to consider re-location of the junior college from Main High School to the Thomas Nelson Page Junior

School's old campus recently vacated in the 400 block of South Alamo Street across from Beethoven Hall. Mr. Fentiman moved, the motion was seconded and carried, and the San Antonio Board of Education stepped forward--however hesitatingly--to approve the location of the former Page property still owned by the District and referred to often as the old site of the German-English School of "yesteryear." It proved to be an historic action, just approving the location, without any further statement recorded as to operations or finances from this point on.

Arrangements for the "new" junior college quarters at the old Page Junior High campus and the discussion of details were shifted to the new superintendent at the regular meeting of the board held on August 17, 1926, with just a month to go before the scheduled opening of the fall semester. At that same meeting, trustees and staff pondered without action a statement for science equipment purchased by The University earlier in the year. The bill was settled on September 7, 1926, and that was the last official contact with The University about the one-year-old "baby" that many said was "abandoned." In October the district bought laboratory equipment and supplies for the institution now officially named "San Antonio Junior College," under "new management" and full ownership of the San Antonio Independent School District serving as foster parent. The name would stick until "Junior" grew up in 1948. That's another story...

President Walter M. W. Splawn
(The UT Institute of Texan Cultures, No. 00621: San Antonio Light Collection.)

Profile: THE GERMAN-ENGLISH SCHOOL CAMPUS

The quaint vintage buildings in the 400 block of South Alamo Street became the second campus for the Junior College. That campus, especially, is well-remembered and loved by former students, but was maligned for obsolescence and delapidation by many who also fought for better facilities. Once housing a pristine German-English school in the later 1850s, the campus buildings had become timeworn even before the junior college made the transition from Main Avenue High School facilities to the "new" home in 1926. Brackenridge Grammar School was a tenant there until the junior high school system came into vogue in 1923. Thomas Nelson Page Junior High School used the campus until 1925, when its new modern campus was built. The hallowed halls-- rather the outdoor porches and stairways--awaited the next tenant!

A bit of history: the "Lateiner" group of 40 intellectuals from German-American families in San Antonio--mostly living in the "Sauerkraut Bend" area known as the King William District--organized a small school with classes which met in a hotel on Commerce Street in 1858. That same year 60 varas (early Spanish/Texas land unit of approx-imately 33.33 inches or about 55 and one-half yards) of property fronting on the 400 block of South Alamo Street were purchased. On November 10, 1859 a cornerstone was laid for the first building and dedicated to the poet Schiller. Two simple stone structures fronted the lot and in 1869 a third two-story building was dedicated to Baron von Humboldt. In 1860 the school was incorporated as "The German-English School of the City of San Antonio."

The school would face constant financial struggles as it offered the equivalent of an eight-year course of study, each term requiring 11 months of applied study by pupils. The usefulness of the school contin-ued until 1897, when--as a culmination of financial difficulties--the campus was sold to Frederick Groos, Mrs. Hulda Groos, and George W. Brackenridge. Mr. Groos had served as the president of the school for 15 years prior to the sale to the individuals. In 1903, the owners sold the entire property to the City of San Antonio and the buildings became part of the City's growing public school system.

Apparently, the junior college classmen were so enamored by the pioneer students who had studied and persevered at the earlier school that on March 10, 1928 the Jaysee students honored former students in an event fully covered by the daily newspapers and enshrined in the first yearbook, *The Alamo*, produced by junior collegians and dedicated to THE Alamo shrine. In 1929, the second edition of the yearbook was renamed *El Alamo*, a name it kept for many years until publication ceased when it gave way to a magazine format. The theme of the 1929 annual was the association students had with the historic buildings where their classes were held.

W. W. McAllister, Sr. was one of the ex-students of the German-English School honored in a 1928 reunion. Later, he was destined to serve as the first Chairman of the Board of the San Antonio Union Junior College District created by an election in 1945, remaining in that capacity until accepting an interim appointment as a City Councilman before serving as Mayor for 10 years.

For a number of years, other reunions were staged for exes of the German-English School by then current college students--such was the affinity demonstrated. Ten years after the junior college settled in the aging buildings, the theme of the college float in the 1936 Fiesta parade was "German-English School Welcome" as bannered above a mock-classroom setup depicting students attired in the clothing of the bygone era as a tribute from the collegians Class of 1936. The float was horse-drawn and quite colorful--even in the black and white photos of the event.

The old campus of San Antonio College is a story in itself and exudes legends that still abound about the life and times of every student who attended classes there: each student can tell a tale or two about experiences recalled from a unique period in time and circumstances that had to be lived to be believed. Esprit de corps was never higher in the minds of students and faculty than the morale and camaraderie of those persons who were thrown together by happenstance during the unique period from beginning of the Fall Semester 1926 on the South Alamo Street campus until January 1951 and the taking up of residence "uptown" on San Pedro Avenue across from the historic park for the Spring Semester 1951. Ask any oldtimer and you will get a testimonial or two.

The old campus of San Antonio Junior College can still be seen by passersby mostly unaware of the history and traditions which are embraced there. Through preservation efforts of the San Antonio Conservation Society, in 1953 title of the property was transferred from the San Antonio Independent School District to the City of San Antonio for use as an annex for offices. In 1964, after a restorative facelifting, the site served as headquarters of HemisFair, San Antonio's World's Fair culminating in 1968. William R. Sinkin, a SAJC student during 1930-32, was one of the organizers and served as the first president of HemisFair.

A four-star hotel leased the site from the City in 1972; more restoration of buildings and landscaping created the hotel conference center. Reunions attracting many students from classes 1925-51 were held in the beautified courtyard June 23, 1990 and another on October 8, 1994. A plaque commemorating the campus of SAJC was placed on the outer limestone wall of the 1859 original building used as the library and a large tablet was erected to trace the chrononology of tenants who occupied the buildings from 1859 to 1992. Both markers were placed on site by alumni of San Antonio Junior College. Kathryn (Kaki) Dial Murray Gueldner was the chairman of reunions and the mainstay in the erection of historical markers. She was cited as an "Outstanding Alumni" during the College's 75th Anniversary Celebration in the year 2000.

Veneration is due the plant which has sparkled as a gem for educational endeavors in the community for 143 years and still counting...

San Antonio College Campus 1926-1951   El Alamo - 1959

3.
SAN ANTONIO
JUNIOR COLLEGE

At Last, A Name and A Campus To Call Its Own--The 1926-1927 academic year was a hallmark. The Fall Semester beginning in September 1926 now brought a different collegial tone among students and faculty under the local governance on a "new" old campus on South Alamo Street six blocks south of the Alamo. The first two buildings on the site had been erected in 1859 before a public school system was thought of in San Antonio. A third building dates to 1869, but reference was made to the "modern Junior College" where students acted like students anywhere with their playful pranks and social activities some of which would become traditions in the Queen's Crown bedecked courtyard.

If Minutes of the meetings of the Board of Education are to be a guide, they did not reflect in the research anything thought to be unusual or outstanding or even newsworthy as reflected in the local press. The tenuous threads of mere survival for the College would be ever-present for years as school officials--both trustees and administrators--sought to nurture yet another school amidst the everyday wants and needs of other schools in the District.

After the first nine months of operation since legal separation from The University of Texas, there was a "slight deficit" problem in meeting the final payroll for teachers. The crisis was met by taking $200 out of the summer school fund. Superintendent Johnston explained to the board members that a number of civic organizations agreed to underwrite the deficit, but he recommended that the District pay the amount as was done.

The 1927-1928 academic year drew a little more interest from the public school trustees who authorized an electrical engineering course of study by providing equipment and budgeting expenses. Students said they wanted an orchestra, so the board approved a request to pay for a director's salary, music and incidentals to a maximum of $250 a year. The library collection was boosted in the Fall of 1927 by $2,500, with the San Antonio Chamber of Commerce offering to pay half the cost of book purchases and the District paying the balance. Deal accepted. Total tuition collections were insufficient to pay teachers' salaries, but trustees approved on May 19, 1928 to meet the payroll for the second straight year.

In the Fall Semester 1928, more science laboratory equipment and supplies were authorized by the board, including one new microscope.

The fledgling institution received a real boost in the eyes of the public when in April 1929 the *San Antonio Evening News* headline "San Antonio Junior College Is Called Good" was welcomed by students, faculty and staff in their search for credibility of the College. Not only was it called "good," the College was "far above the average for junior colleges," according to the official report by J. R. Reid, chairman of the board of examiners of the Texas State Department of Education. The favorable report was released by Director J. E. Nelson who said that Reid had inspected all phases of the work and activity for two days in March. Qualifications of instructors and equipment in laboratories were praised as "better than average" among the 16 accredited junior colleges in Texas. The library contained more books than required, but the registrar's office needed more clerical help. Overall, Reid announced that he would recommend continuing accreditation for San Antonio Junior College.

Newspaper editorial comments were most favorable, urging the support of the community and praising the faculty as doing excellent work of university grade under heavy handicaps.

Newly-elected School Superintendent B. W. Hartley arrived in San Antonio from Louisville, Kentucky the first week in June 1929, succeeding Marshall Johnston who had served four years in the top position before returning to an unassigned principalship. In taking his place in these annals, Hartley said that he comes to the job with no pre-conceived ideas of any kind and does not know what his first work here will be. He had a reputation for work in vocational education while in Kentucky schools. Interviewed by the press, Hartley said that a movement to float a bond issue in San Antonio was in keeping with a general movement in cities of 30,000 or more (*San Antonio Express*, June 4, 1929).

"In Basket" Issue: Abandonment--On his desk was an "In Basket" issue left over from the previous administration concerning continuation of the College in face of deficits in an already strapped District.

Meanwhile, the school board in June 1929 was, in fact, toying with a possible call for a $4 million bond issue, something roundly opposed to by City leaders and businessmen who countered with a proposal for no more than $2.5 million.

42

Sharing headlines in the news of the day, June 5, 1929, was a sub-headline to the main article in the *Evening News*: "San Antonio Junior College Threatened With Abolition at Session" of the school board which had discussed financial figures showing that it has cost the system more each year since the junior college was started in 1925. The estimated cost for the 1928-29 school year was $18,000.

The *Express* bannered the next morning's news with "Junior College May Be Closed--Board of Education Says Institution Proved Too Costly." Trustees Mrs. C. W. Taylor and Mrs. W. H. Quirk both "deplored the expense of the institution" taking funds from the secondary schools.

The Board at this point felt that the Junior College needed to be self-supporting. A study group was appointed by President J. R. Hornberger. Superintendent Hartley reminded everyone at the board table that the problem was strictly financial, not the ideal of providing free higher education.

Bruce Teagarden, attorney for the school district, on June 19, 1929, reversed his earlier, off-hand legal opinion in which he had stated that the Junior College unit was not entitled to support from school district taxes and admitted that he had not read the law prior to giving his written opinion that was issued to trustees on June 4th. He now quoted sections of State law passed by the 41st Legislature to show that junior colleges established and operated before January 1, 1929, are entitled to a maximum of 20 per cent of all money collected by a school district for maintenance and operation. Director Nelson reported to trustees that he needs only $8,000 to $10,000--and certainly not the $350,000 that could be raised under provisions of the law--to operate the College. Only $20,000 had been paid to support the College in the four years of existence, while serving 1,100 students to date and expecting about 300 more enrollees per year (*San Antonio Evening News*, June 20, 1929).

By the August 1st board meeting, Superintendent Hartley had time to become familiar with the problem and made his report on the advisability of continuing--or ceasing--operations of the College. He was "GO" for the 1929-30 session tentatively set to open in just six weeks. The board went along; the faculty was elected for one year, including partial work assignment of Robert Clifton Greenwade, teacher and coach at Brackenridge High School. His salary was set at $900 for nine months to serve as a part-time coach, the first for the College. Salaries for returning instructors were set "same as last year." No incentive or longevity raises were budgeted.

Tuition was set at $115 for five courses pursued for the academic year of nine months. A library fee of $2.50 and a science course lab fee of $2.50 per semester were charged. A caveat in the decision to continue operation of the College held that its future would be determined during the coming winter months.

In a personal letter to English Professor Mamie McLean dated July 26, 1929, Director Nelson assured her that the College would continue to operate and the catalog was going to press.

An advance of the calendar to January 1930 revealed Hartley giving his board members some general and possible options for consideration of a policy dealing with the continuance of the College: (a) establish a free college education plan; (b) provide, operate and maintain buildings with all other costs to be met by tuition income and philanthropy; (c) abandon the College; (d) place responsibility directly on the people through an election. Which one, or none of the above? Hartley clearly favored option "b."

Hartley referred to the San Antonio Junior College position at present (January 1930) as that of an orphan left on somebody's doorstep:

It was left on our door steps after its creation by The University of Texas which was forced to abandon its "child" by a ruling of the Attorney General. Now, it's up to San Antonio one way or another to adopt the child as a member of the family or cast it out (*San Antonio Evening News*, January 22, 1930).

As an outgrowth of Hartley's report, his frank outburst or the discussion which followed caused Board Chairman J. A .McIntosh to appoint quickly a committee to work with the San Antonio Chamber of Commerce--remembering that the Chamber had adopted as one plank of its 1930 platform of activities the development of the Junior College.

A few days later, a meeting was held: representing the District were Hartley, Trustee Leo Brewer and Director Nelson; Porter Whaley was serving as general manager and Dr. Frederick Terrell was chairman of the Chamber; the education committee also was brought in to meet.

Coming off a generally favorable press treatment in the Spring of 1930--when many interesting, informative and otherwise innocuous little stories appeared about activities on the campus--similar headlines bolted in the *Express* and the *News* in the May 7, 1930 editions: **SCHOOL BOARD MAY ABANDON JUNIOR COLLEGE**. The lead paragraph in each story cited the action of the trustees by unanimous vote designated the College as a regular unit of the San Antonio

Independent School District. The College had been maintained without legal status since it was given up by The University of Texas several years ago, the explanation read. That's the good news! Then, in the second paragraph came the warning that the board will consider abolishing the College in a few years if receipts from tuition do not meet the cost of maintaining the school and citing the fact that cost during the past year was about $14,000. In fact, the College was placed on "Probation" by trustees for the next four to five years.

Surviving One Year At A Time--News was relatively quiet during the Depression Years. School officials passed the first "official" salary schedule for faculty assigned to the College on July 1, 1930. Minutes reflect a weak apology that "this salary schedule has been followed for several years, but has never been passed by the Board of Education." It stated:

    (a) Instructor salary range from $1800 to maximum $2200, with annual increments of $100 until maximum reached.

    (b) Adjunct Professor, $2500 to $2800, annual increment of $100.

    (c) If Adjunct Professor receives the maximum salary and obtains a doctor's degree, the salary may continue to increase at the rate of $100 per year until it reaches $3000. Upon receiving the doctorate, the person shall be called "Associate Professor."

The incentive increase aspect was short-lived, however, because exactly a year later the board rescinded the $100 increment and fixed it at $50 per year in accordance with a recent measure granting only half the automatic pay increase to public school teachers.

School board Minutes and daily newspapers continued to reveal little news concerning a routinely functioning two-year college, although many activities involved other units in the developing school district. In a benevolent mood in March 1931, the board granted free use of some rooms at the College to neighboring Herman Sons Fraternal Lodge to conduct German language classes during June and July. A scholarship--first of its kind approved by trustees--was awarded to Main Avenue High School graduate Evelyn Doolittle to attend the Junior College during 1931-1932 (renewed for 1931-1932). Other scholarships were to follow in the tough financial years of the early 1930s.

In the Spring of 1932, the board re-elected 1,200 classroom teachers upon recommendation of the superintendent, but it was August 18th when Nelson and 13 other faculty of the College were re-elected with

130 residual full-time teachers in the grades, making a total of 1,343 professional teachers. Also in August, the board raised tuition $35 to a maximum of $150 for courses in an explained attempt to make the college self-supporting.

Judge O. M. Fitzhugh, former member of the San Antonio Board of Education, made the chicken and peas circuit of civic club luncheons: he spoke to the Lions Club on Wednesday and the San Antonio Kiwanis Club on Friday during the same week in late September 1931, extolling the economic, educational and social values of the Junior College in the community. He traced the short history of the College, saying it is recognized by leading universities yet forced to maintain itself at the expense of students. He urged community support of tuition-free education. He said citizens have provided well for the State University, but the only difference is that the Junior College is at the door of boys and girls, whereas they must go to the university door at greater cost and be thrown into confusion and bewilderment away from home their first two years.

Superintendent Hartley tentatively approached his board in November 1931 to request a loan for the Junior College operation, but withdrew the item on the agenda after "satisfactory arrangements had been made." Trustees voted to reduce tuition by 20 per cent in view of salary cuts made in August 1932.

Mrs. C. E. Barnes, registrar and wife of business instructor Clyde Barnes, was authorized to receive reimbursement for her expenses to attend the convention of collegiate registrars in Dallas in 1932, thus setting a precedent for her successors to attend later meetings and work out smooth transition of students' credits to senior institutions.

In other news items gleaned from chronicles in the next few years:

R. S. Menefee, president of the school board, returned in the fall of 1936 from a trip to Austin where he conferred with state legislators about a special project. Menefee urged local citizens to build a "University of San Antonio" at an estimated cost to taxpayers of $1.3 million to be financed by a public works loan. He predicted the university would attract from 1,000 to 2,000 students and replace the present Junior College.

In October 1936, President Menefee told petitioning students at the Junior College that classes could be held in Brackenridge High School, for instance, if students wanted to move from the delapidated facilities on the South Alamo Street campus.

A number of students and their parents banded together as a Patrons-Student Organization in November 1936, shortly after the students went on strike for improved classroom buildings.

Hull Youngblood replaced Menefee as board president in January 1937, and was not pleased with finances. There was a deficit in Junior College operations of $8,000 in 1935 and $7,000 in 1936 that caused trustees to dip into the maintenance fund in the District to cover the losses. Youngblood warned his colleagues that State law provides that any board member guilty of using any State available school funds for Junior College work shall be liable to a six-months sentence and a $1,000 fine.

Youngblood advised San Antonio taxpayers that if they want a better operated Junior College system they should organize a junior college school district in accordance with State law. He announced at the Board meeting on January 30, 1937 that the rise in tuition of $3 per course, or $30 a year--from $120 to $150 per year--had been necessary to cover the shortfall of $15,000. He said that it had cost the school district $36,628 to operate the Junior College in 1936.

San Antonio Junior College students picketed in front of the campus as registration for the Spring Semester 1937 was underway in January. They carried placards saying "Down with the Tuition Hike" and "Don't Register." During the Fall Semester 1936 just concluded, 317 students had been enrolled, but only 130 students had signed up for the Spring 1937. The student demonstration ended on February 3rd when student leaders became resigned to the fact that the protest would not induce trustees to lower tuition and that students might lose credits if the strike continued. The total registrations rose to 280 that day.

In the up-and-down financial struggle, the school board in February 1937 authorized deferred tuition payments upon students meeting certain conditions and authorized building repairs not to exceed $1,000 at the Junior College.

Trustees at the board meeting on May 24, 1938, decided they should ask the State Attorney General for an opinion defining the status of the Junior College. [No extant evidence of an opinion to that proposed inquiry was found in researching board minutes, press coverage and Attorney General opinions. Opinion No. 3016 on June 13, 1938, advised "that bonds issued by a junior college district are eligible for purchase by the State Permanent School Fund" in response to a question raised by the State Board of Education on May 31, 1938 (Biennial Report of the Attorney General, September 1, 1936 - August 31, 1938).]

Rabbi Ephraim Frisch was the principal speaker at commencement exercises for Junior College graduates held on June 3, 1937 in the Jefferson High School auditorium. He drew wild applause from the patrons in the audience with his suggestion that the College have its own independent school board made up of educators and public-spirited persons with administrative ability, "of which there is plenty of talent in this City" (*San Antonio Express*, June 4, 1937). He also cited "disgracefull conditions" of the present San Antonio Junior College campus buildings.

Board President Youngblood, there to present diplomas, agreed with the rabbi and urged parents to get together and organize an independent school district to operate a junior college.

Director Nelson, on September 15, 1937, foresaw an increase in student enrollment for the Fall Semester because of the reduction in fees from $15 to $12 a course. For the academic year 1937-1938, the Texas Department of Education reported that 9,000 persons were enrolled in junior colleges (for whites) in Texas, a number larger than the combined enrollment of all seven State Teachers Colleges, which had 8,611 students.

The Superintendent of schools recommended the continued operation of San Antonio Junior College for the Year 1938-1939, and trustees approved the wish on June 14, 1938. Sighs of relief, no doubt, went up by students and faculty for their futures received yet another reprieve for another year of study and teaching, at least.

The school board refused to pay a subscription request by the Association of Public Junior Colleges in Texas in January 1939, but did approve Director Nelson's additional request for trustees to go on record to approve backing of a bill in the Texas Legislature calling for State aid for two-year public colleges. Nelson had provided leadership in the Association which worked for the betterment of public junior colleges over many years. In other action at the same meeting, the board allowed for student tuitions to be payable in three installments each semester.

In the Fall 1939, 307 students were enrolled--81 of whom were attending night school classes--and they came from 30 Texas towns and nine other states in the United States, plus students from Spain, Hungary, Germany and Mexico, according to the registrar.

The Texas State Teachers Association's 61st Annual Meeting convened in San Antonio November 30 to December 2, 1939. Director Nelson provided music talent to open the junior college section meeting which featured discussion on library resources and teachers grading, plus other papers at the junior college level.

That activity marked closure of the decade and the first 15 years of operations of San Antonio Junior College...a College on the grow!

"I LIKE YOUR CRUST."

Profile: WILLIAM R. SINKIN

William R. Sinkin may best be described as "BMOC"--Big Man on Campus--as a student from 1930-1932 at San Antonio Junior College. The attributed title is not to be confused with the "Little Man on Campus" cartoons popular among college students during the 1950s and 1960s. Bill left his big mark on the record at the College during the Depression Years, and became an outstanding and contributing citizen for the next 70 years--and is still going...

He was born in San Antonio on May 19, 1913 of Russian émigré parents who left Russia in 1910 to settle in Texas. Bill is a product of local public schools and the synagogue. His father was a dry goods merchant on City Street; his mother was a nurse in the old country. They resided on King William Street and later on East Evergreen Street as neighbors to the Cole family. Mrs. Cole was one of his teachers. Bill knew Robert G. Cole and brother LeRoy. Both parents believed in education and instilled in their son a love for inquiry and achievement. At an early age, he began playing the violin in Hawthorne Junior High School. He was graduated with the last Class of 1930 from old Main Avenue High School where he made the National Honor Society.

Sinkin recalls fondly his counselor role at age 15 at YMCA camp where he selected Christian hymns and joined in singing with the other boys around the campfire.

In September 1930, he enrolled as a freshman at San Antonio Junior College and became active in student activities and campus politics borne of his penchant for forensics; he loved debate. He did not neglect his studies: Bill made the Honor Roll on 30 semester hours completed during the first year; repeated the effort with 30 hours in his sophomore year to gain recognition and membership as one of 14 charter members of the Beta Nu Chapter of Phi Theta Kappa, national junior college honor society, for his scholarship and character. Academic studies came first, but he was heavily involved in leadership roles: advocate of a "blanket tax" to be paid by students to help defray student activities expenses; active debater; an organizer for junior college graduates to become involved in the alumni association; appeared in a drama production; pledged "Etta Bita Pie" fraternity; lead fellow students in a drive to obtain better facilities on campus; writer and an editor on the newspaper staff, and others.

His name and activities are spread over the issues of the weekly newspaper and yearbooks. He was a predominant and popular figure among his peer group and friendly competitors. He was elected President of the Students' Association for his sophomore year 1931-32. His "gifted leadership ability" was well known among these classmates: J. T. Lane, Ed Johnson, Charles Bates, Joe Bates, Henry Dupree, Jr., E. W. Holcomb, Gus Levy, Jay Sam Levy, Herschel Childers, Bill Mayhugh, Earl Arnett, Bill Culmer, Dick Smith, C. W. Martin, Tabor Stone, Joe Briscoe, Glenn Winship, Owen Lancaster, Victor Coose, Max Kahn and Clifford Dismukes.

Also, Margaret Upshulte, Lucille Rock, Pat Webb, Elizabeth Westrup, Bernice Weininger, Nadome Allen, Lewis C. Lee, Marguerite Hammonds, Mary Campbell, Oscar Spitz, Otto Holecamp, Burdette Taylor, Elizabeth Milam, to list a few of his contemporaries whose names appeared in the news.

Sinkin transferred all 60 semester hours of credit earned at San Antonio Junior College to The University of Texas in Austin and completed work for his Bachelor of Business Administration degree which was conferred in 1934. After graduation he worked for his father as a traveling salesman for wholesale dry goods in a territory reaching south from San Antonio to the Rio Grande Valley and to West Texas towns of Wink, Kermit and Odessa near the oil fields. He sometimes slept in his car with only his violin as companion on lonely nights. Practice paid off: in 1937 he became a charter member of the San Antonio Symphony Orchestra playing the violin.

When his father died in 1942, Bill and his brother Sam took over the business. The next six decades, Bill Sinkin would lend his leadership qualities to many local, state and national causes over a wide scope of endeavors all aimed at making San Antonio a better place to live and work. His wife, Fay, and their two sons--one with a law degree and the other with a Ph.D. in history--also are well-known for their public humanitarian interests.

He served as one of the founders and the first president of HemisFair in 1968; was among the founders and elected first president of San Antonio Goodwill Industries; gave years of his financial skills on boards of the San Antonio Housing Authority, Bexar County Hospital District, Our Lady of the Lake University and the National Conference of Christian and Jews. He was honored by the City of San Antonio, institutions of higher learning, the banking industry, Democratic Party, United Negro College Fund, Child Care Council, Jewish Federation, Urban Coalition, food bank, Mind Science Foundation and other organizations.

He ran an independent bank, consulted, and was a political confidant of U.S. Congressman Henry B. Gonzalez for many years. (Gonzalez also was a product of the Junior College, enrolling in 1934 and graduating in 1937 with 72 semester hours. He was cited in 1982 and again in 2000 as an outstanding alumni.)

The Year 2002 found Bill Sinkin behind a big desk in a downtown office serving as Chairman of the Board of Solar San Antonio, Inc., a non-profit organization spreading the environmental virtues of solar energy. He still makes speeches to civic clubs and anyone else who will listen to his persuasive presentation and still wearing a signature bow tie--polka dots preferred--just like he was back on the old campus. Perhaps, he is a step slower; there is no stopping Sinkin as long as perpetual sunlight falls on the octogenerian.

The Junior College had not begun the issuance of diplomas at the time when he completed his courses in 1932, but he regards San Antonio Junior College as his first alma mater. He remains an active supporter of the College.

> Two of the best years of my life were as a student at
> Jaysee. I felt at home there...I had an opportunity for leadership development...any recognition came later...there was no
> hostility whatsoever on an egalitarian campus in those days
> on South Alamo...(from a 2001 interview with the writer).

William R. Sinkin is one of the 75 "Outstanding Alumni" honored by the San Antonio College Alumni Association at a gala in October 2000 as an event of the year-long 75th Anniversary celebration marking the birth and growth of the College. Probably no greater compliment could be paid to him as a humanitarian than borrowing a greeting used by his "Piemen" fraternity brothers 70 years ago: **"I like your crust."**

4.
THE FAILED ELECTION
OF 1941

While it might not be prudent to sustain readers' interest in a story by giving away the climax upfront, it was a well-known fact that the Bexar County-wide attempt to create a separate junior college district failed on November 15, 1941 shadowed by European war clouds which hovered over the nation and especially San Antonio as a military town. Bad timing, perhaps. Three weeks after the slim-margin defeat by voters, Japan attacked and the United States was at war. The outcome of the election and World War II combined to shape the course of local history and would serve the undaunted proponents of a self-sustaining junior college to try again with added vigor in four years as this story unfolds.

The San Antonio Board of Education had tried--mostly in vain--to feed another mouth at the financially-strapped table where sat all the schools in the inner-city school district. Faithfully--although not always willingly--trustees had provided basic sustenance for the Junior College since 1926, when it took over operations on a "tentative basis" from The University of Texas which opted out of the arrangement after an opinion by the Attorney General of Texas. Almost monthly, recommendations were made that a separate college should be created under the statute of 1929 which provided for establishing junior colleges in various territorial models, separate boards and taxing powers.

Credit Leo Brewer, vice-president of the board of education, with suggesting in February 1941 that an election be called within a year to organize a junior college district in urban San Antonio. Dr. James Hollers, a dentist, was board president. Word spread and the Junior Chamber of Commerce pledged support to improve current facilities and urged revival of the ex-students group. Members of the 20-30 Club and the Business and Professional Women's Club met with the Patrons and Students Association to suggest that a 30-acre site at Pine and Astor Streets on the southeast side (bought by the school district as a high school site) be considered for a junior college campus.

On June 17, 1941, Leo Brewer, now elevated as president of the board, made another pitch to "divorce" the school district from the junior college operation and create a separate entity to ensure better educational facilities and to save money. Again, nothing happened.

J. O. Loftin Assumes College Presidency--Notable at this point is a story which appeared in *The South Texan* published in Kingsville (150 miles south of San Antonio) on July 15, relating to the resignation of President J. O. Loftin, effective August 21, at the Texas College of Arts and Industries. His letter had been filed on May 26 with the chairman of the senior college trustees (reportably he had been on active military duty during the early summer) but was not acted upon until the July board meeting in San Antonio. By resolution, the trustees released and lauded Loftin for his accomplishments during a seven-year tenure that brought growth and academic development to Texas A&I College.

Just a month later, on August 12, J. O. Loftin was appointed "President"--in a position name change from the traditional "Director" title--by the San Antonio Board of Education. Only a week earlier the board had received and acted on the resignation proffered by the first and long-serving Director J. E. Nelson. The request was approved "with regret." A delegation of Junior College students had tried to intercede before the appointment of Loftin by petitioning Superintendent I. E. Stutsman to name Clyde E. Barnes, a popular business and economics instructor on the faculty, to succeed Nelson.

Nelson said that he resigned "to devote more time to business interests," effective August 23, but other sources hinted that ill health may have been a contributing factor to the decision after 23 years in the San Antonio Independent School District.

Loftin was no stranger to San Antonio or the school system. He served at several levels in the local district and as Principal at Main Avenue and Lanier High Schools; was nationally known for his model vocational training. His immediate plans called for expansion of the Junior College curriculum to reach more students and to use the facilities of the San Antonio Vocational and Technical School, "Tech" being the successor to old Main Avenue High School.

Still bent on his mission, Board President Brewer on August 9th again called for the creation of a "union district" (meaning two or more school districts either independent or rural or a combination) embracing San Antonio and suburban areas, adding: "Time has come for a junior college district to better serve the people" (*San Antonio Express*, August 10, 1941).

Community "Movers and Shakers" Push District Plan--A strong, dynamic civic leader, O. P. Schnabel--genial insurance agent known for handing out his business card with a Jefferson nickel pasted to it as a reminder that you "never will be broke"--emerged as the chairman of a special committee of 29 members. The list included some of San Antonio's most influential citizens generally respected as "movers and shakers": County Judge Charles Anderson, W. H. Arlitt, W. B. Arnold, Stanley Banks, Sr., Leo Brewer, Chester Chubb, Mrs. Preston Dial, F. F. Doyle, Marion Findlay (a student), Louis E. Hart, Dr. James P. Hollers, Mrs. A. K. Japhet, George Judson, Mrs. Jerome L. Kuhl, J. O. Loftin, Robert Kingston (vice-chairman), John M. Naff (a student), and Dr. P. I. Nixon.

Other members included Herman Ochs, Dr. H. H. Ogilvie (another vice-chairman) Postmaster Dan J. Quill, Mayor C. K. Quin, Louis E. Sein, David P. Steves, Mrs. A. E. Stein, Col. W. B. Tuttle, Temple Wheeler, Mrs. J. S. Crugas and Paul Villaret. Four members were added later: Arthur Biard, Malcolm Bardwell, Dr. Nelson Greeman and Paul Adams (newspaper reports on September 28, 1941).

Things began to move at the hands of these community leaders. At least 500 petition forms were donated by printers Paul Anderson, W. C. Clegg, Benno Clemens, Marvin Hill and Russell Hill (who also provided $1,500 in election supplies). Petitions were circulated in Bexar County with extraordinary results of obtaining 20,323 signatures, when only 3,000 had to be certified as taxpayers by Tax Assessor-Collector P. E. Dickson in order to call an election.

More than 600 people worked to collect names on the petitions. Dickson reported that 43,593 current tax statements had been mailed to property-owning taxpayers.

Based on these figures, nearly half of the taxpaying property owners had signed petitions to call the election. Seventeen local education leaders backed the drive; labor unions were supportive. Early in the campaign at least 50 election workers offered their services free, waiving the mandatory two dollars that each poll worker was entitled to receive. Justices of the Fourth Court of Civil Appeals signed the petition which called for the election to create and finance the operation of the proposed district. Among them were Chief Justice Edward W. Smith, Associate James R. Norvell, Associate W. O. Murray; also signing were District Judges John R. Onion and Everett F. Johnson.

County Judge Charles W. Anderson and three County commissioners signified they were "For" the election call, while District Three Commissioner Robert F. Uhr voiced opposition, holding the opinion that it was the function of the City, not the County, to call the election.

Newspaper editorials at the time all favored the call to allow taxpayers to voice their vote at the polls. The suburban *North Side News*, in its issue of October 10, 1941, wrote that "the present Junior College buildings are a disgrace to the City of San Antonio...the School Board was in dereliction of duty to youth...the Junior College is the Cinderella of the School System."

In flowery, but straightforward, language the editorial continued:

> The gal that sits in the kitchen, eating crusts from the table, clad in rags of neglect, and awaiting the fairy touch of decent housing to burst into "the beauty" of the Public School System. The Junior College has an anomalous standing within the education system of San Antonio and that should be cleared up. It should take its place in the sun.

The Huntress-owned *San Antonio Express* editorialized in favor of the creation of a college district on September 27:

> For 16 years San Antonio Junior College has rendered this community distinguished service...opened doors to numerous young men and women who could not afford to go away to school. Practically without exception, the student body has shown that it appreciated the advantages thus provided.
>
> ...over the entire 16-year period, one third of junior college graduates who have gone to The University of Texas have ranked scholastically in the upper 10 per cent of the student body there...the College has earned a worthy home and an adequate operating budget. Too long it has been an "orphaned" institution--receiving but scant support from the Board of Education.

The editorial also cited the cooperation of civic organizations which combined to give the Junior College more status as a separate college in Bexar County. The newspaper lent its endorsement to an early election call.

The petitions gathered passed muster with the perfunctory review by the Bexar County Board of Education as to being "legal and genuine." The next step in the process was to deliver the petitions to Austin and seek approval by the State Superintendent of Instruction and through him to the State Board of Education. Of the 11 members on the Board, two were San Antonians: Joe H. Frost, Jr. and D. F. Youngblood. It was a huge publicity stunt for the petition drive organizers when they delivered to the office in Austin on October 13th some 20,323 names on petitions so weighty they were carried from cars in a wheelbarrow by 17 Committee members accompanied by 50 Junior College students who made the trip to Austin to show support.

Approval in Austin by the officials as to the need for a free-standing junior college was quickly granted, putting the ball back in the Bexar County court: Commissioners Court, that is. Commissioners toyed with setting the election a week earlier than the Saturday, November 15th date settled on to hold the special election using paper ballots. Now October 16, it left only a month for electioneering.

The campaign was on! There were four propositions in the Special Election of November 15, 1941:

(1) whether a junior college district shall be created in Bexar County;

(2) whether trustees will be given authority to levy and collect a tax of not more than 8 cents per $100 valuation (at three and one-half per cent projected rate of interest from 1942-1971);

(3) whether trustees can issue $490,000 in bonds and levy a tax to meet interest and principal payments;

(4) choosing a board of trustees.

The names of seven trustee candidates suggested by the organizing committee to promote the district creation and serve six-year terms were: R. S. Atchison, labor representative; John P. Classen, rancher; O. D. Drisdale, banker; Dr. Nelson Greeman, optometrist; Robert Kingston, manufacturer; Mrs. Jerome Kuhl, Parent-Teacher Association leader; and Dr. H. H. Ogilvie, physician and surgeon.

A giant pep rally to drum-up public support for the college issue was held on the evening of November 7th in front of the Municipal Auditorium. Brackenridge High School Band Director Otto Zoeller conducted a mass-band concert composed of 550 pieces from seven high schools. Pep squads added color and voice to the gala which attracted an estimated 1,250 high school students in the mass assembly. Junior College President J. O. Loftin led the parade of marchers--including college students and faculty--from assembly on Alamo Plaza to the auditorium circle where they joined the crowd and listened to 10 speakers who had been asked to limit remarks to three minutes each.

All seventeen newspapers published in Bexar County signified support of all the propositions. President C. E. Evans of Southwest Texas State College in San Marcos wrote to Chairman Schnabel on October 1st, saying in his letter made public that the proposed junior college would in no way embarrass or weaken existing colleges. He wrote: "The junior college movement is fundamentally sound, practically essential...strongly influencial upon the whole education movement in your City and County," (*San Antonio Light*, November 10, 1941).

Election endorsements poured in for the new district: Bexar County Medical Society, San Antonio Teachers Council, San Antonio Manufacturers Association, San Antonio Life Underwriters, American Legion Post, barbers' union, P.T.A.'s, Council of Pan American Relations, graduate nurses group, school principals, Junior Chamber of Commerce, plasters and finishers' union, San Antonio Board of Education, music clubs, farm loan association, 20-30 Club, typographical union and more.

The Mexican Chamber of Commerce endorsed the college district idea "100 per cent," vowed spokesman O. L. Trippe. Alonzo Perales, president of Loyal Latin-Americans, was convinced the new junior college would be "most beneficial to our youth, San Antonio and Bexar County." Dr. James P. Hollers, strong former president and still a trustee on the school board of the San Antonio Independent School District, was described as being "warmed" to the tax district proposal on election eve (*San Antonio Evening News*, November 14, 1941).

Adding to the fodder of a "good" press favoring the election was the byline story by Jim Weber--having posed as a student for a day--who gave a first-hand account of the present Junior College's poor physical conditions on campus: drop-socket lights dangling from ceilings on long cords; blackboards that were pitted and cracked; no window shades; pot-bellied iron stoves coal fired; scorch oneself on one side and freeze on the other; no heat in the restrooms; old high-tank toilets; library stacks all the way to a 14-foot ceiling; cracking plaster and drafty classrooms...to name a few (*San Antonio Light*, November 8, 1941).

"I'll vouch for the fact that as far as the physical plant is concerned, the San Antonio Junior College is as near a wreck as it can be without the roof caving in," Weber summarized in his story.

Small, Vocal Opposition Ends District Dream--Almost any political observer or campaign analyst might conclude from the across-the-board support for a separate junior college with its own taxing power was a safe bet, a sure thing, in the bag. Too good for voters to oppose, it all seemed.

But, there was organized opposition--small in numbers, yet certainly not token--very vocal in the final 10 days before the election. The Taxpayers Defense League, headed by Joe S. Sheldon; the Home Owners' Committee; and an anonymous group called "Ex-Service Men," paid for newspaper display ads large enough to get attention of readers with bold and catchy captions demeaning to the creation of a new district for stated financial reasons. Ads cried out in very similar themes and wording bordering on collusion in preparation: "Taxes, Taxes, and more Taxes." "National Defense vs. Local Tax Hike." "Put National Defense First." "The Worst Is Yet to Come." "Sumner Welles Predicts War at Any Time." "To Arms! Taxpayers." "Our Country must have warships, airplanes, tanks and rifles." Ads implied that if one voted FOR the college district formation, it would be downright unpatriotic!

A lengthy and pointed editorial in Hearst's *Light* on the afternoon of the day before the big election was aimed at the opposition groups and castigated them for their "gratuitous insults to the intelligence of voters in the junior college election." The paper took a strong stand against the general anti-vote material of the Taxpayers Defense League, particularly, about its contention that it would not be "patriotic" to vote in favor of the college propositions. The editorial quoted from some of the paid advertising that ran in its own newspaper:

> The security of these United States is the first con-
> sideration of every legal citizen. There are more than 3,000
> counties in the U.S. If each of these counties built a junior
> college costing $490,000, it would divert more than one
> billion dollars from NATIONAL DEFENSE. If it is right
> for Bexar County to do this, it is right for all counties. Do
> you think it would be a patriotic course?

O. P. Schnabel fired right back at the League with his counter that "one per cent of the Taxpayers Defense League is trying to confuse the voters by saying that the small property owners are going to pay the tax." He explained that with an estimated average home valuation on the tax rolls, a taxpayer will pay 80 cents per year to support the college district as outlined. With that off his chest, "O. P."--as he was affection-ately known--and 23 other prominent citizens promptly resigned their memberships from the T.D.L. League President Sheldon declared the resignations would not change his position against opposition of bonds for the college.

Dr. Lee Rice, physician and one of the resignees, sharply criti-cized the League's opposition to the issues and requested that his name appear publicly--newspapers obliged--in a strong stand against "your ideas and attitudes."

A disappointed Schnabel remarked: "Bexar County missed the biggest bargain since Randolph Field was obtained for the County." (Schnabel returned to his day job of selling insurance and became widely known for his real penchant to stop on the streets and plazas of San Antonio and pick up trash; provide free trash barrels downtown; and later lead the Beautify San Antonio Association.)

Schnabel and his cohorts had to lick their individual and collective wounded pride when the final results of the election were tallied and the new district dream had been defeated by a small margin--a very close call!

Creation of the district: FOR, 3,425; AGAINST, 3,508.

Bond issue: FOR, 3,326; AGAINST, 3,485

Maintenance tax: FOR, 3,350; AGAINST, 3,541

Total votes cast: 6,923.

Unofficially, the unopposed trustee candidates endorsed by the district proponents were elected to a paper board--offices in a non-existent school district.

Election Critique Points to Future District Try--An immediate critique of the voting in each of the 195 polling places indicated clearly that all of the propositions lost in the County rural precincts. Commissioner Rudy W. Stappenbach blamed the use of paper ballots as not being secret and that affected the outcome.

Schnabel considered contesting the election because of certain voting irregularities in precincts where he noted 264 illegal votes were cast. J. O. Loftin said to the press that there was a possibility of starting a drive to create a "union district" rather than a county-wide area, leaving out the rural precincts where voters had opposed financing the college. Loftin warned, however, that if a union district (composed of two or more school districts) was to be created, out-of-district residents would have to pay more tuition costs if they enrolled than students residing within the tax district boundaries. Loftin's prediction would come to pass!

A few days after speaking to reporters, President Loftin filed a 10-page, typewritten "Report on the Junior College Election," addressed to his immediate superior in the system, Superintendent of Schools I. E. Stutsman. Loftin began his review with the campaign, citing the formation of the Organizing committee with the initial seven citizens--soon to be enlarged to 32 members--at a call meeting of the Patron-Student Association of San Antonio Junior College. O. P. Schnabel was named chairman. Loftin lauded O. P.'s "untiring leadership."

Loftin verified the fact that during the eight weeks of the campaign, every newspaper in the County endorsed the campaign and ran

117 favorable news stories. Eleven paid notices (ads) were printed in local papers. A list of 25 different "freebies" donated by printers, firms and individuals, including: the petitions for the propositions and candidates for office, various pamphlets, windshield stickers, badges, street car placards, student directories, post card announcements, letters, lists of voting places, etc. Free and paid radio addresses and continuing spot announcements were broadcast over five radio stations in San Antonio.

The sequence of events to call the election was succinctly outlined by Loftin--probably just in case of another go-round--from the first-step approval of the County Board of Education trustees to validation of signatures by the County Tax-Assessor, through the State Superintendent of Instruction to the State Board of Education, then back to the Bexar County Commissioners Court, which was given the mandate to call the election within 30 days.

Besides the work of getting the general petitions signed by property taxpayers to call an election, a second petition was needed for at least two per cent of the qualified voters to sign requesting the names of seven citizens to be placed on ballots as candidates for trustees if the new district were to be formed. The Texas Attorney General was asked and gave his opinion that the County must bear costs of the election.

Loftin wrote in his report that just 10 days prior to the election, the Taxpayers Defense League--after polling about 110 negative votes out of a total membership of more than 400 individuals--"opened a barrage of expensive display advertisements condemning the Organizing Committee as 'unpatriotic' asking for a bond issue during the defense period."

The election was held without supervisors, and in many cases with only two election officials. Irregularities were outlined, for examples: (1) out of 108 of the 136 boxes in the City, 264 names of voters in the election did not appear on poll lists; (2) 65 voters who affirmed property ownership within the precinct had no record of such ownership on the various rolls. Hours polls were open was questioned in four cases; many ballots were thrown out for reasons unknown.

President Loftin made four observations after what he said were several days of post-election reflection and conferences:

(1) Many hundreds of citizens who favored the junior college did not trouble themselves to vote because they thought all propositions would carry without their efforts.

(2) The total vote within the metropolitan area was favorable to all three propositions.

(3) More than 200 net votes were lost in a few rural boxes.

(4) County Judge Anderson, Justice Corrigan and Commissioner of Fire and Police Anderson were conspicuously in favor of the entire proposition.

In his conclusion, Loftin advised Superintendent Stutsman that the College is more favorably publicized now than at any previous period of its existence; growth and field of service is assured; the San Antonio Junior College should carry on under the present control until the most propitious time for the creation of a union junior college-- including the San Antonio metropolitan area, but omitting the rural folks who expressed opposition this time. He ended the text of the report--before attaching six pages of statistics and tables of analysis of the election and comparisons with other junior colleges in Texas--on a rather lofty note:

> The college can and probably will be called upon to offer defense training of technicians, nurses, engineers and basic training for aviators. The teaching staff with some excellent equipment stands ready to serve the community and nation to the full limit of its capacity.

So much, coming from an experienced administrator who had been on the job only three months.

For years after the failed election of November 1941, President Loftin liked to recount a favorite anecdote of an encounter on the far east side of San Antonio--exactly where in the County is dimmed by time 60 years later--when he stopped in at a polling place while "making his rounds" on election day. Two women serving as election officials said by noon that nobody had come in to vote. So, Loftin said he went out and bought lunches and returned to the polling place. Still, no voters. He exchanged a little more banter as the women ate lunch, then left feeling a bounce in his step for the small deed and feeling pretty good about the possibility of picking up at least two "yes" votes from newly made friends. When the votes were canvassed, there were only two votes cast in the particular polling place: both "NO" votes!

Even "Red" Loftin could still chuckle about his folly many years later. Someday someone will actually check the voting places and determine whether there were only two votes cast--two "NO" votes--at an East Bexar County box. Meanwhile, the researcher really doesn't know that detail. Why ruin a good story by a great storyteller and tarnish the memory of Mr. Loftin's amusement in telling it...over...and over?

"ABOVE AND BEYOND THE CALL..."

LT. COLONEL ROBERT GEORGE COLE, USA
Medal of Honor, by the Congress

Miss Mary McGill--diminutive in stature, but not in verve, as she taught Spanish and French at San Antonio Junior College since 1930--kept a personal scrapbook of memories of persons other than herself. Pasted entries were mostly newspaper clippings of stories and photos of events in the lives of hundreds of her former students, *e.g.*, weddings, social activities, military service records and many obituaries.

Two pages of clippings featured Robert G. Cole who was born March 19, 1915 at Fort Sam Houston; he was the son of Army physician Lt. Col. Clarence and Mrs. Clara Hoff Cole. His father died in 1918 at the post as the colonel was preparing to embark for Europe with his laboratory unit. His widowed mother later taught at local schools including Nathaniel Hawthorne and Mark Twain Junior High Schools. Young Cole (Robert to family, "R.G." to friends and "Bob" to others) attended Main Avenue High School and Thomas Jefferson High School where he was graduated in June 1933.

Cole enrolled at San Antonio Junior College in September 1933 and continued studies during the Spring Semester 1934, earning 30 semester hours credit. In addition to Miss McGill's French class, Bob Cole's other instructors included Miss Mamie McLain, English; Lena Koch, history; O. H. Hamilton and J. E. Nelson, mathematics; and James A. Hurry, physics.

His name often appeared in *The Junior Ranger*, especially for his prowess in football and basketball intramural games, but mentioned a few times in the campus gossip column.

Some of his friends and classmates also making the news that year were: Stanley Schmidt, William Arlitt, Roland Crutcher, Jean Longwith, John H. Wood, John Braubach, Woodrow Wendt, Doris Burrows, Marion Longaker, Lois Riedner, John Cary, Starley Alford, John Allen, Louise Kahle, Wyatt Simon, Bobby Byrd, Vic Koenig, Raymond Dowdy, Phyllis Wegner, Wyatt Simon, William Conway, Lorraine Brockman, Paulita Benkendorfer, Jack Hein and Marjorie Kalteyer.

Add the names of Mary Puckett, Katherine Smith, Conrad Kollenberg, Hugh Smith, Walter Lehr, Bill Swearingen, Hugh Reveley, Parr Krumb, Vincent Stucke, Sterling Freeborn and others who were on the campus.

While his attendance of nine months was short, Cole would make his own indelible mark on the world stage and bring great credit to SAJC. Miss McGill was there to clip bits of history about one of her former students: a news story and photos depict his mother and his wife, seen holding the hand of toddler Bruce (at age 18 months) as his mother accepted the Medal of Honor awarded posthumously by Congress from Major General Jonathan Anderson. Some 1,000 soldiers passed the reviewing stand on MacArthur Field at Fort Sam Houston on October 30, 1944. The site was very close to where his life began 29 years before and where he had played as a child.

The significance of that citation has not been lost; moreover, it has been perpetuated. Thomas E. Moseley, himself a graduate of San Antonio College whose career in education included 16 years as the Superintendent of Schools at Fort Sam Houston school district, made sure that every student attending the Robert G. Cole Junior/Senior High School knows the sacrifice and legacy of the school's namesake. The student handbook continues to pay tribute to Lt. Col. Cole for his exploits and bravery in combat. One of those former students so inculcated with the history is Shaquille O'Neal of Cole HS Class of 1989 and professional basketball fame. Another familiar name is Alan Keyes: diplomat, and media personality who made a bid for the Republican nomination for president in 2000. Keyes was president of the Student Council in the late 1960s. Many children of the namesake's West Point classmates also attended Cole.

After attending SAJC, Cole was selected for the USMA Preparatory Academy at Fort Sam Houston/Camp Bullis. In July 1935, he became "Plebe" Cadet Cole at the U.S. Military Academy at West

Point, New York. He confided that his intense grilling in French class by Miss McGill was a saving grace, permitting him to earn the Bachelor of Science in Engineering and to receive his commission as second lieutenant and assignment to the Fifteenth Infantry Regiment. In February 1941, he was selected as one of 20 original regular army officers to staff the newly formed 501st Parachute Infantry Battalion which was the first tactical airborne unit in U.S. Army history. Later that year Robert was in the cadre of officers transferred to the newly-formed 502nd Parachute Infantry Regiment, the foundation unit for the new 101st Airborne Division activated in 1941. He was a pioneer paratroop officer at the genesis of the USA airborne organization. Cole took command of the 3rd Battalion, 502nd Parachute Infantry of the 101st Airborne Division after promotion to Lt. Colonel at age 28 years--just 10 years earlier he had been a student at SAJC.

His battalion arrived in England in September 1943 to begin intensive combat training which lasted until that fateful launch on D-Day, June 6, 1944.

On that same Tuesday--June 6, 1944--the edition of *The Atlanta Journal* provides excellent insight into Cole's place on the stage of world history with a front-page, breaking-news story under the byline of Wright Bryan, 39, managing editor of the paper on assignment in England since September 1943 covering the war. At an Army Air Corps base of the Ninth Troop Carrier Command "somewhere near London" (after censorship was relaxed, it was known to be Greenham Common Airdrome), correspondent Bryan and Robert Cole would have a chance meeting hours before "H"-hour of "Operation Overload."

Stories and photos in family records reveal that General Dwight D. Eisenhower, Supreme Allied Commander in Europe--who had been up since 3 o'clock in the morning checking weather reports before ordering the invasion--visited the marshaling area at about 1900 hours on June 5, talking with troopers, asking names and hometowns, about civilian jobs, hobbies and other tension-diverting chat. He gave the order of the day, which in part told the paratroopers making last-minute checks of their heavy gear: "Full victory, nothing else..." as their airborne armada readied for take off into an uncertain destiny across the English Channel; the commencement of an invasion of immense proportion and complexity.

It was a rare short reunion for General "Ike" and Robert who had served together in the 15th Infantry at Fort Lewis, Washington four years earlier as colonel and second lieutenant, respectively. Both had experienced extraordinary rapid rise in ranks over the intervening years. They were photographed as they talked informally and stood somewhat incongruously with the Supreme Commander attired in Class "A" Winter Service Uniform and the lieutenant colonel battalion commander in combat dress with black-smudged face, but smiling--always smiling, as was his personal trait.

In the pre-dawn hours of June 6th, serials of planes circled in V-formations before heading eastward. Within hours, newsman Bryan and paratroop leader Cole aboard "Snooty"--a C-47 "skytrain" aircraft of venerable design just off the assembly line in California--would become famous the world over. Bryan's news sense recorded flight details and conversations of Cole reassuring his lead "stick" of 18 paratroopers of readiness and asking each man if he needed something. He asked "doc" to give out pills to ward off air sickness; visited with each trooper and urged men to get as comfortable as possible and to sleep a little, if they could. Bryan was perspiring, but Cole said he was "cold" near the rear open door 30 minutes before jump time. An almost full moon temporarily illuminated the gray chop in the Channel; soon empty beaches would be bare no longer. Cole instructed each man to check equipment and static-line hookups before the pilot flashed the green jump-light signal and the chutists cleared the plane in less than 15 seconds. All except one disconsolate whose body was slammed against the door frame so hard that he was dazed and unable to jump.

"Snooty" was over France only 11 minutes, but started picking up tracer fire without hits as it headed for England with Bryan trying to reassure the paratrooper who worried about what his buddies might think because the standing order was that all were to be deployed and no paratrooper was to return to the United Kingdom. Dawn revealed the first wave of Allied naval vessels heading for Normandy.

After "Snooty" landed safely back at the base, Bryan flagged a jeep and made a 50-mile race to London and the BBC studio. Shortly after 9:33 a.m. London time--or 3:15 a.m. in Atlanta where Bryan's wife waited after an alert from the New York studios to tune in NBC radio--he began his 15-minute, eyewitness broadcast preceded by a one-sentence lead-in by the Allied Command and brief tape-recorded statements by King George VI and President Franklin D. Roosevelt.

In a calm, resonant voice with a South Carolinian accent Wright Bryan scooped 600 reporters as the "first man to come back from the invasion and to report to the nation by air" on one of the biggest stories of the century. He mentioned Lt. Col. Robert G. Cole of San Antonio,

Texas several times during the broadcast and, of course, the role played by "Snooty."

"Snooty" survived the war and returned to the United States in August 1945; hired out for flights with several airlines before being honorably deactivated in June 1963, after logging 32,181 hours of service. "Snooty" has been retired to permanent static display at the Oregon Museum of Science and Technology in Corvallis as a principal artifact of the event.

Bryan covered the Allies further advances across Europe; broadcast live the liberation of Paris; was wounded in the leg and captured by the Germans on September 12, 1944. He spent five months in a POW camp in Poland, until freed by Russian troops in January 1945. He returned to *The Atlanta Journal* as editor during 1946 to 1954; edited another paper until he served as Vice-President for Development at Clemson University, South Carolina during 1963 to 1970. It was a proud moment in 1947 when General Eisenhower pinned the Medal of Freedom on Bryan's civilian lapel for services as a war correspondent in ceremony before many of his colleagues in the National Press Club.

Returning to the main subject of this profile: Lt. Col. Cole and his 3rd Battalion, with help from the 502nd PIR of the 101st, encountered intense fighting against the German fortified positions north of Carentan, southwest of Utah Beach on June 11, 1944. History buffs can pinpoint the area because Steven Spielberg's epic war film "Saving Private Ryan" used the famed 101st Airborne Division as the principal characters in the reenactment. Also, the climactic scene at the end of the film--a film, critics warn, not to be construed as a documentary--apparently was based on the unit's defense of Carentan on June 13, 1944. Military analysts say that the battle was not fought against the German 2nd Panzer Division as portrayed in the film, however. Field Marshal Rommel ordered the town to be retaken after giving it up the day before. Carentan was a strategic link to Utah and Omaha beaches. Tom Hanks and his squad in the movie did search for the real-life Private Ryan between June 10 and June 13, roughly.

The digression of military detail and the movie review from the main story serves to set the "real stage" for the quotation from the Medal of Honor Citation for Valor of Lieutenant Colonel Robert G. Cole, General Order No. 79, dated October 4, 1944. The Citation:

> For gallantry and intrepidity at the risk of his own
> life, above and beyond the call of duty on 11 June 1944, in
> France. Lt. Col. Cole was personally leading his battalion

in forcing the last four bridges on the road to Carentan when his entire unit was suddenly pinned to the ground by intense and withering enemy rifle, machinegun, mortar and artillery fire placed upon them from well-prepared and heavily fortified positions within 150 yards of the foremost enemy elements. After the devastating and unceasing enemy fire had for over one hour prevented any move and inflicted numerous casualties, Lt. Col. Cole, observing this almost hopeless situation, courageously issued orders to assault the enemy positions with fixed bayonets. With utter disregard for his own safety and completely ignoring the enemy fire, he rose to his feet in front of his battalion and with a drawn pistol shouted to his men to follow him in the assault. Catching up a fallen man's rifle and bayonet, he charged on and led the remnants of his battalion across the bullet-swept open ground into the enemy position. His heroic and valiant action in so inspiring his men resulted in the complete establishment of our bridgehead across the Douve River. The cool fearlessness, personal bravery and outstanding leadership displayed by Lt. Col. Cole reflect great credit upon himself and are worthy of the highest praise in the military service.

This Citation was signed by President Franklin D. Roosevelt who five years earlier had delivered the Commencement address to Cole's West Point graduating class.

He was the first member of the 101st to be awarded the Medal of Honor. There would be only one other Division recipient of the medal during WWII: Pfc. Joseph Mann who, ironically, died on the same battlefield near Best, Holland and on the same day--September 18th--as Lt. Col. Cole. Mann sacrificed himself when he fell on a live grenade to save the lives of his trench mates. [Cole was one of only two native San Antonians to receive the medal. Staff Sergeant William P. Bordelon, born December 25, 1920, was a U.S. Marine killed in action on Tarawa, Gilbert Islands November 20, 1943. No record was found of his possible attendance at San Antonio College.]

The 502nd Parachute Infantry Regiment was awarded three Presidential Unit Citations and was the first sub-unit to be awarded the newly authorized designation for distinguished action in France. The Division was selected by General "Ike" as his personal honor guard. France awarded the Croix de Guerre with Palm to the regiment citing the heroism of a "splendid Airborne unit" which helped to liberate France. Historian Stephen Ambrose probably had it right when he concluded in *Citizen Soldier* that the 101st Airborne was the best of the approximately 90 U.S. Army divisions in WWII.

After Carentan, the rest of June and into early July 1944, the 101st encountered relatively light offensive action before withdrawing to England on July 11th for refitting and training of replacements. Operation "Market Garden" was the code name for the next battle which began on September 17, 1944, when the 502nd was assigned to capture bridges at Best heavily defended by German troops in the area of Zon-St. Oedenrode-Eindhoven in Holland.

An eyewitness reported heavy artillery fire from the enemy was causing many casualties. Cole called for close air support, but when U.S. fighters strafed the area they began hitting the American position. He ran out to direct the laying of more identification panels to direct the P-47 pilots to the enemy lodgements. It worked. While observing a circling plane from an exposed position, Cole was hit in the head by a bullet fired by a sniper hidden in a house about 100 yards away, according to an obituary written by a West Point classmate, Lt. General Harry W. O. Kinnard of the 101st. Cole's executive officer, Major John Stopka, took command and wrote to Cole's wife Allie Mae in San Antonio describing that fateful day of September 18, 1944, when things seemed "hopeless" to Stopka and the men. As word spread of the "Chief's" death, he wrote, the men were told to "get going"--and they went as if mad toward the enemy.

"The men were so frustrated they overran the German positions, killing 600 and capturing 1,000 in a couple of hours. All this because the men knew this was the way the Chief would want it. We are all very proud to have served under such a great soldier..." (excerpt from *The Screaming Eagle*, January-February issue, 1996).

Lt. Col. Cole's body is interred in an immaculately maintained cemetery in Margraten, Holland. His headstone is specifically identified and of a design reserved for MOH recipients. Margraten contains approximately 8,800 single interments, of which 220 or so are Cole's paratrooper brethren. R.I.P.

United Press War Correspondent Walter Cronkite filed a story on October 24, 1944 reporting that Lt. Col. Robert Cole deserved the MOH for action at Carentan, but that another recommendation should be stacked up behind it for his bravery in Holland. The *Stars and Stripes* issue of November 11 printed that Cole was a hero "twice over" and should be considered for another MOH. The story bore a "UP" attribution and could have emanated from Cronkite's article. Cronkite and other writers apparently were unaware that regulations prohibited multiple awards of the MOH, the presumption being that the medal has unique prestige.

[Note: Personal contact was made in 2001 and continues between Robert Bruce Cole--the toddler has grown into a robustly handsome man greatly favoring photographs of his father--and the writer for the exchange of information. Bruce has made valuable contributions to the profile in the forms of family data and military details. His mother, Allie Mae (Wilson) Cole, passed away in December 2000.

[At the wedding of my brother Robert and his bride Jean Proffitt in Asheville, North Carolina in July 1953, I met Wright Bryan, a first cousin of Jean's mother who was a Bryan. Aware of his background in journalism, we exchanged some newspaper shop talk. Regretably, I did not know then the Robert Cole story or Bryan's connection to him. Fast-forward in time to 1990 when brother Bob sent a war-time tape featuring Wright Bryan to me. The broadcast tape had been laying latently until Ellen (Mrs. Wright Bryan) and son, Bill Bryan, sent it to Bob and Jean Weynand in the summer of 1989. With permission, the tape became a central feature for a program on June 1, 1990 when the San Antonio Kiwanis Club honored World War II service men and other veterans with a "Lest We Forget" theme built around the D-Day invitation. Robert Cole and Wright Bryan were specifically recognized by D-Day veteran Major Frank Prassel (Purple Heart recipient), Cole Superintendent Tom Moseley and Jerome Weynand. A 45-minute, cassette recording was sent to the Bryans with compliments of the Kiwanians. Ellen acknowledged that she and Wright Bryan enjoyed listening to the Kiwanis program which featured his broadcasts and Colonel Cole; that it brought back many memories...They had not known of the namesake school.

[Wright Bryan died in February 1991 at age 85, but not without knowing full well how he helped to bring Robert Cole's heroic deeds to life anachronously. And for that we are most grateful.]

5.
CREATION OF THE
JUNIOR COLLEGE DISTRICT

Loftin's Promise Rekindled--True to his word--in the 1941 post-election critique of the slim-margin defeat of the proposition to create a separate junior college district--President J. O. Loftin had vowed to revisit the concept at "the most propitious time." In that failed election, proponents appeared confident that taxpayers would vote "FOR" the establishment of a stand-alone college district with tax options to be governed by its own elected trustees on a county-wide basis. That is, everyone except that 93-vote majority of the 6,923 voters who went to the polls and voted "NO" on the district plan. Loftin said it was the rural voters who defeated the issue.

His concept in the Fall 1944 was the same theory he outlined in the November 1941 review to the school board and the general public in the summary that follows: shrink the area of the proposed district to the metropolitan core and omit rural precincts from the plan to combine multi-school districts to enhance a victory. World War II was still raging in the European and Pacific Theaters, but Loftin sensed that it was time now to enter a joint election with public schools, county and city--all of which were proposing other "post-war" development projects.

Members of the San Antonio Junior Chamber of Commerce, the energetic generation of "pushers and shakers," again put their full support as hardworking individuals and sponsorship as an organization to begin a petition drive to get signatures of property owners and to inform the general public in an election campaign. O. Z. Gulledge served as Jaycee president and Jimmy Rogers was the chairman of the education committee during this crucial period in 1944, and continuing for the next year until the election was held. In retrospect, the 1941 district and bond election proponents had only a few months to inform and garner support from the public.

Loftin advised all planners and various constituents that the same procedures followed in the 1941 call would be necessary to follow at the local and state levels with one addition: clearance would be needed from a new agency called the "Post War Planning Board" composed of directors representing the City of San Antonio and Bexar County. The board had the mandate to review various bond issues for improvements in streets, sewers, and buildings sought by governmental entities. The Taxpayers' Defense League again posed as a watchdog over unnecessary taxation and spending. Meetings were not always harmonious. As far back as the summer of 1944, Loftin and School Superintendent I. E. Stutsman had succeeded in getting a resolution passed by the Board of Education to attach an additional $1 million to the total bond package being considered by the SAISD, but to be used solely for improvements at the junior college after the establishment of an independent San Antonio Junior College. The resolution was discussed and rejected by the Post War Planning Board.

The issue remained latent without any further action until the school board passed another resolution on July 24, 1945, going a step further, to include the key word "support" to a junior college bond call (*San Antonio Express*, July 25, 1945).

President Loftin revealed on October 4, 1944 that petition forms for signatures of property owners were being circulated as the first step in calling an election for the formation of a new junior college and to issue bonds in the sum of $940,000 for buildings. He outlined to the press that the Junior Chamber of Commerce was seeking 10 per cent of the qualified voters within the proposed district to lend their signatures in support of an election call that included electing a board of trustees authorized to levy and collect annual taxes not to exceed 8 cents based on each $100 on the County valuation for the purpose of maintaining a junior college. Trustees also would be authorized to issue bonds, to be amortized over a 30-year period with interest rates not to exceed 2 per cent per annum, for the construction of the college.

The proposed district--and target area for taxpayers within--was comprised of the San Antonio Independent School District, Alamo Heights, Los Angeles Heights, South San Antonio, and Harlandale Independent School Districts; also included were Common School Districts Numbers 9, 11, 16, 25, 41, and 49, more commonly known (not in order) as Olmos Park, Serna, W.W. White, Hot Wells, Edgewood and Kirby Common School Districts. The area within the metes-and-bounds district was about 154 square miles.

The petition drive was an outgrowth of Loftin's request made to the Planning Board directors that a new junior college should be included in their overall postwar plans. The board considered the project "meritorius," and referred the proposal to its finance and engineering committee for consideration and report, said E. A. Baugh, the manager of the board at this stage (*San Antonio News*, October 4, 1944). [A year later--on October 3, 1945--Baugh resigned just before the election, but with no cause to believe there was any connection between the election and his departure.] Some notable leaders on the board during 1944-1945 were Alex Thomas, C. W. Miller, John Zeller, H. B. Zachry and Mayor Gus Mauermann.

On December 16, 1944, it was announced that in two months 5,700 signatures (more than enough) of taxpayers within the proposed district had been collected on the petition. Stacks of sheets bearing the signatures were turned over to the Bexar County Board of Education for initial validity checks by County Superintendent R. W. May, Board President C. G. Carter, and Board Vice-President Andrew H. Young. Petition forms then were handed to the County Commissioners Court; in turn, sent to the County Tax Assessor-Collector for determination of property-owner qualification; finally, the petition arrived in Austin for a last look by the State Board of Education.

Loftin profusely credited and praised all who had hit the streets in the signature drive; he especially singled out students at San Antonio Junior College and St. Philip's College (which also had an interest in the outcome of the election) for assistance to the Jaycees and who accounted for at least 2,000 signatures on the petition. He told the students that he regretted that any future building construction would be delayed beyond their short terms spent on the campuses. But, he said, they could take great pride in knowing they had a part in building it and seeing other students benefit by expanded and elaborate facilities envisioned.

"Start now talking to your friends, urging them to be busy on that election day," (*The Junior Ranger*, February 8, 1945), he added.

Loftin used his weekly column, "Our President's Message," in *The Ranger* to further the call to action by voters at the proposed election. He wrote of his aspiration to provide new facilities to better serve students at San Antonio Junior College and St. Philip's College as follows:

> Students will be interested to know that all hurdles have been made which are necessary to get the new Union Junior College proposed before the voters of Greater San Antonio. There are four propositions, namely (1) Shall a new Junior College District be formed comprising Greater San Antonio? (2) Shall a bond issue be voted? (3) Shall a tax rate of eight cents on the County valuation be voted? (4) Shall there be a Board of Trustees? (*The Junior Ranger*, March 5, 1945).

He foresaw the proposed issues to be decided in a joint election with public schools, the city and county, which also are proposing post-war projects. The President called on all Junior College faculty, students, and parents to work quietly among their friends so that a large favorable vote may go to the polls on election day, which he predicted could be as late as June 1945.

"Now or Never!" Battle Cry--Students immediately picked up on the call to action by their president. They understood that benefits of a new and finer campus would come to fruition after they had completed their time at SAJC. An editorial appearing in *The Junior Ranger* issue of April 28, 1945, outlined that in "not many weeks hence, the qualified voters of San Antonio and contiguous territory will go to the polls to approve an expansive program for San Antonio Junior College."

The editorialist commented on the careful and intelligent planning and hard work; the diligent labor of several groups of people; the definite plans and cost estimates that have been drafted; business, industrial, and professional leaders support the program and the nominal tax needed to realize the need of the young people in the community to be trained in skills and technical work beyond the high school level; the program emphasizes just as strongly the cultural education of youth in the liberal arts and professional fields.

This expansive program for the Junior College is imperative...Our present facilities are no longer adequate...We have reached the limit of possible expansion under our existing setup. With us it's **Expand or Contract--Now or Never!**

[The staff of the weekly campus newspaper was headed by Editor Geraldine Long and Associate Editor Joyce Vance, either or both of whom may have written the editorial. Their newsroom colleagues who may have had a part in the editorial stance were reporters Barbara Winterborne, Marjorie Wynkoop, Bobbie Willis and Pat Loftin (daughter of J. O. Loftin). The sports writer was Charles Anderson (who had just received his appointment to West Point and a future as colonel); he was the son of County Judge Charles W. Anderson. Herbert Haynes served as business manager. Faculty sponsor was Lillian M. Nelson, English professor and wife of former Director J. E. Nelson.]

With the year-long wait now over, the election was set for October 30, 1945. The Junior Chamber of Commerce billed the case before the public as a "Post War Project" in the two-sided, eight-panels brochure entitled "A New Junior College for San Antonio." In it they posed questions and gave the answers to inform the voter as to the need, plans and proposed buildings for San Antonio Junior College and St. Philip's College; outlined the location aspects and cited the organization's sponsorship of the project to bring a "Class A" junior college to greater San Antonio.

The campaign flyer also listed endorsements by the San Antonio Board of Education, Bexar County Board of Education, State Board of Education, and the San Antonio and Bexar County Planning Board (which was credited with financing plans and cost estimates). All that was needed at this point, the Jaycees said, was approval of the property owners as voting citizens within the 11 school districts comprising the proposed Union Junior College District. (See Appendix P for the full text.)

Decals for use on notebooks or automobiles were distributed on the campus. The four-inch diameter sticker with orange print on a white background simply read: "San Antonio's JUNIOR COLLEGE Needs Buildings."

On October 15, 1945, two weeks before the election, a one-page outline of the needs of the SAISD was addressed to parents and patrons of San Antonio's inner-city school district. The "laundry list" of items included additional classrooms to relieve crowded conditions; correct bad sanitary conditions in some schools; add health and physical education facilities; expand cafeteria services; provide more shops and laboratories to offer vocational and technical training; improve lighting, ventilation, and heating in schools. Trustees had worked more than a year with staff to settle on a total need package of $2,186,000 to make these improvements. The bonds would be amortized at a cost of 5 cents for each $100 valuation.

The SAISD proposal had the approval of the Planning Board. Paul Adams, acting president of the San Antonio Board of Education, signed the letter. (Adams had served as vice-president until he succeeded Randle Taylor, a short-term president who resigned on July 25, 1945, stating that he had moved outside the district to a residence in Alamo Heights.)

Just a week before the election, Loftin and the Jaycees conspired to issue their own letter of appeal as follows:

SAN ANTONIO JUNIOR COLLEGE
October 22, 1945

Dear Friends:

The San Antonio Junior College numbers you among the many friends who have sent their sons and daughters to its campus.

You, more than any one else, realize the splendid school advantages that have been afforded the San Antonio youth for many years at the old German-English plant on South Alamo Street. You also know the handicaps under which the college faculty have labored because of the antiquated buildings.

On October 30, an opportunity for a new building and a greater program will come through an election to be held jointly with the San Antonio schools and a new Junior College organization.

May we count on you to vote and influence your friends to vote for the new Junior College and Public School improvements?

San Antonio Junior College Faculty
By J. O. Loftin, President

San Antonio Junior Chamber of Commerce
By Jimmy Rogers, Chairman, Educational Committee

Election Results: Big Win for Students--If there is such a good thing as knowing how or when to select the right climate in which to hold a school bond election, the Fall 1945 was not the best of possible times, politically speaking. Two special county elections had been held on July 25 and August 25 without much fanfare.

The City of San Antonio was next up at the polls and held a public works bond election on September 25th, barely to eke out wins in five of the six major proposals with a total price tag of $5.7 million. Fewer than 12,000 property-owning voters cast ballots with final tallies as follows: city's share of an inter-regional highway won by 878 votes; airport expansion passed by 348 votes; streets and bridges construction won by only 30 votes; new garbage incinerator was favored by a margin of 683; four new fire stations won by just 128 votes, but the fire alarm system failed by a mere 10 votes (*San Antonio Express*, October 4, 1945).

There was a long, bickering feud over election results that smoldered, but was kept alive in the press from September 26 until November 1, when a petition contesting the election was filed with Bexar County District Court Clerk Hart McCormick. Names on the petition were G. J. Lucchese, H. H. Theis, and E. H. Maddox, the fronts for about 25 more protesters. They set forth charges regarding 556 voters who had not paid their 1944 poll tax; complained about 3,318 "illegal and void" votes that were cast on voting machines and another 54 votes cast on paper ballots that were suspect; the general mishandling of absentee ballots; assailed action of the City Council to sit as a canvassing board and objected to the council calling in certain election judges to amend official vote counts.

City Tax Commissioner Alfred Callaghan spearheaded the opposition to the improvements package. The in-fighting and the whole issue was a distraction, at least, to the proponents in the campaign for school bonds and, perhaps, to the public.

[Especially disheartening was the Callaghan-led opposition to defeat at the polls an item to finance a memorial to World War II dead (*San Antonio Express*, November 2, 1945).]

Another distracting, pre-election issue was aired in newspapers on October 2, when County Commissioners Bob Uhr and Sam Anderson objected to the County paying for the election costs of the SAISD and the junior college elections at polls outside the school district limits because the County lacked funds. County Judge Charles W. Anderson believed the County should assume some obligation and pay its share.

The SAISD had wanted the County to pay expenses for all voting machine stations. Schools use of voting machines was not at issue.

Bexar County Commissioners' Court--made up of the judge and four precinct commissioners--passed the coveted order calling an election for October 30, 1945 to permit voters to consider creation of a San Antonio Junior College District. The vote was unanimous after L. J. Gittinger, assistant district attorney, advised the court that the election was legal after a question had been raised whether validation of the bonds, if voted, would be legal. Gittinger also assured the court that the voters' petition held since December 1944 was still valid. The court passed an order permitting the SAISD to have rental use of 20 voting machines; the County agreed to pay the cost of the junior college election in the 10 boxes located outside the school district boundaries.

Distractions of a different sort in the form of money drives in the postwar awakening were noted as follows:

Almost daily reminders appeared in the three daily newspapers-- some as display ads paid for by Joske's of Texas and Frost Bros. stores-- urging San Antonians to "please" buy E-Bonds" and to support the local Community War Chest. During October, plaintive cries by notable leaders called for citizens to make their commitments to the 57 agencies who faced budget shortfalls because the fund drive was off by over $300,000 toward making the Chest's goal of $830,000. Just 10,000 more pledges at $20 per person would meet the challenge for charities, campaigners said.

Victory in Europe came in May 1945, a month after President Franklin D. Roosevelt died April 12, 1945; victory over the Japanese in late summer was finalized in the surrender treaty September 2, 1945. Uncle Sam still sought $11 billion to be raised by December 8 to help pay for WW II costs through loans now called "Victory Bonds" rather than the previously named "War Bonds." Bexar County was asked to raise $18.2 million of the $43.6 million goal to be raised in 55 South Texas counties. The drive was to be the eighth and "last one" by the United States government.

Banks and building and loan associations ran newspaper ads to attract applicants for Federal Home Administration backed loans, now that war-time restrictions had been removed for would-be homeowners.

Amidst all these offers to spend their money, property owners received a reminder of the approaching election in the biggest headline, yet, which appeared in the *San Antonio Express*, October 14, 1945, as follows: "Seven Junior College Trustees To Be Named in School

Election." The storyline outlined the proposal for $940,000 in bonds and the levying of an 8-cent tax rate to be decided in the ballot on October 30th in the San Antonio Junior College election.

The article informed the public that the Junior Chamber of Commerce had pre-selected seven candidates whose names were proffered to the Commissioners' Court on a separate petition containing 1,400 signers. The candidates were as follows:

Ernest A. Baetz, 134 Cedar St., near Brackenridge High School, a banker (and former president of the national Junior Chamber of Commerce organization); Leo Brewer, 107 E. Gramercy, near northside residence, attorney, and former trustee and chairman of the San Antonio Board of Education; Lee A. Christy, 231 Cardinal in the Alamo Heights suburb, building contractor; Jesse N. Fletcher, 102 Thomas Jefferson Drive (at the corner of Wilson Drive across from Jefferson High School), insurance agency manager (who served as president of the local Jaycees in 1936 and named Outstanding Young Man in San Antonio in 1938, and a former student at SAJC); E. H. Keator, 114 Geneseo Road in Terrell Hills, an independent oil operator and president of the San Antonio Symphony Society; Walter W. McAllister (Sr.), 138 E. Huisache, near northside, building and loan association executive (and an emerging leader in the development of San Antonio); and G. S. McCreless, 1028 Drexel Avenue, in the Highland Park area of the southeast side of San Antonio. These men all knew each other and, in some cases, were good friends; three were fellow members in the Kiwanis Club of San Antonio.

If elected--there was no opposition to the slate drawn by the sponsors--trustees would draw for staggered terms of two, four and six years.

Three days before the election, a press release by the College made it to print on October 27th in the *San Antonio Express*, extolling the fact that "Students from San Antonio Junior College enter The University of Texas equipped to maintain higher grades than those averaged by grades of other junior colleges," according to a letter sent to President Loftin by E. J. Matthews, registrar and dean of admissions in Austin. He cited a study of records over the preceding six years and determined the average made by SAJC was higher than the state average.

"We have always thought well of San Antonio Junior College and are glad to receive its students. We are greatly interested in the campaign now going on for improvements and we wish for it the highest degree of success," Matthews wrote in the letter.

Following the chronology as found in the *Express*, a lengthy editorial was printed on October 24, expressing much of the same material previously published, but citing the belief held by J. O. Loftin as chief administrator of the college that the junior college would cost the owner of a $3,000 house less than a dollar a year in tax. The editor had not sensed any opposition against the bond proposal going into the final week of the campaign.

A second editorial, this time in a prime spot on page one of the *Express*, dated October 29 and boxed in a 2-column by 5-inches deep border, promoted votes "FOR" both the junior college district and bonds and the public school bond program. In part the editorial read as follows:

> It is high time that this community redeemed its many promises to give San Antonio Junior College the adequate, modern plant which the institution has earned and which San Antonio's credit and reputation demand.

> During the 20 years of the Junior College's life thus far--struggling against the handicaps of old, small, shabby buildings and insufficient equipment--and particularly during the war years--it has served the young people of the San Antonio area well. Many of its graduates have achieved outstanding records for scholarship in the universities and senior colleges. Besides, a great many boys and girls here, who, for financial reasons, could not have gone away to such institutions for two years or longer, have acquired the sturdy groundwork of an education at San Antonio Junior College.

The editorial outlined how $940,000 in bonds and the creation of an independent district would serve to help San Antonio Junior College and St. Philip's College--"whose service record is likewise admirable"-- and also the educational, economic, and social services in the community. The editor pressed for support of the $2,186,000 in improvements slated for the SAISD. "Remedial action by the taxpayers is a 'must' for both causes," the editorial concluded.

Another--but this time shorter--boxed notice appeared on page one of the paper on election morning and summarized (1) creation of the independent district; (2) issuance of the junior college bonds; (3) the need for the $2.186 million city public school bonds. A well-placed story on the same front page called readers' attention with the headline that read "Vital Service of College Is Outlined." The sub-head stated that "Bond Issue Vote Due to Carry, Officials Say."

Loftin was optimistic--just as he had been when on the job three months in the failed election of 1941--that voters this time would respond favorably to the needs as expressed. He noted a "warm feeling" of support in the suburbs. San Antonio would become the second large city in Texas to form a municipal junior college, after the University of Houston founded as a junior college in 1927, he challenged. There were 250 students--35 of whom were veterans--enrolled on the South Alamo campus, but within three years, the College could expect 1,000 students, Loftin predicted. Public school officials also proclaimed their faith in the passage of bonds for improvements.

Thirty polling places were announced by the San Antonio Board of Education which supervised the simultaneous elections. Officials urged any person who has property listed on the tax rolls and whose property lies within the SAISD of the old, six-mile square (36 square miles) city limits, to vote on the school improvement issue. Voters on the junior college issue were required to be property owners in the San Antonio school district or the specified adjacent school districts.

And, well they might have placed their trust in the patrons who, by Tuesday night of October 30th, had voted favorably on all of the propositions, both inside and outside the SAISD boundary. The candidates of junior college trusteeships outlined earlier, were elected.

The early count--total from 27 of 30 precinct boxes reporting--indicated the creation of the junior college district passed by a vote of 3,003 to 1,404 against; the maintenance tax passed 2,886 to 1,461; the bond issue was approved by 2,887 votes for to 1,396 against the proposition. Only 5,077 votes were tallied election night, with three more boxes to come.

The public school repair and renovation package fared well with 2,677 to 917, still missing the votes from the three precincts not reporting.

STOP THE PRESSES! The usually routine procedure to canvass and arrive at official returns, which had been scheduled for the Friday after the successful election on Tuesday, now faced delay. A protest was made at the Friday meeting of the Commissioners' Court by R. S. Menefee, representing himself as a "citizen, taxpayer, and a member of the Property Owners' Protective League," (*San Antonio Express*, November 3, 1945).

Arley V. Knight, legal counsel for the just-created junior college district, sought an immediate vote by the Court, but presiding Judge Anderson granted a postponement of the hearing until Monday, November 5, to allow the seven elected trustees to meet and to organize within the seven days allowed under law. The law also required election returns to be canvassed and certified within 10 days. Knight contended that Menefee had no grounds for his claims of illegality of the election and that the Commissioners' Court was not the proper court for his grievance. Judge Anderson said the canvass was a legal duty of the court.

The district attorney's office entered discussion and ruled that no legal question was involved in Menefee's protest. Opinions were tossed back and forth by all parties in the dispute until the commissioners huddled and completed the tabulation. Total numbers were set for presentation and official action set for 8:30 a.m. Monday, November 5.

Judge Anderson appeared ready to announce the results at the Friday meeting, but held off at the request of Commissioner Sam H. Anderson after he was opposed to immediate action. Students and faculty would have to wait another weekend to be certain that they were going to get a new junior college.

Good to his last words of the previous week, Judge Anderson convened Commissioners' Court Monday morning November 5, and, after taking care of two business items, the next order was to act on the returns of the election: to open, read, examine, and canvass the 6,145 votes on the four propositions in the junior college election. Com. Rudy W. Stappenbech, Sr., moved, the motion was seconded by Com. Sam C. Bennett, and the presiding judge called for a vote to approve passage of the order, resulting as follows: AYES: Commissioners Anderson, Bennett, and Stappenbeck and Judge Charles Anderson. Not voting; Commissioner Uhr. The order was duly carried and passed as summarized in the tallies as follows:

(1) FOR creation of the District	3,594	
AGAINST	<u>1,765</u>	
	1,829	majority
(2) FOR the maintenance tax	3,443	
AGAINST	<u>1,704</u>	
	1,739	majority
(3) FOR the issuance of bonds and tax	3,460	
AGAINST	<u>1,745</u>	
	1,715	majority

(4) FOR TRUSTEES:

Lee A. Christy	3,036 votes
E. A. Baetz	3,227
Jesse N. Fletcher	3,103
E. H. Keator	3,010
W. W. McAllister	3,169
G. S. McCreless	3,147
Leo Brewer	3,156

(Source: Commissioners' Court *Minutes*, October Special Term, November 5, 1945, Vol. 18, pp. 641-642.)

Also present at the meeting of the court were J. O. Loftin, president of the current San Antonio Junior College; Arley V. Knight, attorney for the junior college; S. Benton Davies, assistant Bexar County District Attorney; and R. S. Menefee, member of the Property Owners' Protective League, was also true to his protest that a contest would be made over election results--in fact, he now said a law suit would be filed "soon." (San Antonio Express, November 5, 1945). [By all accounts, Menefee acted as an individual; press reports never identified him as a representative or spokesman for the League.] Menefee had contended that having only 30 consolidated precincts out of 171 was not proper; that the Court had no authority to canvass the votes, and other technical points cited. The election stood.

After the busy morning in the Bexar County Court House to seal the creation of the district, action on the district's organization continued at 419 South Alamo Street on the junior college campus where trustees convened to elect officers and do other business relating to SAJC and St. Philip's College now under their control. Only five of the seven trustees-elect were present, they were Christy, Baetz, Fletcher, Keator and McCreless. McAllister and Brewer were out of the city.

Leslie C. Merrem, a junior college professor and a notary public, administered the oath of office to the five men present. A story and photo featuring the new district and the swearing-in ceremony ran on page 8A of the *San Antonio Express* the next day. Ernest Baetz, banker, who had received the highest number of votes (58 more than McAllister), nominated McAllister in absentia to serve as president; seconded by McCreless; with no other nominations, the motion passed by unanimous vote. Fletcher, who was presiding, called for nominations for vice-president. Christy nominated Fletcher, Baetz seconded the motion; no further names advanced; Fletcher was elected unanimously.

McCreless suggested that in addition to the president and vice-president positions--only offices provided in the law regulating organization of junior college boards--a secretary was needed. His motion prevailed and was the first Resolution (of the thousands more to come) recorded in the *Minutes* of the few-minutes-old board. Christy became secretary, and all three officers served in their positions for many years.

Next in order was to appoint their legal counsel Arley Knight as attorney for the district. President Loftin was asked by the board to prepare and recommend for consideration a business manager and other employees. Discussion was held on contracts for employees hired by the SAISD, but action was postponed until all seven trustees could attend the next meeting. The operation of the junior colleges as part of the public school district would continue for the current academic year which would end August 31, 1946. Then, the ownership and operation would pass to the junior college board.

"Expressions of good will and congratulations" from School Superintendent I. E. Stutsman and Angus Cockrell, 1945-46 president of the Jaycees," prefaced the initial college board meeting," (*San Antonio Express*, November 6, 1945).

***Returning Servicemen Impact Growth*--**Veterans' discharge certificates were being recorded at the rate of 60 to 70 daily in the Bexar County District Clerk's office in October 1945. Since May, Clerk Fred

Huntress had put on three full-time clerks to handle this free service. Already, 2,350 veterans, who wanted to keep a safe record of their honorable discharges which would be needed for educational and other benefits, were the forerunners of thousands more ex-GIs returning to the area.

An "advance party" of over 30 veterans had enrolled in January 1945, in time to start the spring semester of classes at San Antonio Junior College and using their educational benefits earned while in the armed services. Hundreds more would follow the point men in the next two years. The "welcome aboard" sign was put up by students, faculty, and administrators led by President Loftin. He cited the opportunities for veterans to blend in with the existing student body and pledged full assistance from everyone on campus. He said the following:

> The Government has done a generous and yet very
> fair thing in returning men to college who have had their
> work interrupted in the armed services. In our aspirations
> for both veterans and non-veterans, we are thinking con-
> stantly of a new college plant (*The Junior Ranger*,
> February 8, 1945).

The chief of the Veterans' Administration at Waco, Mortimer Woodson, had visited the SAJC campus in October 1944 to interview qualified veterans interested in the "G.I. Bill of Rights," under Public Law 346, to receive a college education. A veteran would be entitled to receive $50 a month if single, or $75 a month if married, while attending college full-time. All connected expenses, such as tuition, fees, books and supplies, would be paid by the Veterans' Administration, he said.

In a public statement aimed at veterans and appearing in the press, Woodson invited those who might be dubious of their rights under the recently enacted "G.I. Bill" to see him on campus for further information.

"The colored soldier will find equal privileges under the Bill," Woodson said, in the invitation for anyone interested to visit the administrative offices and enroll at St. Philip's College (*San Antonio Evening News*, October 5, 1944).

Trustees of the SAISD at their meeting November 14, 1944, quibbled over a title change and pay increase for a coordinator to advise and assist returning veterans who resume their studies in the public schools. Superintendent Stutsman recommended the employee--who had done similar work for the past five months in addition to regular duties--be given a 10-month contract pay increase from $2,807 to $3,600. Action was deferred after President Leo Brewer questioned giving the man a $900 pay increase for handling duties outlined for the job.

[A year later Brewer, an attorney, would don the hat of a junior college trustee--one of seven elected at large in the new district on October 30, 1945.]

Brewer said more about veterans as follows:

> I am in favor of the San Antonio schools doing everything they can to help returning veterans. I am in favor of spending money until it hurts to aid returning veterans, but I am opposed...to the increase in salary on the coat-tails of this humanitarian resolution (*San Antonio Express*, November 15, 1944).

It rained and rained on the first day of classes in September 1946-- after the San Antonio Union Junior College District assumed control of the college on September 1--to the extent that downtown flooded and classes were canceled. It was a disappointment to some veterans, at least, eager to get to work and make up for lost time. Enrollment reached a high in that Fall Semester when 650 students, about half of whom were World War II veterans, crowded the little campus. And, men once again outnumbered women for the first time since the war began in 1941.

One exemplary veteran--a very popular role model among fellow students and admired by faculty--was Blair (Bruzzie) Reeves. He was paralyzed from the waist down since 1945, when a Japanese sniper's bullet tore through him even as he attempted to retrieve the body of a fallen buddy during fierce fighting on Okinawa. A Jefferson High School graduate, the stalwart Marine sergeant was now confined to a wheel chair when he began pre-law courses in the Fall 1946 at the J. C. There he met the attractive Betty Armstrong; the romance began, and they were married by the time of graduation in May 1948.

Reeves went to St. Mary's University Law School and was graduated in 1951. The next year he was bitten by a political bug and at the age 28 he handily (by a vote of 1,785 to his opponent's 619) won the Democratic primary for election as Justice of the Peace in County Precinct 8. It was his first political victory, but Reeves was destined to shape his legal career from private law practice to judgeships, including probate judge; served several terms as Bexar County Judge; appointed, later elected as an Associate Justice, then elevated to Chief Justice of the Fourth Court of Civil Appeals sitting in Bexar County. He retired from the active bench ca. 1993, with full honors from judges, attorneys, and civic leaders from all walks. Judge Reeves largely is credited with creating the Bexar County Hospital District, a real political challenge that he survived.

Throughout his adult life he was confined to a wheel chair, but that did not slow him down. He used a specially-equipped auto at first, but then had a converted motorcycle with a custom-made sidecar-type platform attached, enabling him to operate the conveyance while still seated in the chair.

Betty succumbed first, then his death on March 23, 1999 brought to a close the work of a dedicated jurist. Uncle Sam made a good investment on the relatively small amount of dollars paid through the G. I. Bill to one Blair Reeves, Sgt., U.S.M.C. Next to his smiling photo in the 1948 edition of *El Alamo* is the notation that he was a member of the Veterans' Club and Speechcrafters. The traditional yearbook epithet speaks loudly about this ultra-distinguished alumnus when it records for eternity: "Fortune favors the brave."

Truett L. Chance, himself a veteran of the South Pacific Theater, began teaching at the College in January 1947 to the overflow of ex-GIs with whom he could identify when he served as sponsor of the Veterans Club, and one of Bruzzie's instructors.

Registration in the day school in the Fall Semester 1947 saw a leveling off and a trend for future veterans' enrollment, according to Registrar Glynda Bess Brown. She reported in the lead story of *The Jaysee Ranger* (note the recent change in name of the newspaper) on October 1, 1947, that veterans no longer dominated the class after last year's peak. She gave exact figures that showed 264 "civilian" to 226 veterans enrolled. Also, the number of girls had increased, much to the liking of single veterans.

Unfortunately, the World War II vets were not the last phase of GIs. Armed services men and women returned home and swelled the ranks at San Antonio College after their tours ended in the Korean and Vietnam wars. Other male students sought draft deferments on the basis of full-time study (minimum of 12 semester hours) using Selective Service Form 109 certified by the registrar and filed with draft boards.

[Ironically, President Loftin was accused in January 1955 by State Representative Pearce Johnson of Austin, chairman of the House Appropriations sub-committee on higher education, of "recruiting" active military personnel to become students at San Antonio College and St. Philip's College under the Army and Air Force information and education programs. Minimum tuition was based on a student's residence within the tax district; a slightly higher tuition rate was charged to Texas residents living outside the District; non-residents of Texas were subject to even higher tuition. Johnson alleged that Loftin was making money collecting non-resident fees from military personnel who were stationed in Texas. Loftin denied the charges and replied that the lawmaker had not "acquainted himself with all the facts because I feel sure he is a reasonable man," (*San Antonio News*, January 28, 1955).]

"Junior" Grows Up: San Antonio College--A precursor to the name change, the college weekly newspaper in October 1947 omitted the "Junior" in the long-standing title and called itself the *Jaysee Ranger*. Editors explained that "Jaysee" meant "J.C.," a common reference used on campus that meant Junior College, but the "Junior" was gone! San Antonio Junior College, the legal name used since 1926, became known officially as San Antonio College by a resolution of the Board of Trustees in 1948. Official grade transcripts requested by students transferring to other institutions or wishing a document in support of job applications had to be altered on the so-called, alteration-proof, check stock which remained in large supply with "Junior" still in the title. Not to waste expensive paper, it was decided to blot the word "Junior" using India ink. [For this important job and other tasks, Registrar Glynda Brown paid this writer 50 cents per hour as a student assistant in the summer session 1949.]

After "Junior" matured into San Antonio College, the San Antonio Union Junior College District in 1978--with blessing of the state Coordinating Board--dropped the "Union Junior" names from its title and became known for awhile as the San Antonio Community College District, much to the chagrin of some old-line professors who sincerely believed that the "Community" label denoted a lesser academic mission of the two-year college. Public two-year colleges across the nation were by then using "Community" in titles to describe their perceived expanding roles to serve the needs of people in their--you guessed it--communities.

Still another change in the title was made in 1982, but this time the name was welcomed by the on-campus people and the public. Nary a word was heard opposing the new title as the District soon would be enlarged from the old, metes-and-bounds, gerrymandering, boundary lines encompassing approximately 154 square miles to a County-wide tax district.

Alamo Community College District is the first listed on the State's roster of two-year colleges. The "ACCD" monicker is an easy acronymn for use by everybody, including the press.

The San Antonio College *Catalog* for 2000-2001--the 75th year edition--reported an average semester enrollment of 21,000 credit students and an average annual enrollment of 16,000 other-than-credit students. San Antonio College is the largest single-campus community college in Texas and one of the largest in the United States, according to statements in the *Catalog* (pages 15-16).

Indeed, "Junior" has matured well over the years.

The "Hein" memorial pecan tree leafing out
Spring 2002 on the San Antonio College Campus.

"Like leaves on trees the race of man is found... Now green in youth, now withering on the ground..."

--Alexander Pope

Profile: HENRY M. HEIN, A.S.

One of the most poignant stories about a graduate of San Antonio Junior College is the "All-American" youth story of Henry M. Hein, who left behind his legacy on both the old South Alamo Street campus and the new site on San Pedro Avenue in the simple form of a native Texas pecan tree.

Henry attended Edgar Allen Poe Junior High in Southeast San Antonio. He was a Boy Scout. He liked athletics. On Saturday mornings he caught the bus downtown to take accordian lessons at a music store. That is how he met Charles Ford, who lived on the shallow East Side and attended Ralph W. Emerson Junior High. Charles started guitar lessons, but switched to the accordian. Sometimes after lessons--if they had a dime each--they would go to the matinee double-feature at the State Theater on Main Avenue. The boys bonded over similar interests and became buddies at Brackenridge High School which carried on through junior college days. Both played in the big band and were second lieutenants in the ROTC band.

Young Hein played the French horn and belonged to an accordian combo of five organized by Director Otto Zoeller. Ditto, Ford. Hein was president of the German Club and a member of the National Honor Society. Both were graduated in the Class of 1942. The tale will focus on Hein's profile.

After a one-semester go of it at Texas A&M, Henry returned home and enrolled at San Antonio Junior College in January 1943, completed the Spring Semester and earned more credits during summer school. He continued studies at SAJC for the 1943-44 academic year when he served as president of the student body. Among his fellow students--along with best-friend Ford--were Betty Abel, Jim Knox Loftin, Charles F. Kalteyer, William Faulkenberry, Willard Judson, Herbert Spiro, Lucille Hildebrandt, Lorraine Layer, Harold Eiserloh, Barbara and Charles Anderson (the last two children of County Judge Charles W. Anderson). And Dorothy Nye, whom Henry dated.

Hein and Ford were among leaders of a petition-drive asking school officials for better facilities. The pair on their own started a "book store" on campus whereby students could buy and sell or exchange textbooks to save money which students--not the entrepeneurs--shared. The two inseparable friends pledged Etta Bita Pie, a non-Greek fraternity organized in 1931 to promote the love of pie. Membership was limited to eight men. Initiation required pledges to stand on the outdoor water fountain and sing the EBP song; to erase blackboards and push pennies on the sidewalk with their noses. A pledge knew when he was accepted because a member smashed a cream pie in the initiate's face. The guy then ran around chasing girls to plant sticky kisses, much to the delight of the girls. Each week a co-ed was selected as "Pie Girl," with the privilege of taking pies to Thursday afternoon meetings where girls were not included.

Ford, 77, retired as a businessman and resides in New Braunfels, can relate other anecdotes of student life and church activities with Hein. Ford remembers that everybody liked Henry who never said an ill word about a person. He worked in his father's Goliad Street Pharmacy across from Waitz Market. The parents, Henry and a younger brother, Robert, lived above the drug store.

During his junior college days, young Hein was instrumental in obtaining trees to plant in a campus beautification project. It might have helped that his father, Henry F. Hein, was the elected Commissioner of City Parks and Recreation in those days of San Antonio's mayor and four commissioners form of government. The San Antonio Independent School District--still the owner of the college campus buildings and land--easily gave permission for City workers to plant trees at the site. One of the trees, a three-year-old native Texas pecan was uprooted from Maverick Park at Broadway and Ninth Street, and transplanted on the campus. It survived and bore nuts after Hein received his Associate of Science degree on May 26, 1944, knowing that he had left the old German-English school site prettier than he had found it. The commencement program listed 120 names of Junior College boys serving in the military. Henry too soon would join their ranks. (Appendix M.)

Facing the summer after graduation, Henry Hein was subject--like many others his age and fitness--to the draft by one of the local boards of the Selective Service System. He had shown an interest in pre-med; it was suggested that Henry might seek his father's political influence or intercedence in placing him for training as an army medic. He refused to seek special favors and said he would take whatever comes. A small group of family and friends saw him off to the military at the train station. He trained at Fort Hood and later was assigned as a private to rifle Company K, 328th U.S. Infantry Regiment in the 26th Division which wound up as part of General George Patton, Jr.'s Third Army.

One could easily assume that, with four million allied troops who would serve on the Western Front in the European Theater of Operations, Hein's military unit at the company or regimental levels would be lost in the shuffle trying to identify his combat actions. (It is reported that about one-third of the men in the U.S. Army were of German-American origin, as he was.) But, thanks to tomes of the depth and breadth of Charles B. MacDonald's, *The Last Offensive*, and military historian Stephen Ambrose's prolific writings, the 328th is traceable in movements covering the period September 1944 to May 1945. Combat actions of a sister Company G (not certain if K Co. and G Co. were in the same battalion) are well-documented in Ambrose's books, *Citizen Soldiers* (1997) and *The Victors* (1998), both historical accounts often relying on eye-witness stories by a staff sergeant and a lieutenant.

Original units of the 328th Regiment had arrived on Utah Beach September 8, 1944, three months after D-Day of Operation Overlord. "Repple Depple" (military jargon) company replacements joined the 325th and were soon thrown into breaches along the Siegfried Line in France. By November 6th units were on line and engaged in first combat with the Germans on November 14th east of Nancy in the Province of Lorraine. Hein's unit was a part of this battleground. The "Battle of the Bulge" commenced on December 16th, but on December 20th action of the regiment containing Hein's company was centered on German-occupied Arlon, Belgium. The town was in a holiday look: shoppers and workers went about daily business; streets and stores were decorated and Christmas trees reminded troops of home. Intense fighting occurred on Christmas Eve and Christmas Day. The area was heavily wooded; rains caused a mire; but the greatest concern of the soldiers were booby traps and land mines hidden by the enemy in houses and roadways. The small Schu mine--one-fourth pound of TNT in a small wooden box about the size of a box of kitchen matches with a nail as detonator--caused horror among the men moving about in snow and mud, survivors related.

On December 21, military records show that Headquarters of the 328th issued an order that "No SS troops or paratroopers will be taken prisoner, but will be shot on sight." Apparently, this was in retaliation for the Malmedy Massacre on December 17th, when some 150 U.S. artillery troops that had been captured by German panzers were mowed down by machine-gun fire in one of the most brutal acts perpetrated by Nazis forces in World War II, historians say. Fighting did not let up during January and February for Hein's outfit east of Metz.

As best the family could learn was that Henry was leading a group under enemy fire near Saarbrücken in the Saarland region of southern Germany when he jumped into a shell hole or crater for protection only to suffer the impact of an explosion from a booby trap or a mine. His body was never recovered, according to Robert Hein.

First "word" was received by the Hein family in San Antonio on February 16, 1945, that Private Henry Hein was listed as "Missing in Action." However, 10 days later some hope was revived when a notice came that Hein had died in a hospital from wounds received in action in Germany. Robert Hein discounts that report although it appeared in a newspaper account dated February 26th.

In July 1945, in a telegram that Robert Hein keeps, the actual grim "Official" notice was received from the government by Mr. and Mrs. Hein and little Robert, about 9 at the time. Hein's parents died in 1975 without experiencing full closure of their son's death.

Years later, Robert Hein visited the cemetery at St. Avold in France, about 5 miles south of the German border. There is no white cross, but Henry Hein's name is inscribed along with other's listed as "MIAs" in a wall of the cemetery.

If Company's G's statistics are typical of similar units in the 328th Infantry Regiment, what began as a company strength of 187 enlisted men and 6 officers in September 1944, by May 8, 1945 had recorded a total of 625 men having served with 51 killed, 116 suffered trench foot and 51 disabled with frost bite.

Author Ambrose interviewed thousands of military survivors of WW II and has favored at least one, Bruce Egger, of Idaho.

"There is no typical GI among the millions who served in Northwest Europe, but Bruce Egger was representative." Egger rose from private to staff sergeant with battlefield promotions. He and his Lieutenant, Lee Otts, collaborated to write *G Company's War*, a vivid account of the rifle company's campaign in the Ardennes and the Battle of the Rhineland. Egger wrote that he was miserably cold, exhausted and scared to death most of the time:

"Not a man among us would want to go through it again, but as we are proud of having been so severely tested and found adequate, the only regret is for those of our friends who never returned" (*Citizen Soldier*, p. 469). Egger got his college degree and served in the U.S. Forestry Service for 29 years.

Henry Hein is "representative" of all the brave young men who attended San Antonio College and served in the military. One can only ask what might have been in Henry's promising career had he lived. Doctor Hein?

A memorial tree was planted at City Hall with Mayor Gus Mauermann presiding, Charles Ford playing the accordian accompaniment for 17 Jaycee Rangerettes in uniform who sang at the dedication. The photograph is extant.

There is that other tree, the same Texas pecan tree mentioned earlier--now 10 years old--that was uprooted again on February 7, 1952 on the old campus and moved carefully to the new campus San Antonio College first occupied in February 1951.

"First Tree on New College Site Dedicated to World War II Dead," was the headline of the feature story which appeared in the *San Antonio Express* on February 8, 1952. Commissioner Hein, now in his waning days before the City would vote in Council-Manager form of government, and College President J. O. Loftin are pictured in the photograph guiding the balled tree being lowered from a crane into the ground in front of the Science Building in the 1300 block of San Pedro Avenue. Mr. Hein remarked:

"Let this be a memorial to the war dead, particularly those who attended San Antonio College."

A lone pecan tree still stands vigil in the front courtyard of San Antonio College. The tree was leafing out in green finery in the Spring of 2002.

[This reporter and others who attended the brief ceremony that day felt in our hearts that this really was Henry M. Hein's own tree because he had helped transplant it just seven years earlier while he was student body president and a member in good standing of Etta Bita Pie.]

> "As of the green leaves on a thick tree,
>   some fall, and some grow."
> --Ecclesiasticus xiv.18

6.
SAN ANTONIO COLLEGE
MOVES "UPTOWN"

The move of the San Antonio College campus from the German-English school site on South Alamo Street across Nueva Street from historic La Villita to the "uptown" address opposite equally historic San Pedro Park with its ageless oak trees and flowing springs where Comanches and Buffalo soldiers once camped--but not at the same time--was exciting for students and faculty anticipating the transition.

San Pedro Park was the city's oldest and a landmark gathering place for generations. It featured a swimming pool, softball fields, and tennis courts for day or night recreation. There were two permanent buildings on the grounds: one was the Little Theater and the other a branch of the city library which fronted the 1300 block of San Pedro Avenue. A portion of the park was among priority property considered by the San Antonio Union Junior College District a year before the City Council nixed the idea and trustees settled on the purchase of the San Antonio Transit Company's vacated maintenance shops and "bus barns" in the 1200-1300 blocks of San Pedro Avenue facing the branch library.

Board president (chairman) Walter W. McAllister, Sr. announced the purchase price of $142,000 for six acres "with improvements" (*San Antonio Evening News*, April 5, 1949). Other future campus sites had been visited and for reasons not acquired.

New Site Considerations--Since the establishment of the junior college district as a free-standing, tax district with seven trustees approved in the election of October 1945, board meetings were held in McAllister's office at the San Antonio Building and Loan Association, 401 Navarro Street, across from the Nix Professional Building. On September 1, 1946, the San Antonio Board of Education on schedule relinquished control of San Antonio College--and St. Philip's College--to the full operation by the new trustees. Almost immediately, the board's planning turned to locating a suitable site for the proposed campus of San Antonio College. Suggestions and even stronger recommendations were received by McAllister and Loftin. Among the properties actually considered--not in exact order or priority--by the board were the following:

1. The first five floors of the Transit Tower (aka Smith-Young Tower) after Sears, Roebuck & Co. vacated the premises and moved to Romana Plaza at Navarro and Soledad Streets.

2. The United States Arsenal property on South Flores Street-- located a few blocks south of City Hall and the Courthouse--was declared surplus by the government on June 30, 1947. Loftin had seen the closure coming as early as December 1946, and was interested. Although local opposition mounted to keep the World War I era facility in San Antonio, the arsenal was moved to Texarkana, Texas. Loftin had eyes on 14 buildings (monolithic, multi-story concrete buildings; almost windowless) which, he said, he could convert into classrooms in a week.

The University of Texas and the Texas Legislature also showed interest at the same time on the arsenal site. Loftin and the trustees voluntarily withdrew the district's bidding and supported efforts to locate the university's medical branch on the property. The legislative bill to create the medical school in San Antonio died a natural death on the last day of the session. The Federal Works Agency kept the buildings for use as offices and military reserve training centers. Eventually, the Howard E. Butt grocery headquarters took over some of the old arsenal grounds.

3. "The site most suitable for the Junior College is in the northeast corner of San Pedro Park...it meets every standard with few if any objectionable features," Loftin outlined eight advantages and savings by using the land in an address to the San Antonio Optimist Club February 11, 1948. He told the Optimists (Loftin was a Kiwanian) that a "group of fine women" in the San Antonio Conservation Society had a right to question the use of a piece of the park because "that was their reason for existence." He cited 10 instances where the City of San Antonio had allowed use of park properties, including the museum on the Alamo grounds, present site of City Hall, Witte Museum and Pioneer Hall in Brackenridge Park, the Little Theater and branch library in San Pedro Park and other examples.

Clearly, by his stump speech and other comments, the San Pedro Park acreage--north and east of the extension of West Dewey Place and Angle Road (later closed to traffic) that cut through the park--was Loftin's favorite. The Ex-Students' Association tried to help by sending an open letter dated February 19, 1948 urging citizens to express their feelings favoring the site to the City Council and to allow the district to purchase the parcel. The Letter was signed "For a better college, Robert O'Connor, president." [Judge O'Connor later served as a federal magistrate in San Antonio.]

Loftin was devastated (to put his reaction mildly) when City Council turned down by a vote of four to one the district's request to purchase the small acreage (where the McFarlin Tennis Center is located today). C. Ray Davis, tax commissioner, moved to deny the San Antonio Union Junior College District use of the land. Mayor Alfred Callaghan and Commissioners Raymond South (fire and police), and James W. Knight (streets), sided with Davis. Ironically, Henry F. Hein (parks and sanitation) did not oppose the sale, explaining "I've got a good reason not to..." he explained without amplification (*San Antonio Light*, February 27, 1948). [His son Henry was president of the student body when he was graduated from SAJC in May 1944; later killed in action February 1945 as an army private in Germany's Saarland.]

4. In September 1948, college officials showed interest in a triangular tract of property known by oldtimers in the city as "Swiss Plaza" as a likely central location for a new junior college campus. [The site was bounded by 5th Street, Avenue B, and 7th Street near the San Antonio River just north of First Baptist Church complex. The area later was developed as Valero's twin towers.] Trustees considered taking an option on the property and even offered $80,000 to owner Peter Trease. McAllister cited a title controversy and put the transaction "on hold" (*San Antonio Express*, September 15, 1948).

In December 1948, Trease sued the District for breach of contract. Trustees authorized Arley V. Knight, attorney for the district, to defend the suit and counter sue to recover $2,500 in earnest money paid. The plan was abandoned.

5. Turning to the city's southeast side, another site considered was several square blocks of vacant land known as the "Pine-Astor" property owned by the San Antonio Independent School District for a possible future high school. The public school board later divested the property and built Highlands High School farther to the southeast than Pine-Astor. The college board in 1948 had offered to buy Brackenridge High School on South St. Mary's Street a few blocks from downtown if the school board built a new high school on the Pine-Astor site.

6. The high-rise Aurora Apartments-Hotel building, facing across Crockett Park to Main Avenue and bordered by Cypress Street on the near-northside of downtown, was mentioned during early planning but not really given much consideration by trustees. [Today, SAC students park near the old Aurora and ride a free shuttle bus to get to classes on the campus.]

There were other properties--San Antonio Vocational and Technical High School, Tech Field, the Drought home, Halff Building, even stay at the present German-School site--but the six detailed earlier were given the most consideration by the trustees searching for an inexpensive and centrally-accessible tract for the future campus. The election of October 1945 did not contain a provision for land purchase. College leaders thought before the joint election they had a verbal understanding with the public school trustees to help in providing a suitable location for the college. The original college trustees were still bent on building a new plant for the predicted surge in enrollment, the need to expand the facilities, and to vacate their lease on South Alamo Street.

In the end, the San Pedro "Uptown" property was selected by trustees as offering the best possible "location...location...location," often said to be key tenets of real estate.

Construction Begins--The San Antonio Transit Company had relocated its offices, shops and bus parking facilities a block west of the old site in the 1200-1300 blocks of San Pedro Avenue. Only recently it had acquired Tech Field owned by the local school system--the same site that the college district had shown an interest. It was south of San Pedro Park on West Myrtle Street and extended southward to near Five Points. (Tech Field was the former leased-home of the San Antonio Missions, minor league baseball club.) The old bus-barn site now had to be readied for its new tenant, San Antonio College.

The "improvements" included in the purchase price of the property consisted of a few frame buildings surrounded by asphalt paving. It was obvious, the college's physical plant would have to start from the ground up to provide a modern campus promised to the people.

On July 21, 1949--just three months after purchasing the property--the board authorized the retained architectural firm Phelps & Dewees & Simmons to proceed with plans for the first building on the San Pedro campus. The "building fund" amounted to $1 million. Groundbreaking was held in January 1950. A master plan had been developed by the same architects to house 2,000 students in the red brick with white mortar chosen for the buildings. (The firm had for years been the major architects for the SAISD; some buildings on the college campus might look similar to public schools.) With the first three buildings on the drawing boards now ready for entertaining bids by contractors, the completed projects would represent about one-third of the master plan.

Bids for construction of building number one--consisting of classrooms, library, small auditorium and administrative offices--ranged from $418,000 to $520,000 in November 1949 (*The Ranger*, November 23, 1949). Enrollment in day classes reached 521 students and night school had 706 part-timers in the Fall 1949. Library holdings totaled 10,000 books.

The contract was awarded to Joe Joeris with his final bid of $461,000, allowing for 275 calendar days to complete. Pouring of concrete on the first section of the administration building was completed on March 6, 1950. President Loftin acted as a "sidewalk superintendent" and made almost daily trips to the construction site to check progress.

Final revised plans for the new science building were completed in February 1950. J. C. Worcester was the contractor whose bid of $244,035 was accepted in May. He began construction on a promise to complete within 275 calendar days. W. E. Simpson & Co. did the engineering. The two buildings were connected on two levels by a covered arcade, giving the enclosure a U-shaped appearance looking from San Pedro Avenue towards the front elevation. That phase was well along when construction specifications were being prepared in August 1950 for a health and physical education building--something the college had lacked since 1926--to be located in the 1200 block of San Pedro Avenue at the corner of Locust Street. First, however, the district needed to buy four properties which ranged in price from $10,000 to $20,000 each. The option for a 70-foot indoor swimming pool was accepted at the added cost of about $70,000. J. C. Worcester, with his construction crews working just across the street on the science building, received the go ahead on the modern gymnasium (the pool area enclosed) with a completion date expected by the Fall semester 1951 at a cost of $200,000.

The Move--Construction had been slightly delayed and the two buildings were not completed as the "M-Day," originally scheduled late January in time to begin spring semester classes, approached a critical time. Classes remained on the old campus as a new target date for the move was set for February, then to start classes on February 26. A delay had been partly due to recent ice and sleet storms, it was reported in *The Ranger*, February 15, 1951. Rooms still lacked doors and finishing touches were being made in the main building. Full completion of the science building called for another 90 days. Meanwhile, the combination health-gymnasium-pool building construction was on schedule. Physical education activities would take place outdoors in the spring 1951.

President Loftin had been telling students all along that the new campus was "quite accessible" for bus transportation. Students with cars "will find ample parking space," he was quoted as saying (*San Antonio Light*, August 6, 1950). The library would seat 200 students and ample shelves for current holdings of 15,000 volumes and room for expansion.

San Antonio College students were eager and ready to pack up books and belongings on a Saturday at the old campus and report fresh and ready to start day and evening classes at 1300 San Pedro Avenue in the "ultra-modern school," as reported on February 21 in the *San Antonio Express*. The board already had met for the first time in the joint boardroom-president's office a few days earlier and got a preview of the facilities. Unfortunately, Walter McAllister, who had worked for years to launch the new college facilities, was not present because of ill-ness. Jesse N. Fletcher, vice-president, presided. Other trustees present at the meeting were Travis Moursund, G. S. McCreless and G. J. Sutton; James V. Graves was absent. Loftin was there to herald the "fine com-munity college building that has long been sought by San Antonio."

A United States flag, gift from American Legion Post 366, was raised on the 42-foot pole centered in a rose bed at the entrance to the first building built on campus (later named G. S. McCreless Hall with its sometimes fast, sometimes slow clock facing San Pedro Avenue and motorists) during a ceremony on March 10, 1951. President Loftin and Dean Moody received the flag from Post Commander U. D. Filizola and Legionnaires W. R. Merrill, Lloyd M. O'Neal, Herbet H. Frey, Wilmer Krueger and Francis Burgess. Robert Peace, president of the student body, also attended as a member of the official party.

Dedication: "A Dream Comes True"--That's what the *San Antonio Express* (backer of a new campus for 10 years) in Section A on May 7, 1951, called the reality of moving into a modern junior college campus on San Pedro Avenue. The eight-columns wide, banner headline proclaimed as follows:

A Dream Comes True As San Antonio College
Will Dedicate New Plant Friday

over the full-page story and five photos. The text included a short his-tory of the College's struggles for facilities and space for expansion since 1926. (The byline named Jerome F. Weynand, Staff Writer.)

The official Dedication and Open House was planned as an affair for students, faculty, and the general public to inspect the campus on guided tours after the 7:30 p.m. ceremonies on May 13, 1951. Loftin invited Clyde E. Barnes, educator and lawyer now living in Jasper, Texas, to give the dedicatory address. Barnes had been the popular choice of students on the former campus to succeed the first Director J. E. Nelson when he retired in July 1941. Loftin was named "President" by the Board of Education in August 1941 (as reported in Chapter 4).

Barnes was one of the original faculty members (his wife was registrar) and served for 18 years at SAJC teaching courses in speech, government, economics, and accounting--plus practicing law on the side. Later, he became dean of men and then dean of the college when it was on South Alamo Street. He resigned on March 31, 1945. He had been a civic leader serving as president of the San Antonio Optimist Club in 1933-1934; was a member of Travis Park Methodist Church; a Mason and Shriner. (He was "welcomed back home" at the dedication.)

Platform guests included the following:

Board of Trustees, public school administrators, representatives of local colleges, members of civic clubs; also, City, County and State officials; military representatives from local bases; architects and builders; alumni association members and guests from other cities completed the official party. Edison High School band provided a concert under the direction of Jean Sarli. President Loftin introduced guests before the San Antonio College chorus led by James Gambino gave a presentation. Dr. C. C. Colvert, pioneer professor in junior college education at The University of Texas who served as consultant in the planning stages, brought greetings to the assemblage. After the address by Barnes, Chairman Walter W. McAllister representing the trustees, faculty, and students responded; Jerome F. Weynand, representing the SAC Alumni Association, also responded, before the Rev. Chess Lovern pronounced the benediction and the audience adjourned for tours. The alumni gathered in the new Small Auditorium. (See Appendix N.)

Commencement Exercises of the Graduation Class of 1951 were held under the stars on May 30th in the same courtyard setup used at the dedication on May 13th. Dean Wayland P. Moody presented the class as the first students to have the honor of graduating on the new campus after about 12 weeks of attending classes there. President Loftin conferred the various diplomas accepted by those attending of the 85 students listed in the program, including 10 graduates who had completed the requirements after the Fall Semester 1950-51 and were invited to participate in May. A class photo made the news on page 30 of the *San Antonio Express*, May 15, 1951. (See Appendix O for graduation program.)

San Antonio College turned to advertising as a recruiting method by running a half-page display ad on August 5, 1951, featuring the new buildings ready to serve San Antonio's educational needs as noted: an air-conditioned library, paved parking area, an indoor swimming pool, new gymnasium, and new science laboratories--"All for $30 tuition each semester." Day and evening courses of two standard college years will be offered leading to the Associate of Arts degree, or students may enroll in terminal courses leading to entry jobs in business and industry. Registration was set for September 10-11.

Different makeup and wording appeared in a half-page display ad published in the *San Antonio Express* August 8, with the addition of several photos of new buildings to attract students who were urged to visit the Registrar at 1300 San Pedro Avenue or call Pershing 8172 for information.

***"Good News": Finally, Accreditation Granted*--**Students and faculty had endured a long wait to move into new plant facilities, but even a longer period until the universal stamp of approval would come in the form of regional accreditation. Since the establishment of San Antonio Junior College in 1926, students who transferred to other institutions of higher learning were accorded full credit for college level courses passed with a letter grade of "C" or better. Grades of "A" and "B" were not automatically changed to "C's" by the receiving college or university despite the prevailing myth circulated. Valid credits were recorded the same way for junior and senior college transfers in that no grade points usually were assigned to incoming credits whether a San Antonio College student or a student from Rice University transferred to The University of Texas, for instance.

The articulation process for transfers had run smoothly since the 1930s at SAJC, and continued until formal accreditation was granted, although the poorly-housed junior college did not have accredited status from the college division of the Southern Association of Colleges and Schools in Atlanta, one of six regional agencies in the United States. Accreditation meant that transfer of credits from member schools in Texas were acceptable in the 10 other states in the Southern Association and generally at institutions nationwide.

The familiar adage, "Just as clothes don't make the man, neither do fine buildings make colleges," was used by Director Nelson in the earliest years of the fledgling college explaining the fact that the Southern Association had not allowed membership of San Antonio

Junior College because the buildings were so rundown. He continued in the news story with comments aimed at convincing students, faculty and the public that credits earned at SAJC were of the highest scholastic type; that Jaysee graduates enter The University of Texas, Rice University, and other schools without loss of credits. Registrar Matthews said at that time that credits of SAJC transfers would continue to be accepted at face value by the University of Texas (*San Antonio Express*, February 9, 1932). [Matthews used the same terms in a letter to President Loftin just days before the second election try to create the district in October 1945.]

Nelson stuck to his contention that the Southern Association's refusal to accredit SAJC was based on the location and construction of the 1859-era buildings, problems in lighting, heating, and sanitary conditions--all of which did not meet minimum requirements of the Division on Colleges of the umbrella Southern Association of Colleges and Schools [to which every self-respecting college, university, elementary and secondary school aspired to belong].

About the time Nelson was attempting to explain accreditation, or the lack thereof, the San Antonio Board of Education (Minutes of March 15, 1932 meeting) noted that the junior college had lost affiliation because the school lacked proper housing and that it could be moved to Brackenridge High School and re-affiliation arranged. [Note: the SAISD did not lose accreditation for its schools. In response to this researcher's inquiry in March 2001, a spokesman for the Commission on Colleges of the Southern Association replied that there was no record of any junior college affiliation with that group until 1952. If the junior college had tried to be accredited under Brackenridge High School or use its buildings under the public schools umbrella, it would have dealt with the Commission on Schools. No further inquiry was made on this issue.]

The accreditation trail was cold until December 1950, when President Loftin personally carried a written report as backup to his verbal plea to the membership committee of the Commission on Colleges of SACS meeting that year in Richmond, Virginia. He reported back home that the Commission, made up of college peers from other states, found no deficiencies in the report and the application for membership. He repeated earlier assurances to students and patrons of the college that, while transfer credits have been accepted by colleges and universities, "accreditation added prestige to the institution," (*San Antonio Express*, December 18, 1950).

The two-year application process continued during the construction phase of the buildings on the San Pedro Campus and culminated to everyone's relief in the recommendation for accreditation first accorded by the Commission on Colleges and the final approval of SACS. Dean Moody had attended that pivotal meeting in Memphis, Tennessee, and when he returned to San Antonio he wasted no time in quickly announcing the "good news" to students and faculty first, then to the public (*The Ranger*, December 5, 1952).

[The year before, in December 1951, President Loftin was successful in obtaining Southern Association accreditation for St. Philip's College.]

[Every 10 years, each accredited college and university must undergo a self-study of its mission, curriculum, faculty, finances, library, facilities and other major components; then, receive a visiting committee which spends three days on campus before making their "eyes and ears" report with suggestions and recommendations for improvements where needed to meet requirements in some 22 areas. The detailed written report is filed with the Commission for review and another vote for reaffirmation. Every periodical self-study and review by the college itself and the visiting delegation have passed muster since 1952. The College enjoys hearing the "good news" of full accreditation and enjoying the prestige brought on by diligence.]

"A BUNDLE OF SOUTHERN SUNSHINE"

Profile: *BERNICE TAYLOR*

Bernice Taylor was an institution within an institution. Her first job title was "maid" on the South Alamo campus of San Antonio Junior College where she began--on a part-time basis--according to the archival records in September 1940 and remained as a permanent fixture until she retired on August 31, 1974. Her friendly, personal services to students over 34 years went well beyond her job description when she served as unofficial counselor, mentor, consoler of the love lorn...she was ubiquitous, gregarious, and inquisitive with students, faculty, and administrators.

Bernice was an "ambassador-at-large" without official portfolio, but always smiling and helpful as she cleaned her assigned areas and preened the flowers on the first campus. She was assigned to the administration building on the San Pedro Campus after San Antonio College moved in February 1951, but her peripatetic nature took her to other hallways, the library, student center, etc. for chats with students. She took care of the rose gardens before the college employed a grounds keeper.

One of a number of tributes to "Bernice--Confidant, Pal," appeared in *The Junior Ranger*, September 30, 1946, when sophomores were inculcating new freshman students on finding the answers to questions. Simple, the "encyclopedia" was Bernice, all-seeing, all-knowing source of study helps and "out-of-the-way" facts of the college.

"It is even rumored that the officials would not dare to make a decision without first consulting Bernice, who probably knows more news than (Walter) Winchell..." She was given the unofficial title of "Assistant Dean of Women" by students. Bernice was deemed "indispensable and intelligent" in the article for her aid to students in various subject areas, i.e., Spanish, English, and mathematics.

The Ranger on April 1, 1953--no April Fool's joke--featured her in a story headlined: "Bernice Taylor, Everyone's Friend, Always Extends Helping Hand." She was described as "A bundle of Southern Sunshine who laughs and works all day." She could help in any subject from calculus to Spanish to love, the article continued.

Born in Pollok, Texas, Bernice Centers attended high school in Tyler and was graduated at age 15 years. Later, she attended St. Philip's College with an interest in sociology. Reportedly, she also attended a college in Austin and did not lack many hours to complete a bachelor of arts degree. According to the feature story, Bernice said she gave up her college career in order that her nephew, George, could continue his education. She married Fernando Taylor at an early age before she moved to San Antonio.

Widely read, a good talker--and a good listener--Bernice Taylor knew and was known by every student on the small campus. Over the years she signed many yearbooks with little messages to students that nearly always ended with the simple phrase, "Your maid, Bernice."

Illness probably brought on her retirement which was against her will. She lived for nearly 12 years before she passed away on June 18, 1986. Funeral services were held at St. Paul United Methodist Church with a large gathering paying respects [including the writer].

Bernice reared a daughter, Vanessa Taylor Antwine, and instilled in her the love of helping people through teaching. Vanessa earned a master's degree and taught in Virginia schools, but later returned with her family to San Antonio where she was in 2002 teaching in an elementary school. Her daughter is attending college; her twin boy and girl were age 11 in April 2002 and are aware of their grandmother's love and life of service.

Bernice will be remembered also by "her students" and all of the photographs and mentions that she received in many issues of the school newspaper and yearbook. A byline story by Sue Doerr in *The Fourth Write*, May 1968 issue (the successor publication to *El Alamo*) clearly underlines Bernice's legacy as a super maid on the payroll, but an ambassador-at-large for San Antonio College when the journalism student wrote:

> Everyone seems to profit from having known her. Bernice states that she finds it hard to "try to live up to the nice things people say." In the eyes of those who know her, she has.

7.
THE OLD DOCTRINE:
"SEPARATE BUT EQUAL..."
IS OVERCOME

San Antonio Junior College students must have appeared aghast when they read in the weekly *Junior Ranger* the bannered headline: "Wealthy Negro Buys College." The story predicted how miserable life would be for students after this unfortunate event. Sarcastically, the writer described the new owner as a highly-educated man with 14 years in school who will graduate to the second grade next year. The date was April, 1931. April Fool!!

Such pranks may have been typical of college students and possibly indicative of racial humor in the 1930s-1940s era of Amos and Andy on radio. No other evidence--in publications and interviews with students of that period--points to any racial slurs at the Junior College. But the future implications of such attempted wit were no joke in a segregated city, state and nation. In 20 years, San Antonio and San Antonio College would actively be involved and divided over the long-abiding doctrine of "separate but equal" in many facets of society, including educational opportunity.

After many years, when all of the political rhetoric and legal threats had run their courses and the imbroglio resulted finally in action, President J. O. Loftin could claim one distinction for San Antonio College. It was the first public college in Texas to admit Negro students in June 1955 in compliance with the U.S. Supreme Court's decision and order to integrate schools "with all deliberate speed." Other higher education institutions and school districts would soon follow San Antonio College's historical lead to integrate black and white students in what appears 50 years later to be so matter-of-fact policy taken for granted by people.

[But, not to be taken lightly by someone who first reported on the embroilment 1951-53, then was cast as a player in college administration only to utter the "no comment" dodge about rumors that Negroes had been admitted to San Antonio College in June 1955.]

At Mid-Century, It Was a Tense Time--Racial tension affected all concerned Americans: transportation, restaurants, hotels, theaters, neighborhood housing, amusement parks, swimming pools, ballparks, restrooms, drinking fountains, churches and schools...remained segregated in San Antonio and much of the nation. In some northern states, a few athletes and entertainers were among the first to break color barriers in their professions.

Willie Howard Mays--born in 1931 in Westfield, Alabama--at age 20 was a rarity in major league baseball when he joined the New York Giants as a centerfielder and became the National League Rookie of the Year in 1951 under Manager Leo Durocher. Mays played 22 seasons with the Giants and Mets, and in 1979 the "Say Hey Kid" was elected to the Baseball Hall of Fame. He was drafted in the Army and served 1952-53 before returning to baseball. "I don't make history, I just catch fly balls," he quipped.

Another athletic hero who made integration history was William Felton Russell, born in Monroe, Louisiana in 1934. He experienced racial segregation of the "Deep South" as a child, but at age 9 years he moved with his parents to an integrated housing project in Oakland, California. He failed to make a sports team in secondary schools, but played basketball and ran track at the University of San Francisco on a work-scholarship. He played on a U.S. Olympic basketball team and won a gold medal before playing for the Boston Celtics in the NBA for 13 seasons. After the 1965-66 season when his coach and mentor "Red" Auerbach retired, Auerbach made Bill Russell head coach of the Celtics.

These are only two good examples of young men who with exemplary athletic skills helped to break color barriers. They suffered prejudice and indignity at home and on the road because of their black color. Southern racism, especially, was still a national story in the 1950s and was attributed to the doctrine of "separate, but equal" generally followed in thought and deed by many Southerners to be the law of the land for nearly 60 years.

To better understand this period, one must look to the celebrated case of Homer Plessy, a black man from Louisiana who challenged the constitutionality of segregated railroad coaches in state courts and fought it all the way to the U.S. Supreme Court. In the *Plessy v. Ferguson* landmark decision of 1896, the U.S. Supreme Court found that the doctrine of "separate but equal" concerning segregation in public facilities did not violate the Constitution. Separate schools for whites and blacks became a basic rule in Southern society, legitimized in this doctrine that legalized segregation. The Supreme Court upheld the lower courts: separate railroad cars provided equal services and the 14th Amendment was not violated.

In the 1950s, the "time had come for America to examine the color of its soul," as the narrator recounted on "The Rage Within" segment on the History Channel Classroom program in April 2001. Historians estimate that 15 million blacks were living in the United States early in the 1950s, but during the next 10 to 15 years, some 6 million of them left the South to head north for better jobs (better than picking cotton and cutting cane), being especially attracted to the Chicago area.

Discontent Reaches San Antonio and the Colleges--There was about this same time a discontent among some Negro leaders in San Antonio, a smoldering fire that had been fanned twice in a year: (1) the move of San Antonio College from the rental campus buildings ca. 1859, to the modern campus on San Pedro Avenue in February 1951; (2) discussion by college district trustees in May and June 1952 of a proposed bond election of unspecified amount to expand San Antonio College and part of which monies would be earmarked for land expansion, buildings and needed repairs at St. Philip's College. The future of San Antonio's only Negro school of higher learning was at stake.

At a regular meeting on May 6, 1952 of the Board of Trustees of the San Antonio Union Junior College District--which had jurisdiction over San Antonio College and St. Philip's College--Trustee Travis Moursund, an attorney, offered a motion that the District buy three houses and lots to "fill out" the St. Philip's campus. Trustee G. J. Sutton, a black and a mortician, strongly objected to the routine motion on the grounds the additional property was not needed and, furthermore, the District should go "all out to improve St. Philip's College or close it down by May 31st." Sutton also called for more discussion at the next meeting in two weeks, to which Chairman W. W. McAllister, Sr. agreed.

McAllister went on record as opposing mixed education "unless the Supreme Court forces us" to have a common school. Later, he expressed his hope that after the District fixed up the St. Philip's campus, Negro students would--at this time--rather have their own school.

J. O. Loftin, who served as president of both St. Philip's College and San Antonio College, said "It won't be long before the Negroes will be allowed to enter every white school, judging from recent Supreme Court decisions evolving challenges of separate but equal facilities for education" (*San Antonio Express*, May 7, 1952).

At the May 7th Board meeting, Miss Artemisia Bowden, dean emeritus of St. Philip's College and a revered community leader, was asked to comment on the one- or two-school concept. She said:

> You must either fix it up or close it down. People in Houston and right here in San Antonio have told me the repair of the school is disgraceful (*San Antonio Express*, May 7, 1952).

She continued her remarks, that if something isn't done soon the board will have the citizens on its hands "because there is a restlessness." The elderly educator said that Negro students didn't want to attend the new San Antonio College, even if allowed. She said she had heard San Antonio College students also had been polled and the feeling there was against admitting Negro students.

Loftin and other college officials denied the report that a survey had been taken. He said current graduations from the two Negro high schools were not conducive to increasing the small enrollment of day students at St. Philip's College. San Antonio College, on the other hand, he explained, was fed by 31 institutions. After all the talk, Moursund withdrew his motion to buy property to expand the St. Philip's campus.

At the May 21st meeting the SAUJCD Board was urged in a resolution, also released to the public, by the local chapter of the National Association for the Advancement of Colored People (N.A.A.C.P.) to abolish segregation among St. Philip's College and San Antonio College and to "integrate all students into one institution on a non-segregated basis, irrespective of race." The organization said that its suggestion was in line with the national association's campaign to eliminate segregation from public education.

The N.A.A.C.P. resolution was a prelude to a motion offered by Sutton to abolish St. Philip's College at the end of the school year and admit Negro students to San Antonio College in September. The motion died for lack of a second, but the matter would be up for discussion again in two weeks. McAllister responded:

> I feel it would be a great mistake to close St. Philip's College. It would be doing the Negro people great injustice. What we need is public approval of a bond issue to meet the needs of St. Philip's College over the next five years. This we must get in the very near future (*San Antonio Express*, May 21, 1952).

More than 40 Negro citizens showed up at the meeting and forced a move from President Loftin's office and the small board table to the San Antonio College Library on the second floor of the Administration Building. Persons who said they represented the local chapter of N.A.A.C.P. were led by the Rev. C. W. Black who told trustees it would take at least a million dollars to bring St. Philip's College up to par with San Antonio College. He voiced that it was a moral obligation of democracy to provide a total, integral program for the college district.

Trustees G. S. McCreless, a businessman, and Lee A. Christy, a general contractor, wanted more time for study and to determine what the public wanted before making decisions. The Rev. Black asked President Loftin about a recommendation and Loftin replied:

> That's a good question...the $64 question...I think a common school is coming, but when the white people are forced into it, they will accept it more graciously than if we invite them (Negro students) in (*San Antonio Express*, May 21, 1952).

Loftin never did give a recommendation, but went on to outline that cities of Wichita Falls, Amarillo and Brownsville either couldn't afford or didn't want to provide equal junior college facilities for a dozen or so Negro students, so they were admitted to white schools. Loftin then read results of a questionnaire of students and faculty at St. Philip's College which showed that the majority did not favor a merger. Dr. Ruth Bellinger, a physician on the East Side, countered by saying that St. Philip's College administrators, being so economically connected, are inclined to be in accordance with the Board.

The SAUJCD Board passed a contested motion proffered by Vice-Chairman Jesse N. Fletcher, insurance manager, which called for a bond election to enhance property and buildings at St. Philip's College. Fletcher outlined that he neither favored or objected to segregation, but only had in mind the welfare of the Negro students and the duty of the board to provide equal education. Sutton cast the lone dissenting vote, as expected, on the resolution and the follow-up offer made by Chairman McAllister to enlist Sutton to serve on a three-member committee of trustees to study school needs and cost estimates. Segregation and integration--and the ultimate fate of St. Philip's--appeared to hang in the balance of a public vote on a future bond election. Fletcher also explained to the audience that the State Constitution made it incumbent upon the trustees to maintain separate and substantially equal facilities for Negro students. Fletcher and Sutton quibbled over whether St. Philip's College students were "happily attending" their college, as

Fletcher had mentioned. After Sutton's request to delete the word "happily," the resolution was approved. The emotional meeting toned down at the end, but during the course of heated debate involving Loftin and Sutton, Sutton--low-voiced and of slight build--stood on a table in the Library to be seen and heard better by the crowd.

The next month--at the July 3rd Board meeting--junior college trustees unanimously proposed a $2.5 million bond issue based on hasty study and a recommendation from a 25-member citizens Committee on College Improvements chaired by Fletcher. Sutton referred to the members as "hand-picked and not representative of the community." With no East Side factions present, Sutton agreed to at least submit the proposition to a public vote, but reserved the caveat that he opposed the issue as a "waste of money." While he had the floor, Sutton continued by saying that he was taking his stand in the belief that the courts will abolish "Jim Crow education."

Financial arrangements and fine-tuning for the bond election were cleared by trustees in August 1952; the first week in September the board officially set September 30th as election day on the proposed $2.5 million bond issue.

Integration Just a Matter of Time--About 9 a.m. on Tuesday, September 9, 1952, three Negro youths sought admittance to San Antonio College for the fall semester, but were denied by President Loftin. Applicants were accompanied by their parents. Two of the boys recently had been graduated from Phyllis Wheatley High School and asked to take courses in architecture. A female co-ed who had attended St. Philip's College last spring semester sought enrollment in medical technology courses. A few hours later a fourth student appeared with his father asking Loftin for entry into business administration classes there because "classes are crowded at St. Philip's College," the President quoted the boy as saying.

All of the students--after being denied admission to the all-white student body--indicated that they probably would enroll at St. Philip's College, also under Loftin's administration. The enrollment attempts were not a surprise to Loftin or the board because of notification a month earlier by U. S. Tate, a Dallas lawyer, that several students would apply for admission to exhaust legal remedies before a law suit was filed. Tate served as a counsel in the historical *Sweatt v. Painter* case at The University of Texas in 1950, a case ultimately decided by the U.S. Supreme Court to admit Negro Sweatt to the Law School in Austin

114

under the equal protection clause of the 14th Amendment of the U. S. Constitution.

Also, Loftin and others at the College were mindful that in September 1951, 10 students had been denied entry into various elementary, junior and senior high schools in the San Antonio Independent School District.

Loftin was quoted as saying after the short interviews with the four students and their parents that "they left with apparent satisfaction. I told them I was sorry we have no option in the matter since the State law requires separate schools and we have them" (*San Antonio News*, September 9, 1952).

Less than a week later Harry V. Burns, N.A.A.C.P local chapter president, released a statement he had drawn recommending (1) that St. Philip's Negro College be closed and all students integrated into San Antonio College, and (2) opposition by voters to the proposed $2.5 million bond issue up for election (*San Antonio Light*, September 14, 1952). [Burns, a civil service executive, later sat as a trustee on the Board of the San Antonio Community College District, as irony would have it.]

Burns also made the arguments in his resolution that the Board has admitted the Negro campus is inadequate and in non-compliance with federal law; that local Catholic colleges admitted graduate students two years ago and admitted Negroes at the undergraduate level in September 1951; that Central Catholic High School admitted a 15-year-old Negro boy in September 1952; and that Negro students are now attending formerly all-white junior colleges in Corpus Christi, Amarillo, Brownsville, Wichita Falls and Lubbock.

On the eve of the election, the *San Antonio Express* and the *News* editorialized in favor of the passage of the bond issue labeled as "a sound investment." The Huntress publishers were close friends with Miss Bowden, now retired as leader of St. Philip's College, and the editorial lauded her distinctive services to the community and the State. As a frequent visitor to the newspaper offices, it was not known if she was an influencing factor in the publishing company favoring the bonds.

[True story: after covering an event at St. Philip's, Miss Bowden asked "off the record" (as she was sometimes wont to say) if she could ride with me downtown? As I opened the passenger door she hesitated a moment, then sat in the front seat. We traveled in that 1947 Plymouth on East Commerce Street to the Joske's store at Alamo Street where she got out expressing thanks for the ride. It was a big moment for me to act as chauffeur for a person I greatly admired.]

The *San Antonio Light* on September 29th also endorsed the bond issue in a shorter editorial. It allowed that 25 per cent of the bond monies would be spent at St. Philip's College which operated on a smaller scale than the main junior college (SAC); furthermore, "this is proper, both on moral grounds and to conform with the Supreme Court's ruling..."

Board Chairman McAllister, on the speaker's stump, reacted to the N.A.A.C.P. advocacy to close St. Philip's College in his address before San Antonio Kiwanis Club colleagues on September 12th: "We whites are not yet conditioned for integration; the Negroes aren't conditioned either," he ventured. He outlined three types of education and training offered by San Antonio College and St. Philip's College: (1) first- and second-year college work for students preparing to attend senior colleges; (2) two years of college training for those students who want training beyond high school; (3) adult education. He reported to the civic club members that St. Philip's College in May 1952 had 200 day students and 300 enrolled in evening adult education classes. A recent survey, he said, had shown that 75 per cent of the 200 day students preferred to remain at St. Philip's if facilities were improved on a par with the new San Antonio College campus on San Pedro Avenue. San Antonio College had 600 day students and 1,800 night school attendees for the same period. Increases were expected at San Antonio College in the fall semester which was set to begin within days of the talk. In closing, he urged Kiwanians to support the bond issue on September 30th.

The Taxpayers League of San Antonio--the same organization that had strenuously opposed the failed election in November 1941 to create a separate junior college district--decided unanimously at a meeting in the St. Anthony Hotel days before the election to throw support behind the proposal for the benefit of St. Philip's College and San Antonio College.

Two East Side leaders, Dr. C. A. Whittier and the Rev. S. H. James approached Board Vice-chairman Fletcher as chair of the improvement program committee for his assurances that more than $624,000 talked about would be spent on St. Philip's College upgrading. The Negro people wanted explanations of just how funds would be spent before they vote, the men said, although they pointed out they were not representing or sent by any particular group. Fletcher answered that figures were based on estimated costs by architects and that it was the Board's plan to take care of the needs at St. Philip's first, then apply the balance of money to further expansion of a growing San Antonio College.

News was mixed in the final days before the election as all three metropolitan dailies carried stories about the San Antonio Council of Parents and Teachers urging passage of the bonds at its fall meeting attended by 300 teachers and parents in the Municipal Auditorium. Loftin (then serving as president of the San Antonio Kiwanis Club) and Leon Taliaferro, principal of Horace Mann Junior High School (another Kiwanis leader) spoke at the meeting in favor of the improvement program. Mrs. J. W. Miller presided; Mrs. Manfred Gerhardt, a member of the San Antonio City Council known for her work as a P-T.A. leader on the Southside, attended the meeting.

While this "favorable press" was welcomed by the bond proponents, headlines in the newspapers from September 23-25 were lead-ins to stories about legal action looming from Loftin's refusal to admit the four Negro youths to the white college under his control on September 8th because of their color. Tate, now regional attorney for the N.A.A.C.P., requested an appeal hearing on behalf of the applicants. He had previously advised Loftin and trustees that if they would close St. Philip's College and integrate Negro students, the District could save costs. There were other reports that the bond election may well prove to be "academic" in view of reported promises by the N.A.A.C.P. to tie it up in court in connection with San Antonio College.

The *San Antonio Register*, Valmo Bellinger's respected clarion for the East Side residents, on September 26th ran side-by-side arguments "For" and "Against" the bond issue, giving adequate coverage to the oft-repeated messages by Loftin and the trustees and the views of the N.A.A.C.P., in opposition. It was a fair presentation; no recommendation was evident, leaving it up to the voters to decide. However, the *Register* published in the same edition an architectural rendering of proposed buildings at St. Philip's College. The photograph already had appeared in other local newspapers and drew the ire of Sutton who labeled the rendering "unauthorized and designed to mislead the Negro voters and is purely election propaganda" (*Register*, September 26, 1952).

With all of the exchanges between proponents and opponents, voter apathy was apparent when observers revealed only a "scant" 14 absentee votes were cast. College trustees, except for Sutton, paid for a last-minute political ad which ran on election day urging voter turnout: "The Junior College Bond Issue Affects You...Your Children...THEIR Future. Vote 'Yes'." In smaller text the message read that the Board of Trustees was bound by the State Constitution to maintain separate schools for Negro and white students, but held sympathy with the Federal Court ruling that such separate schools must offer equal opportunities. The stated amount of the bond issue was $2,500,000; the maximum tax rate on the County valuation was fixed at 25 cents per $100; it was estimated that the owner of a home of $10,000 value on the taxroll would not pay over $7.50 yearly in taxes.

The voting was restricted to property owners and was conducted with only one voting machine at each of 41 polling places from 7 a.m. to 7 p.m. on September 30th. Voting was considered "light" by election officials who tallied 2,587 votes in favor and 1,993 against the bond issuance, a slim 594-vote majority for passage. As predicted, voters at the Northside and the Southside polling places in the greater San Antonio area favored the bonds; voters in the East and West precincts voted to defeat the bond proposal. After trustees canvassed the election results the next day, they wasted no time in preparing for the sale of the $2.5 million bond issuance by setting the date October 20 for bid opening. The actual date to issue the bonds was fixed as November 15, 1952. McAllister, as expected, was "elated" over the results. Sutton said with all the money other trustees spent on boosting the bond election, "they didn't win by a great majority" (*San Antonio Light*, October 2, 1952).

A week after their bond vote victory, trustees turned to other business at hand and set October 20th as the date to give formal audience to Attorney Tate acting on appeal by the four Negro students denied entry to San Antonio College. Sutton saw the hearing as the last legal remedy before "going to the courts." He foresaw the alleged racial discrimination and unequal educational facilities suit to be filed in Federal District Court. McAllister agreed that all administrative means must be exhausted before the petitioners can approach the court.

Trustee Moursund, himself an attorney, called for immediate action by the Board that had granted the request, heard the appeal and denied it. He said to send the Minutes of the meeting to Tate: "There's not any use coming back in a week or two weeks from now and doing what we all know we'll do" (*San Antonio Express*, October 15, 1952). Arley V. Knight, attorney for the District, said that Tate wants to put on evidence and obtain a stenographic record. The Board then voted to give Tate a formal hearing. Sutton said Tate represented the four students and took exception to references that Tate was representing the N.A.A.C.P. It was going too far, Sutton continued, to say that Tate wants a hearing only for court reasons. The students want to know whether they will be admitted to San Antonio College, he concluded.

It surprised no observer that on October 20--after trustees emerged with Attorney Knight from an executive session that had been closed to the public and press--trustees upheld Loftin's refusal to admit the four students. Then, in another action, denied the August 19th petition to close St. Philip's College. No formal hearing was held because "U. S. Tate, counsel for the N.A.A.C.P. told McAllister in a telephone conversation that formal appeal was unnecessary" (*San Antonio Light*, October 21, 1952).

***Law Suits Filed To Admit Black Students*--**Tate, with associate counsels W. J. Durham of Dallas and Harry M. Bellinger, young and articulate San Antonio attorney, wasted no time in filing injunctions against the San Antonio Independent School District and the San Antonio Union Junior College District seeking to restrain the barring of eight named Negro students because of race and color from attending Burbank High School (for specialized agriculture courses) and San Antonio College, both so-called in the suit as "white" institutions.

Co-counsel Bellinger personally filed the law suit on November 24, 1952 in the very presence of Judge C. K. Quin (former Mayor of San Antonio) in the 57th District Court sitting in Bexar County. Recall the earlier citation that Bellinger in 1951 had sought admission of a total of 10 students denied entry to Burbank High School, Jefferson High School, Tech and Lanier High Schools, Washington Irving Junior High School and Fannin Elementary School. He had taken up appeals before the San Antonio and the Bexar County Boards of Education; both denied admission requests and the status had been latent for the past year.

[Friendly Attorney Bellinger telephoned reporter Jerome Weynand--who had been following the segregation/integration story for the past two years for the *Express* and *News* as the education reporter--giving the time, date and place where he was going to file the injunctions. When asked later if the N.A.A.C.P. was instigator or in any way behind the suits against the local school and college districts, Bellinger replied: "All legal facilities, personnel and financial aid of the N.A.A.C.P. are available when and if needed in these cases," as I duly reported the next morning in *The Express*.]

Judge Quin set hearings in both suits for January 19, 1953.

The first week in December 1952 there arose in the local press an awareness based on a tip-off from a national spokesman for the N.A.A.C.P. that five cases aimed at breaking segregation barriers of public education would be argued before the U.S. Supreme Court on December 9-11, 1952, a month before the local hearing date set by Judge Quinn. Outcome, no doubt, would have direct bearing on the two injunction suits filed by Bellinger on November 24th. At the time of filing, Bellinger said he would not ask the judge for a postponement of the January 19th hearing date.

The press release from the N.A.A.C.P. cited three of the cases to be heard by the high court as among the most important the Association had handled in its 43 years of existence. The three cases backed by the Association came from Clarendon, South Carolina; Topeka, Kansas; and Prince Edward County in Virginia. Two other companion cases had originated in Delaware and the District of Columbia. All five cases were based on the issue of the validity of state statutes and constitutional provisions pursuant to which Negro and white children are segregated in public elementary and secondary schools; that segregation, per se, is discrimination.

For history's sake, *Brown v. Board of Education* was the collective title for the five separate cases that were heard by the U.S. Supreme Court during the period 1952-1955. Each sought a decision to end segregation in public schools because of the contention that "separate educational facilities are inherently unequal." To refresh one's memory:

Linda Brown had to ride a bus five miles to a school although a public school was located only four blocks from her home in Topeka, Kansas. The nearby school wasn't full and the girl met all requirements to attend, except one--Linda Brown was black!

Back in Bexar County, Texas, six College trustees--all except Sutton--voted on December 2, 1952 to make a formal answer through Attorney Knight denying all allegations as stated in the segregation injunction suit filed against them and President Loftin. Moursund suggested that Sutton could file his own dissenting answer.

During the period that the Supreme Court was considering arguments on the *Brown v. Board of Education* litigation, the Texas Attorney General Price Daniel issued an opinion on December 14, 1952, in which he held that State Education Commissioner J. W. Edgar had no jurisdiction to hear appeals from decisions of governing boards of junior colleges. Edgar had sought the opinion after being asked to hear an appeal by Negroes denied admission to Texarkana Junior College. A federal court had agreed with Texarkana Junior College arguments that the Negro students had not exhausted their administrative remedies to the Commissioner and the State Board of Education. It appeared that the

120

Texarkana student applicants would have to seek relief again through the federal court if administrative remedies were not open to them in the State system. The San Antonio Junior College case stood to be affected by the ruling, if Judge Quin had not passed the suit "indefinitely" on January 16, 1953, just days before the scheduled hearing. Attorneys for both the plaintiffs and the defendants agreed to the action pending a decision in a similar case still before the U. S. Supreme Court.

While court action was pending, work continued on construction of a two-story classroom and administration building, a student union building, and an auditorium for St. Philip's College--all scheduled for occupancy by the fall semester 1954 at a cost of $700,000.

Before St. Philip's College students and faculty could move into the new and expanded buildings, Justice Earl Warren delivered on May 17, 1954, the U. S. Supreme Court's unanimous ruling in the landmark civil rights case in *Brown v. Board of Education* of Topeka, Kansas, summarized here:

> State-sanctioned segregation of public schools was a violation of the 14th Amendment and was, therefore, unconstitutional. This historic document marked the end of the "separate but equal" precedent set by the Supreme Court nearly 60 years earlier and served as a catalyst for the expanding civil rights movement during the decade of the 1950s.--National Archives & Records Administration

[Recall that the 13th Amendment to the U.S. Constitution outlawed slavery; three years later in 1868, the 14th Amendment guaranteed the rights of citizenship to all persons born or naturalized in the United States, including due process and equal protection under the laws. The 15th Amendment protected voting rights.]

The latest decision clearly was a victory for the N.A.A.C.P. that had been formed in 1909 to champion the black civil rights movement-- namely, elimination of lynching and to obtain fair trials--which in the 1930s focused on the complete integration of American society and to force admission of blacks into universities at the graduate level, especially. Thurgood Marshall in 1938 had become the general counsel for the N.A.A.C.P.'s Legal and Defense Fund. He won the *Sweatt v. Painter* case against The University of Texas, previously cited.

Integration Comes to School with Calmness--On May 31, 1955, now Chief Justice Earl Warren issued a follow-up ruling, known as "Brown II," on how the May 17, 1954 decision would be imposed. He instructed the states to begin desegregation plans "with all deliberate speed."

Local news accounts sensed few problems were envisioned for the Alamo City schools as they moved to comply with the edict against segregation handed down by the U. S. Supreme Court. Religious leaders in the area greeted the decision as being in keeping with Christian and American principles. Rabbi David Jacobson of Temple Beth-El, adjacent to the San Antonio College campus, cited "Thou shalt love thy neighbor as thyself," in lauding the decision to proceed with integration.

School officials predicted no difficulties in making "adjustments" and abiding by the law. Attorney Bellinger also anticipated no problems as far as students were concerned. Roman Catholic Archbishop Robert E. Lucey was reported to be "elated" upon hearing about the news.

The San Antonio Independent School District had at this time a census of 4,391 Negro children registered in its schools: 2,880 in elementary schools, 940 in junior highs and 571 in senior high schools. Outlying districts reported fewer Negro pupils. The County superintendent reported some 161 Negro students in rural schools.

Miss Muriel Forbes, president of the San Antonio Teachers Council, said that she was "surprised," but added that the law would be followed in Texas and predicting the State will not secede!

President Loftin said that he was "not surprised and certainly not disturbed. We've worked for this day and not against it" (*San Antonio Express*, May 18, 1954). As chief administrator of two schools soon to be integrated, he saw no reason for St. Philip's College students suddenly to transfer, but acknowledged that some San Antonio College students had voiced interest in attending vocational courses offered only at St. Philip's. He allowed that the decision and implementation order would result in an overall saving to the college district by combining some classes.

Meanwhile, San Antonio Negro leaders joyfully hailed the law of the land decision banning segregation in schools and predicted that the change-over could be made with little or no friction. S. H. Gates, 78-year-old retired high school principal and veteran of 40 years as a teacher and administrator in the segregated San Antonio school system, said the decision was something that he expected and was heartily in favor of it.

Sutton, now off the College board but for six years an elected trustee and outspoken champion of integration, hailed the decision as "justice," but still objected to the current building project at St. Philip's.

He branded the improvement program--now nearing completion--as "underhanded." [Years later the Board would name the Sutton Center in his honor; his widow would serve as a local Representative in the Texas Legislature.]

Mrs. O. M. Whittier, wife of a physician, had been an unsuccessful candidate for a place on the board in the May 21st election, said she expected the outcome as "inevitable."

Even with all the elation expressed by San Antonians across the spectrum of the community, junior college trustees on May 28, 1954 delayed voting on non-segregated admissions at San Antonio College and St. Philip's College pending further study. Despite the Supreme Court's opinion, no definite legal action had taken place. The Texas Commissioner of Education ordered continued segregation in Texas public schools for the coming 1954-55 school year.

Integrating the City's segregated nine swimming pools was the next target of the local chapter of N.A.A.C.P. Harry Burns and his members had just succeeded in convincing the City of San Antonio officials to allow Negroes to use for the first time municipal golf courses, tennis courts and playgrounds, ending many years of enforcement of unwritten law.

A new City ordinance ordering segregation in city swimming pools was passed hurriedly by the San Antonio City Council in June 1954, only days after six Negroes took a dip in the Woodlawn pool. Police guards were set up at some pool gates, but the N.A.A.C.P. put out the word that it would not violate the ordinance in an attempt to force Negroes into pools designated for whites only. Local chapter members, however, indicated that a law suit would be filed to overturn the ordinance. City Manager Ralph Winton, a retired F.B.I. special agent, reacted by saying: "That's what we want them to do. Everybody agrees with them in principle, but we need a final court ruling" (*San Antonio News*, June 21, 1954).

During the remaining summer months of 1954, Harry Bellinger made several more attempts to persuade the San Antonio Board of Education to integrate classes in September 1954. No luck.

President Loftin in October 1954--on the eve of the dedication of improvements at St. Philip's College--caught people off guard when he floated the idea to expand that college to a four-year Negro school to provide even greater opportunities for Negroes in Southwest Texas. Current enrollment at the two-year college was placed at 400 students. Whether or not his "idea" was done tongue-in-cheek, the recommendation never reached serious study. But, Loftin's recommendation to name the new Classroom/Administration Building after Dean Bowden was heartily approved by the Board.

> Economic considerations, as well as those of justice and decency dictate that local school authorities fritter away no further time in devising schemes to thwart, or even unduly delay, the integration process...It should be done calmly, reasonably, sensibly--but upheld it should be.--(*San Antonio Express* editorial, June 2, 1955).

Calmness and good sense did prevail in the integration of white students entering St. Philip's and Negro students enrolling at San Antonio College. At San Antonio College, led by President Loftin, Dean Wayland P. Moody and Registrar Jerome Weynand all declined to talk about rumors that Negro students had quietly enrolled, pending an official policy statement to be issued by the Board (San Antonio News, June 11, 1955).

Finally, Loftin announced a few days after the fact, that two Negroes had been admitted to the first summer term at San Antonio College in June 1955: (1) Hubert F. Lindsay, 27, an Army veteran originally from Pennsylvania, married and with two children was credited as the first enrollee. He worked as a civil service employee at Fort Sam Houston and had been a student at St. Philip's College before being permitted to enroll in biology and bacteriology courses which met evenings at San Antonio College; and (2) Linus Dietrich, who said only that he entered "through Fort Sam Houston," enrolled in an elementary course in German. He declined to give other personal information. The Associated Press picked up the story for statewide distribution.

Three Randolph A.F.B. airmen were identified by Loftin as the first white students admitted to St. Philip's College. All enrolled in evening classes: A1/C Eidsell C. Obenshain and M-Sgt. John Claude Beckett, both sought a course in radio and television repair; and S-Sgt. Darvin E. Sachtleben took a class in auto body and fender works. Dr. Clarence W. Norris, dean of St. Philip's College, welcomed the new students with open arms, it was reported:

> Frankly, I'm glad to see segregation breaking down. Prejudice shouldn't stand in the way of young people's growth and development and education (*San Antonio Express*, June 10, 1955).

The Huntress papers both had "words" to say against how the college officials had agreed to "sit on this thing" even to the point of refusing comment on the known facts of integration. But, in the end, they had good words to print:

The *News* said the San Antonio College Board and President Loftin "did the right thing the wrong way in using hush-hush secrecy." Another comment:

> The end result--if not the method employed--by San Antonio College in taking the lead for integration locally, receives this newspaper's commendation...(*San Antonio Express* editorial, June 10, 1955).

This chapter on the integration process involving San Antonio College is at the end. There was still a long way to go before the color lines were erased completely. The nation soon focused on other cities, especially in September 1957 on Little Rock High School in Arkansas. President Dwight D. Eisenhower sent troops from the 101st Airborne Division (that will be remembered as LTC Robert G. Cole's old outfit) to ensure that nine teen-age Negro students' civil rights were upheld and they could enter the school. The "Screaming Eagles" soldiers had fixed bayonets, jeeps with mounted machineguns, and patrolled the halls...In June 1958, one male student of the original nine was graduated. Martin Luther King Jr. attended the graduation ceremonies.

Another milestone in the colorful history of San Antonio College had been overcome.

San Antonio College Official Seal
adopted in the mid-1950s.

"MR. MONEY BAGS"

Profile: *VERNON VICTOR LaBAUVE*

Vernon LaBauve, the first and long-time financial administrator in the San Antonio Union Junior College District, came into his position coincidentally with the change of the guard from the San Antonio Board of Education to the operation and control of San Antonio College and St. Philip's College by elected trustees for the new tax district that had been approved by taxpaying voters in October 1945. He brought to the job wide experience in education, finance, and military service. He kept the books, wrote the minutes of official board meetings, deposited the money, issued the payroll and other tasks. He served in positions of great trust as business manager, comptroller, and administrative assistant to the president of the colleges in the district for 43 years before retirement.

When the student enrollment was smaller and dollar income was less, Vernon LaBauve made his daily trips alone to the bank depository carrying a small money pouch and encountered no problems for many years. After the move to the larger campus in 1951, he maintained scheduled trips to the bank until forced to use an armored car service because of the increased flow of money. Years later he would lose his nickname, "Money Bags LaBauve," but Vernon didn't mind the loss of his moniker as he did the problems after armed robbers made a heist of an armored car loaded with thousands of dollars of college funds collected during a heavy registration period.

Born December 31, 1911 in Pleasanton (Atascosa County), Texas, he attended public schools and was graduated in 1934 with a bachelor of science degree from Southwest Texas State Teacher's

127

College in San Marcos. He and Ann Lee Rhode were married in 1936 in Charlotte, Texas. Vernon began teaching in a one-room school. In 1934, he received a master of education degree in finance from The University of Texas; then, he spent his early years in education as teacher and principal in Frio County.

His career took him to a stint serving on financial assignments in the U.S. Air Force. After discharge, LaBauve returned to teach business administration in South San Antonio ISD schools. He was teaching an accounting course at Trinity University in the summer of 1946 when President J. O. Loftin employed LaBauve to take the financial helm of the District.

Students on the GI-Bill after World War II recall the efficient manner in which Business Manager LaBauve and a small staff assisted in processing requisitions for book vouchers and certifying stipends for the veterans. He was variously described by students and fellow workers as a model administrator: diplomatic, friendly, gentlemanly, dedicated, dependable, and soft-spoken, among other attributes. His entire tenure was one of financial services to the District and to the students, faculties, and staff of the colleges. He toiled without complaint in a largely unsung-hero role as one of the pioneer and top administrators.

His civic duties included serving as Councilman and Mayor of Balcones Heights, a bedroom city. He was a member of the Optimist and Lions International Clubs, providing further community service.

LaBauve voluntarily and honorably retired in 1979 never dreaming, he told colleagues, that the college district would grow as large as it had become. Before the onset of a debilitating illness that would curtail his travel, LaBauve--accompanied by Ann and a nurse--revisited his old haunts and office on the campus of San Antonio College and was warmly received by friends and co-workers. With a wry sense of humor--and possibly a little twinge of sadness he still felt over retirement--used a good ol' country-boy adage as cover saying:

"This is better than sliced bread" (San Antonio College *Ranger*, February 21, 1992) in an expanded obituary written by students. He died on February 3, 1992 at the age of 80 years age. Friends eulogized him at a memorial service that was held at Manor Baptist Church where he had been a member, Sunday School teacher, and deacon. Survivors include his wife, son Daniel and daughter Mary Ann.

[Vernon: this belated recognition is for you!]

128

8.
PRESIDENT WAYLAND P. MOODY
SUCCEEDS LOFTIN

Dr. Wayland Pelton Moody, 53, was "in the wings"--so to speak--for more than eight years when he was suddenly elevated to the presidency of San Antonio College by a unanimous decision of the board of trustees at a special called meeting held on Monday morning, January 2, 1956.

He succeeded J. O. Loftin, 68, who, with his wife Matilda, died as a result of an automobile accident on the western outskirts of Kerrville, Texas about noon on December 31 as the couple was returning to San Antonio from their ranch northwest of Junction.

Moody and his wife, Lillian, were among guests at the deer-hunting camp for two wintry days before returning home Friday evening. When news reached him of the tragic deaths, it was a bittersweet moment for Moody--prepared by education and experience, groomed, and no doubt the man expected one day to replace Loftin as chief administrator--that he would become president of the flourishing institution on the morning before the Loftins' funeral services were held that afternoon.

Loftin had spent the last 14 years of a long and varied career in public education at all levels and seemed destined to help create a junior college district and develop San Antonio College and St. Philip's as their enthusiastic leader.

Transition Runs Smoothly--Loftin and Moody had shared one small office on the South Alamo Street campus. The front of their desks abutted causing the administrators to face each other. An aisle and a counter separated them from the registrar's office. The business manager had an office upstairs; the librarian was down the long open porch. A dozen faculty had offices scattered about the buildings. Moody had been hand-picked by Loftin and joined the College as the dean and administrative assistant in September 1947. He brought to the position broad experience as an educator with college and military backgrounds.

His assignments included teaching psychology. Dean Moody quickly established rapport with students on the intimate campus, knew most of their names, and his personality carried over to the larger student body when the campus was moved to the San Pedro site in the spring 1951. (See "Profile" on Moody, Appendix D.)

Trustees recognized his worth to the college in the hurried transition period and raised President Moody's salary to $12,000, a boost of $2,240 a year over what he was earning as dean--which left some growing room to the $15,000 paid Loftin. Salary was not the issue for Moody; after abruptly losing a friend and mentor, having to lead two colleges was the challenge.

As he assumed leadership, President Moody had the backing of a businessmen's board of trustees with whom he had worked. Walter W. McAllister was still president (chairman); Jesse N. Fletcher, vice-president; Lee A. Christy, secretary; G. S. McCreless, James M. Goodman, Travis B. Moursund and Manuel C. Gonzales. The familiar names of McAllister, Fletcher, Christy and McCreless were noted earlier as original members elected in October 1945 and each had 10 years of experience.

At this juncture in the life of San Antonio College, enrollment data for the academic year 1955-1956 (as noted in the *Catalog* for 1956-57, p. 113) are summarized as follows: head count for the Summer Session 1955 had been 973 in Day and 1,437 in Evening Division. For the Fall 1955 and Spring 1956, there were 3,738 students enrolled.

In the 1956 Summer Session, the first under Dr. Moody's administration, there was a total headcount (i.e. counting each student only once) of 2,309, about evenly spread between day and evening classes. In the Fall 1956 and the Spring 1957 there were 1,750 students in day classes and 4,732 enrolled in the evening program. Added to those totals were thousands of adult distributive education students enrolled in short-term courses leading to certificates.

The first year had been a smooth transition from the Loftin to Moody administrations, everything considered.

Administrative and Faculty Lineup--The new president had kept most of his experienced administrative team in place and all of the department chairpersons to lead some 110 full-time faculty and hundreds more lecturers in the evening classes.

The board also acted with dispatch approving the call-up of Clyde R. Nail, director of the booming Evening Division, to fill the position left vacant by Moody. His new title became "Vice-President and Dean." Nail had been with the college for five years, building the late afternoon and night classes from an enrollment of some 190 students on the old campus to 2,847 in 26 courses in January 1956, making it one of the largest evening programs in the Southwest. He coordinated at first 13 instructors; now he led 128, and that was just the beginning.

Dr. Nail (he received an honorary Doctor of Laws degree from Howard Payne College in recognition for his many years of educational leadership and community involvement) was the Number 2 administrator. Nail's slot was filled by Edwin S. Keasler who began employment on January 16, 1956, having previously worked for the Veterans Administration in Dallas and San Antonio, where he was chief of vocational rehabilitation and education division of the regional office. Immediately prior to taking the evening director's position, Keasler had taught part-time at Trinity University and at San Antonio College, and was a counselor in the Northeast school district. The masthead of Moody's administration entering the academic year 1956-1957 appeared in the *Catalog*, Vol. 28, No. 2, June 1956, as follows:

ADMINISTRATION
Dr. Wayland P. Moody, President
Clyde R. Nail, Vice-President and Dean
Jerome F. Weynand, Registrar
Vernon V. LaBauve, Comptroller
Edwin Keasler, Director, Evening Division
Charles U. Breeden, Assistant Director, Evening Division
Dr. Lester Beals, Dean, Student Personnel Services
Dr. Lois G. Morrison, Dean of Women
James O. Wallace, Librarian
Dr. Omar Roan, Physician
Ernst & Ernst, Accountants
Arley V. Knight, Attorney
Phelps & Dewees & Simmons, Architects
John Gano, Plant Superintendent

DEPARTMENT CHAIRMEN FOR 1956-1957
Mrs. Margaret Peavey ....Art
Mr. Elmer A. Jones ....Biological Sciences
Mrs. Nina Olson.............................Business Administration
Dr. Josephine McAmis ....Chemistry
Mr. Carl Atkins ....Drama, Speech

Dr. Lester Beals ....Education, Psychology
Dr. Mary Tom Osborne ....English, Journalism
Mr. Edward A. Bell, Jr...........................Foreign Languages
Mr. John O. Gibson, Jr. ....Geology
Mr. Wame J. Hallmark ....Mathematics
Dr. Marjorie Walthall ....Music
Mr. Bill Candler ....Physical Education
Mr. Leo S. Duke ....Physics, Engineering
Mr. Truett L. Chance ....Social Sciences

---

FACULTY
Day Division

The following full-time faculty members are listed without professional rank or discipline identification:

John Aeikens, Carl A. Atkins, Kathleen R. Barnard, S. W. Bass, Lester Beals, Edward A. Bell, James David Bennett, A. Chesley Bowman, Bill C. Candler, Loren C. Caraway, Truett L. Chance, George V. Casey, Julian Cooke, Paul R. Culwell, Leo S. Duke, Merle Dulin, Eileen Elliott, William F. Fleming, John O. Gibson, Perry E. Gragg, Wame J. Hallmark, Maria Hanau-Schaumburg, Leone C. Harding, Charles L. Herndon, John H. Hicks, Millicent S. Huff, John Igo, Charles William Jenke, Elmer A. Jones, Warren Paul Kohls, Charles A. Lewis, Ava Josephine McAmis, Roy McCollum, Mamie F. McLean, William R. Mabe and Frederick E. Maples.

Also, Lois G. Morrison, J. B. Olson, Nina M. Olson, Mary Tom Osborne, Margaret Peavey, Floyd M. Roland, Vivian Adams Rudisill, William Samelson, Cole Smith, Charles Stone, Muriel B. Storer, William P. Snyder, Dorothy Jean Taylor, Elaine Tomlinson, George Towns, John A. Wagner, Miriam Wagner, James O. Wallace, Marjorie T. Walthall, Henry B. Webb, Helen Wheeler and La Nell Wilson.

One hundred ten instructors were listed in the Evening Division, a large number of whom became full-time faculty within a few years and remained until retirement.

When the campus move was made in February 1951, Moody was dean of 800 students in three buildings. He focused on enlarging the curriculum and working with Loftin on the building plans to accommodate increases in enrollment each year. The nursing building, technical building, administration building, chemistry-geology building with attached planetarium, and the new learning center--all were completed under Moody's guidance. The physical plant had increased in value to $25 million at the time of his retirement in 1973. At that point the enrollment had peaked at 19,560. At no time during his 17 years as president had the district operated in the "red."

In January 1971 Moody, at age 68, signaled the board that he planned to retire in "about two years." Trustees did not have a formal rite of succession plan, but clearly saw in Clyde Nail the attributes of the man they wanted to succeed Moody when he asked to retire. It was prudent, trustees felt, to name Nail to a new position as "President-elect" when they extended Moody's contract for two more years, giving Moody a salary increase of $8,000, making it $36,000 a year--the growing room previously mentioned. Nail's health was the main reason that he was unable to fulfill his goal to lead the colleges into the future. He had lots of plans, but the indefatigable worker was beginning to slow down, on doctor's orders. He notified Moody in March 1971 that he would resign effective August 31, 1971 for health reasons, and not be available to assume the role of President-Elect on September 1. (Dr. Nail died November 27, 1980.)

Retirement Brings Honors to Dr. Moody-- It was nearing the end of an era when President Moody submitted his letter of request to be retired effective August 31, 1973. The agenda listed 28 items of business at the Regular Meeting of the Board of Trustees of the San Antonio Union Junior College District called to order at 11 a.m. May 18, 1973 by G. S. McCreless. Several items pertained to Moody. Item XVII was his request for retirement that was granted, albeit with regret. M. C. Gonzales came prepared with a two and one-half legal pages, single-spaced Resolution which he presented to the board tracing Moody's life and pioneering contributions to education and his leadership of the local colleges in a span of 50 years. Recognition of the highest order, it read, is hereby ordained to designate Wayland Pelton Moody the first "President Emeritus of the Colleges," effective upon his retirement from active service to the District on August 31, 1973.

But the board was not through: it decreed that the Library-Classroom Building at San Antonio College be known, henceforth, by all people as the "Wayland P. Moody Learning Center," in lasting recognition of "the man who has nurtured the colleges through extraordinary periods of change and growth in students, faculty and physical plant and in singular dedication to the man who has so far given the best fifty years of his life in serving others, Wayland Pelton Moody..."

The vote was unanimous, of course. With a little more house-keeping in order, Moody was granted unused sick leave pay in Item XIX; and the last item on the Agenda, XXVIII, trustees endorsed the title of the car Moody had been using to his personal ownership upon retirement.

Dr. W. W. Jackson, past president of the State Board of Education (recall his quotation on Page One, "In the Beginning,") addressed the board, thanked the trustees and President Moody for the "many fine accomplishments of the District under their administration."

There was one other agenda item of some significance: #XXVI, By Mr. Gonzales:

> BE IT RESOLVED that Dr. Jerome F. Weynand be, and he is hereby elected as President of the Colleges of the District for the period September 1, 1973 to September 1, 1976, at a salary of $30,000 per annum and full use of the President's home, 415 West Ashby Place. This motion was seconded by Mr. Steen. The chairman then called for a vote the same resulting as follows:
>
> Ayes: Mr. Gonzales Mr. Steen Mr. Conway Mr. McAllister,
>   Jr. Dr. Nielsen Mrs. Oppenheimer
> Noes: None

So, another change in administration...another transition would begin in September 1973. Filling the shoes of Nelson, Loftin and Moody would be impossible--but that is another story to be told by other writers at another time...

THE
END

ENDNOTES

1.
In the Beginning...

1. Jackson, W. W. An Address given by the Chairman, Texas Board of Education, to the Faculty of San Antonio College, September 6, 1961, summarized in the Minutes of the General Faculty Meeting of that date.
2. Weynand, Jerome F. "The Role of Public Junior Colleges in Texas as Viewed by Their Presidents and Board Members." Unpublished doctoral dissertation, The University of Texas, Austin, June 1963.
3. Knudson, Marvin C. "President's Report." *Junior College Journal*, Vol. 30, No. 9 (May 1960).
4. Gleazer, Edmund J. Jr. "Annual Report to the American Association of Junior Colleges." *Junior College Journal*, Vol. 31, No. 9 (May 1961).
5. "Focus on the Two-Year College." A Summary of a Conference of the Two-Year College," held Dec. 5-6, 1960, Berkeley, Calif., co-sponsored by the American Association of Junior Colleges and the Center for the Study of Higher Education of The University of California at Berkeley.
6. Gardner, John W. "Quality in Higher Education." *Current Issues in Higher Education 1958*, G. K. Smith (ed.). Washington D.C.: Association for Higher Education, 1958.
7. Knudson, Marvin C. "The Junior College in the Decade Ahead." *Junior College Journal*, Vol. 30, No. 6 (February 1960).
8. Gardner, John W. "The Elite and the Masses. "*College and University Business*, Vol. XXIV (May 1958).
9. Parker, Franklin. "The Community College--*Enfant Terrible* of American Higher Education: A Bibliography of 225 Doctoral Research Dissertations." *Junior College Journal*, Vol. 32, No. 4 (December 1961).
10. Medsker, Leland L. *The Junior College*: Progress and Prospect. New York: McGraw-Hill Book Co., Inc., 1960.
11. Ibid.
12. Weynand, Jerome F. "Some Factors in Career Choice of Freshman Students in a Metropolitan Junior College." Master's Thesis, Trinity University, San Antonio, Texas, 1959.

13. "Junior Colleges: A Low Cost Answer to Crowded Campuses." A Special Report in *U.S. News and World Report*, Vol. XLIV (May 2, 1958).

14. Colvert, C. C. "The Organization, Function and Services of the American Association of Junior Colleges." An Address by the professor and consultant in Junior College Education The University of Texas, 1956.

15. "St. Philip's College: 75 Years of Tradition...An Unlimited Future." Booklet celebrating the Diamond Jubilee of St. Philip's College, San Antonio, Texas, Spring 1973.

16. Op. cit. Weynand, Note 2.

17. *Junior College Directory 1961*. Association of Texas Colleges and Universities Bulletin, VI, Austin.

18. Graham, R. William. *Instant College*. Boston: Branden Press, 1971.

19. Valentine, P. F. (Ed.). *The American College*. New York: Philosophical Library, Inc. 1949.

20. Richardson, Richard C. Jr. *Student's Guide to the Two-Year College*. New Jersey: Prentice-Hall, Inc., 1968.

21. Cook, Dan. "Slocum is taking raps he doesn't deserve." Column, *San Antonio Express-News*, Feb. 17, 2001, page 1C.

22. *The Handbook of Texas Online*: Lon Morris College. Joint project of the General Libraries at UT Austin and the Texas Historical Association, 1999.

23. Whisenhunt, Donald W. *The Encyclopedia of Texas Colleges and Universities*. Austin: Eakin Press, 1986.

24. Op. cit. *The Handbook of Texas Online*. "The Junior College Movement."

25. Ibid. "Dallas Baptist University."

26. *Annual Report and Directory 1979-80*, Texas Public Community/Junior College Association, Austin.

27. San Antonio Board of Education Minutes, meeting on Jan. 24, 1939, Vol. 9, p. 244.

28. DeYoung, Chris A. *Introduction to American Public Education*. New York: McGraw-Hill Book Co., Inc. 1955.

29. Eby, Frederick. *A Study of the Financing of Public Junior Colleges in Texas. Austin*: Univ. of Texas, 1931. Bureau of Research in the Social Sciences, Booklet Study No. 1.

30. Reid, J. R. and Marrs, S.M.N. *Texas Municipal Junior Colleges*. Austin: Bulletin of State Department of Education No. 25-5, Vol. 5, No. 5, June 1929.

ENDNOTES

2.

The University Junior College

1. *The New Handbook of Texas*, Vol. 6, p. 31. Austin: The Texas State Historical Assn., 1996.
2. San Antonio Board of Education MINUTES, June 16, 1925, Vol. 5, p. 159.
3. Ibid. October 6, 1925, Vol. 5, p. 227.
4. Smith, Charles Aubrey. *Fifty Years of Education for Business at The University of Texas.* Austin: College of Business Administration Foundation, 1962.
5. Shelby, Thomas Hall. *Development of Extension Education at The University of Texas 1909-1952.* Austin: The University of Texas Division of Extension, 1952.
6. *San Antonio Express*, Thursday morning, September 24, 1925.
7. *San Antonio Evening News*, Saturday, October 3, 1925.
8. Ibid. Monday, September 21, 1925.
9. Ibid. Friday, September 25, 1925.
10. *San Antonio Express*, June 15, 1925.
11. Moody, Dan. *Biennial Report of the Attorney General of the State of Texas,* 1924 to 1926. Austin: Von Boeckman-Jones Co., 1927.
12. Ralson, Hugh Ellsworth. "History of the San Antonio Junior College." (Unpublished master's thesis) The University of Texas, Austin: 1933.
13. Pollard, Claude. *Biennial Report of the Attorney General of the State of Texas*, 1926 to 1928. Austin: Numbers Printing, 1928.

APPENDICES

APPENDIX A

Roster of First Students to Attend "The University Junior College" *(San Antonio Junior College)*
1925-1926

(Under the supervision of The University of Texas)
Alphabetical list of students compiled from Instructors' Grade Reports:

Harry S. Affleck
Florence Ahr
Bertha G. Allen
Roy E. Anderson
Reynolds L. Andricks
Amy Adrienne Arno
Francisco Asunsula
Alex August

Janie C. Bell
Luther C. Berry
O. Biglow
Alton Blumberg
Eleanor F. Boldt
John B. Bomer
Elmer L. Bonham
Ruth Bourke
Philip Braubach
Anne Breese

Paul Campbell
Mary E. Cannon
John Carriere
Charlton H. Carrol
Inez W. Casey
Hugh Caterson
Carlos Chavido
A. C. Chrone
Robert Chrone
Macke Cockrell
Julius Conrads
Anthony J. Correon
F. A. Covington
Eula Mae Cox
Watson H. Crane

Beulah Daniels
J. B. Daniels
William G. Darley
John D. Dashiell
Lewis Dilworth
T. R. Dixon
Frank J. Donaldson
Norman F. Dullnig
Grady E. Durham

Benjamin E. Edwards
George Elam
Almer C. Engle
Frank Judd Engle
Julia Evans
Mrs. Zula Hale Evans

Thelma Fitzwater
Jesse Newton Fletcher
Theodore Flint
J. B. Folts
Charles A. Forbes
Allen C. Franklin
John Neil Fredrick
W. J. Fredrick
Lucille Fullwood

Arthur L. Gardner
C. J. Garland
Fred Gembler
George G. Geyer
Myrza Gillis
Charles Giraud
Ethel Glenny
Charles E. Glover

Mrs. Sara Jo Goddard
Thea Goldschmidt
Lucille Goodwin
Eula Grantham
William B. Green
Mary Belle Gresham

Avis Halbert
Edward Allen Hall
John C. Hamilton
Ben E. Hammond
Shirley E. Harding
Albert W. Hartman
Leroy H. Haverlah
Hugh Montgomery
   Hawthorne
Marshall Hays
Judson Henderson
Robert L. Henry
Jarvis Hilje
Agnes Hirsch
Martha A. Hodgin
Christine Ethel Horn
Dorothy Houston
M. Edward Howard
John C. Hudnall
Mrs. G. B. Hundley
John V. Huntress

Olive Laverne Johnson
Leah Jones
Henry Murray Jones
Robert Knox Jones
John Knox Jones

141

John C. Kennedy
Vann Kennedy
Alva King
W. A. King
Margaret King
Martha King
John Lewis Kirby
Jack Burke Krueger
Thomas P. Kelly
Ethel Kessler
Montford A. Klewer
Mrs. Lillian H. Kirk
K. C. Kocyan

Lucien Jean B. LaCoste
Louise Leckie
M. C. Lefshutz
Joseph P. Lessor
Sidney Lester
George Lewis
Leo Lewis
Lucian D. Lewis
Clyde Wyatt Lightfoot
Anna M. Lipschulz
Mary Ann Lipshutz
Louis Little
Anna Lock
Georgia Locke
Hal A. Long

Ruby V. Mangham
Louis E. Marshall
W. B. Martin, Jr.
John E. Miller
G. E. Mitchell
Philip J. Montalbo
America Moore
Luther Moore
Ophie Moore
Anna Sue Morehead
Mrs. Ruth H. Mounts
Herbert Mueller
John McCollum, Jr.
George McIlhenny
Homer D. McKee

M. W. McLellen
Richard W. McMahan
Walter C. McMahan
Richard McMahon
Ethel McMillan
Jo C. McVea

J. Nayfac (?)
S. Henry Needham, Jr.
Louis Newton
Mary Newton
Margaret Newton
Charles F. Nichols
Annie R. Norich

William M. O'Hair
Catherine E. Owens
Dorothy K. Owens

Donald L. Pardue
A. B. Parker
Bruce Parker
Robert B. Parker
Hal Parks
Elbert H. Pfeiffer
O. A. Pfeiffer
Lillian Phelps
H. L. Pickler
Irene M. Piggot
George Lewis Porter
Lucy Porter
Elizabeth Prothro

Carroll Rabon
Julius Racusin
Vergie M. Ratliff
Genevieve Bess Redding
Mrs. Warner Reid
Nell H. Reislinger
Oberon Reynolds
Fenton C. Rice
Lee E. Ricks
Vinna Robinette
Sanuel A. Roelofs
Dorothy Rooke
Sterline C. Russ

Ella Savage
George W. Scallorn
James D. Scarborough
J. S. Schattenberg
Arthur E. Schram
Elmer Schram
Paul Herman Seeliger
Mary Helen Self
Jose L. Serna
Yale M. Shafer
Lemuel Shaw
Gwendolyn Shepherd
Harry M. Shklar
John Simmang
Mrs. R. Smith
Mildred Snell
Charles Lee Sowell
Irwin Stoker
Herman G. Stromberger
Annie B. Sutherland
James M. Sutton
G. B. Swain

Maude M. Taylor
Paul Taylor
Hope Thompson
Hugh Marvin Tiner
David A. Todd
Jack Tolar

Daniel A. Uhr
Helen Upschulte
Fernando Uribe
Ruth Utz

Meredith Wagner
Homer E. Walker
Albert Walker
William Walker
Frank R. Wallace
G. E. Warren
Vivian L. Waters
Fred Watkins
Paul Watkins
Juanima Wells

Lea Smith Wells
Orin Whitley
Carroll Williams
Wilfred Winship
Harry B. Wise
Genevieve Wood
Jane Wood
Beth C. Worthington

Arthur Zucht

NOTE: Name spelling variations were found among 46 individual Instructor's Grade Reports examined

Miss Beth Worthington was the first to enroll in the new Junior College in September 1926.
(The Institute of Texan Cultures, No. 0091-B: San Antonio Light Collection.)

APPENDIX B

Excerpts from Catalogue of The University of Texas - May 1926

University of Texas Bulletin
No. 2617: May 1, 1926

CATALOGUE

OF

THE UNIVERSITY OF TEXAS

1925–1926

With Announcements for
1926–1927

PUBLISHED BY THE UNIVERSITY FOUR TIMES A MONTH, AND ENTERED AS
SECOND-CLASS MATTER AT THE POSTOFFICE AT AUSTIN, TEXAS,
UNDER THE ACT OF AUGUST 24, 1912

San Antonio Junior College

The San Antonio Junior College is a coöperative enterprise carried on jointly by the Board of Education of the San Antonio Independent School District and the Division of Extension. Entrance requirements are the same as those of the Main University, and the work covers the freshman and sophomore years of the College of Arts and Sciences. The course of study is determined, the faculty selected, and the work of the college supervised by the University. The work is on the semester basis. A course which requires the full session at Austin is completed in a semester in San Antonio. Recitations are held each day.

The College is conducted at present as an afternoon and evening school, beginning at 4 o'clock and continuing to 10 o'clock. Students who complete the course there are admitted to junior standing in the College of Arts and Sciences.

San Antonio Junior College

JOSEPH EDWARD NELSON, *Associate Professor of Mathematics; Director.*
    B.A., Texas, 1907.
NAASSON KELLEY DUPRE, *Dean of Students.*
    B.A. Southwestern, 1922; M.A., Texas, 1923.
WILEY JULIUS CARNATHAN, *Associate Professor of History.*
    B.A., Birmingham-Southern College, 1911; M.A., Vanderbilt, 1918.
WILLIAM PHILIPP UDINSKI, *Associate Professor of Chemistry and Physics.*
    B.S., Illinois, 1918; M.S., 1920; Ph. D., 1922.
JANE FEILD BASKIN, *Adjunct Professor of English.*
    B.A., California, 1919; M.A., 1921.
REBECCA SWITZER, *Adjunct Professor of Spanish.*
    B.A., Texas, 1912; M.A., Columbia, 1924.
CLYDE ERNEST BARNES, *Instructor in Economics and Business Administration.*
    B.A., Texas, 1920; M.B.A., 1924; LL.B., 1924.
MRS. JESSIE WOOD NANCE, *Instructor in Education.*
    B.A., Texas, 1910; M.A., Columbia, 1923.
MRS. LILLIAN MARTIN NELSON, *Instructor in English.*
    B.A., Texas, 1910; M.A., 1922.
NISSON SZAPU, *Instructor in Latin and German*
    Maturity Degree, V. Gymnasium, Lemberg, Poland, 1906; Absolutorium, University at Vienna, 1918.
MRS. EVELYN KERNS TAYLOR, *Instructor in Botany.*
    B.A., Texas, 1920; M.A., 1924.

APPENDIX C

"He's a dreamer, but a practical man, too..."

Profile: James Otis Loftin

President J. O. Loftin was the central figure in the development of San Antonio College from August 1941 to December 1955, when he died tragically in a one-car automobile accident in Kerrville, Texas. His long-time career as an educator was on a "roll" before it so abruptly ended his dream to build a Class A junior college on the foundation he had laid. The San Antonio community was shocked at the death of this leader. He envisioned continuing academic enlargement and physical plant expansion of the College which had moved to the new campus on San Pedro Avenue in the spring 1951.

A whole book could--rather should--be written about him, but some highlights of the life of J. O. Loftin are as follows:

Born July 19, 1887 in Thornton, Texas, he was a son of Sam R. Loftin, a pioneer teacher, and Lila McLellan Loftin. Young Loftin was reared on a farm and attended rural elementary schools of Limestone County; he was graduated from Kosse High School in 1905. He was graduated with a diploma from North Texas State Normal School in 1907; began teaching that year in Seymour High School; during 1908-09, he taught at McLean High School, then served as superintendent of Floydada High School 1908-11; then, he held a similar position with Estacado schools from 1911-12.

Loftin continued his moves when he became a mathematics and science teacher at Corpus Christi High School from 1912-15, before his arrival to teach in the public schools of San Antonio.

He was bent on continuing education which enabled him to obtain a bachelor of arts degree in 1925 at Southwest Texas State Teachers College in San Marcos; later he received his master of arts degree at Colorado State University at Greeley; later, he took advanced courses at The University of Texas, Texas A&M College, and the University of Mexico, D.F.

His leadership became apparent when he was appointed principal serving Sidney Lanier Junior-Senior High School and San Antonio Vocational and Technical High School until 1934. It was a career jump to higher education, after his stint in San Antonio, to become president of Texas Arts and Industries College in Kingsville, Texas in 1934. That was his last post before resigning in the summer 1941, and answering a return call from the San Antonio Independent School District to become "President" (former position title of "Director" had been held by J. E. Nelson since 1925) of San Antonio Junior College in August 1941. [In 1942, the SAISD embraced St. Philip's College as a public junior college unit and Loftin became president of both schools.]

Loftin was the author of magazine articles, mostly on industrial education for which he was noted. He held state and national education organization memberships; served as president of Phi Delta Kappa, a men's fraternity in education; president of Southwest Texas State Teachers College Ex-Students Association; president of the San Antonio School Administrators and had the distinguished honor to serve as president of the Texas State Teachers Association, an organization of 40,000 teachers, at that time.

He was president of the Kiwanis Club of San Antonio in 1952; a Mason and a Shriner; a member of First Baptist Church. Mr. Loftin had two children by his wife, the former Texas Mary "May" Cotton (who died ca. 1936 in Kingsville); James Knox Loftin was a pilot in WWII; a business man in San Antonio; later, business manager of a church. For many years, until his retirement in January 1987, Jim managed the bookstore in "The Cave" of the Loftin Student Center on the SAC campus. Patricia "Patsy" Loftin Sutton attended San Antonio Junior College after her brother, Jim, before making her permanent home in Albuquerque, New Mexico, where she was a home economics teacher until retirement.

Among Loftin's many interests was the devotion to his family; the love of the cultural arts; gardening; lapidary buff; a skilled hunter and fisherman.

He had been president for nine years on a six-day, regular work schedule. On the morning of Wednesday, November 22, 1950, the chief administrator and Librarian Matilda Glidden Fuller reported for work as usual. The unusual being they left their posts shortly after noon, apparently getting the jump on the four-day Thanksgiving holiday enjoyed by faculty and students. They had good reason: to make final preparations for their marriage later that afternoon in the home of Mrs. A. J. Parker on East Mulberry Avenue. The marriage came without announcement on campus and to the surprise of many friends of the couple (*San Antonio Express, San Antonio Evening News*, November 23, 1950). It was the culmination of a congenial friendship.

He was age 63 and she was younger. Matilda, a native of Fredericksburg, had been the librarian at the college since 1939. She finished the fall semester and continued to work through the spring

148

semester before she resigned in May 1951 to become a homemaker.

They had been married just five years when J. O. and Matilda Loftin died as a result of the accident about noon on December 31, 1955, when their station wagon swerved to the right side of Highway 27 and crashed into a deep culvert within the western city limits of Kerrville. He was 68. Mrs. Loftin died about 3 p.m. at Sid Peterson Memorial Hospital in Kerrville. Their cocker spaniel survived.

The Loftins were returning to San Antonio after two days of deer hunting at their ranch northwest of Junction. Their guests were son Jim (whose wife stayed home to be with children); Wayland and Lillian Moody; and Jerome and Adrienne Weynand. Dr. Moody had driven home safely those members of the hunting party on Friday evening. The Loftins closed camp and headed home Saturday morning. They traveled as far as Kerrville.

Miss Mamie McLean, professor of English at San Antonio College since 1926, beautifully expressed the total essence of James Otis Loftin in the eulogy of his life and with appreciation on behalf of students and faculty in a full-page memorial in the yearbook, *El Alamo* 1956. She closed the tribute with the reality that with the sudden passing of Mr. Loftin, "the old order changeth leaving place to new."

W. W. McAllister, Sr., active chairman of the board of trustees--although he divided his time between San Antonio and Washington, D.C., where he held a government appointment--lauded Loftin for "a magnificent job in building the school...his death will be a tremendous loss to local educational and civic development" (*The Ranger*, January 13, 1956).

On New Year's Day 1956, the *San Antonio Express* ran the traditional "Happy New Year to You" banner across the top of page one, but the bold, black headline spread across eight columns of the front page of Sunday's edition announced the deaths of the Loftins to the community.

The board was called into special session and acted quickly on January 2--about eight hours before the funeral--to name heir-apparent Wayland P. Moody, dean and administrative assistant to Loftin for about eight years, as president of the colleges. That was the new order about which Professor McLean had written in the eulogy.

Little did students, who wrote in these words of praise of Mr. Loftin six months before he died, realize it was an epithet:

He's a dreamer, but a practical man, too...and he envisioned a greater San Antonio College for San Antonio, he set about to make it a reality.

--El Alamo-1955

J. O. Loftin

President

Diploma – North Texas Teachers College
A.B. – Southwest Texas Teachers College
M.A. – Colorado College of Education

El Alamo - 1948

THE SAN ANTONIO JUNIOR COLLEGE

J. O. LOFTIN, President

SAN ANTONIO 5, TEXAS

Greetings,

The San Antonio Junior College is experiencing its second year of growth under its own governing board. The student group is becoming more homogeneous -- of like tastes -- and in consequence, college life seems to be more attractive this year.

The adults who have planned and executed the present economic world have left a sorry heritage of turmoil, debts, and international suspicions. They have provided, however, educational facilities whereby you may equip yourselves to so live and work as to leave to the next generation a better world than you shall enter after college days have passed.

This living and preparation for living with your fellows are beautifully portrayed in the 1947-48 yearbook. Everyone should secure and preserve a copy for the future years when retrospection becomes such a pleasant diversion.

President

El lamo - 1948

151

APPENDIX D

"He was the faculty's administrator..."

Profile: Wayland Pelton Moody

There was a period of shock and mourning after the deaths of Mr. and Mrs. Loftin on December 31, 1955. A few days later, a memorial service was attended by students and faculty in the Small Auditorium of the main building. Another student assembly was held during that bleak time and the new President Wayland P. Moody addressed the gathering to memorialize his predecessor. He said that the students who attended SAC on the South Alamo Street campus when the school was small had gained something which the students on the larger campus did not have.

"They had the opportunity to know Mr. Loftin personally," he explained (*The Ranger*, January 13, 1956).

He might have been saying that he wanted to get to know the students better in the ever-increasing student body on the same basis that he had established rapport on the old campus. Moody was also telling the students that he missed his mentor and friend and wished for them to know him as he did.

Dr. Moody joined Loftin as his administrative assistant and dean in September 1947 succeeding a dean who had served the initial year of operation of the college under the newly created junior college district. Prior to coming to the San Antonio Junior College, Moody had been the chief of the education and training division of the Veterans Administration in San Antonio since July 1945. The Moodys moved to San Antonio in 1942 when he was a newly commissioned first lieutenant in the Army Air Corps stationed at the San Antonio Aviation Cadet Center (later named Lackland A.F.B.). He was released as a major in 1945 and took the civilian job with the VA.

Wayland Moody was born October 7, 1902 (the 10th born of 13 children) in Watt, Limestone County, Texas (ironically, J.O. Loftin hailed from Limestone County), a son of William M. and Melissa Moody. His father was a landowner and bank president who, as a child, had come from Alabama to settle in the area east of Waco, Texas. The family had moved from Watt to Tehuacana so the kids could go to school. Westminster College had a college preparatory school which Moody attended and was honored as the valedictorian when he was graduated in 1921.

153

He earned a bachelor of arts degree in social sciences at The University of Texas in June 1923, and began at age 20 teaching French and Spanish at Westminster College at Tehuacana in the town where he was reared. He and the pert piano teacher, Lillian Pierce of Cooper, Texas, were married on September 15, 1925.

For two years--1928-30--he taught and was principal in the Ferris High School. After he received his master of arts degree in educational administration from Southern Methodist University in 1930, he returned to Westminster in the depths of The Depression which affected the survival of students and the college. From February 1935 into 1940, Moody served as dean and business manager at Lon Morris College in Jacksonville. In the fall 1940, Moody returned to the classrooms as a student this time to work toward his doctorate and to teach for income. The Doctor of Education degree (Ed.D.) was conferred by The University of Texas in June 1942, when he joined the Air Corps.

When he became president of San Antonio College and St. Philip's College on January 2, 1956, he focused attention on enlarging the campuses to cope with rising enrollment. Eight major buildings were completed during his tenure, but he never lost sight of the needs of students and faculty.

> Moody's greatest strength as an administrator was he thought as a faculty member. He was the faculty's administrator rather than an administrator's administrator. He was forever faculty oriented...when he was in total disagreement, he sat and listened and understood...he would think about what you said and come back to you and say, 'No, here are my reasons.' --Professor John Igo, *The Ranger*, April 19, 1985, a week after Dr. Moody died at age 82.

Many trustees and faculty voiced opinions about Dr. Moody, here are some descriptive words: He fought for better faculty pay; you could always talk to him about problems without agreeing; he was hot-tempered and autocratic, but just; he was angered by any infringement on academic freedom; sometime he acted like the head janitor, picking up trash on campus; he had interests in all facets of the junior college, but especially liked music, art, drama and sports.

Dr. Moody tried to learn at least a new word every day and use it in conversation. He kept a huge, unabridged dictionary on a stand in his office that provided plenty word-fodder.

Magdalena Garces Saldana had been a student, worked as a student assistant in administrative offices, and became his secretary for 18 years. She remembers well his work towards financial aid for students, just sitting down with students in the Loftin Student Center to have discussion over a Coke.

Coach Bill Candler recalls Mrs. Moody faithfully attended basketball games and rooted from the bleachers in her unique style of whistling or letting an official know he made a "bad call."

Among Dr. Moody's leadership roles were serving as president of the Association of Texas colleges and Universities, president of the Southern Association of Junior Colleges, and secretary of the Board of Trustees of the Texas Education Television Council which operates KLRN-TV.

President Moody retired August 31, 1973 at age 71, after 50 years of pioneering leadership in education. When he came to San Antonio Junior College in 1947, there were 200 students; fewer at St. Philip's College. When he left in 1973, there were 22,000 regular credit students enrolled at the two colleges. He referred to the end that the success was because of the open door policy, "a people's college where everyone gets a chance."

After leaving the President's Home on West Ashby Place, Wayland and Lillian Moody sold their personal home in San Antonio and returned to their roots in Wortham to live in retirement. Lillian Moody, who had lived a rich full life as his wife for 59 years, chief supporter, and gracious "First Lady," died May 15, 1984, a day shy of her 82nd birthday. Dr. Moody had severe health problems after her death and he died on April 13, 1985. They were laid to rest in Tehuacana.

They are survived by son Wayland Pierce Moody and his wife, Annette, and two grandsons. Young Moody played on the 1947 Brackenridge High School football team that won a state championship. He completed two years that culminated in an Associate of Arts degree in May 1951, graduating with the first class to hold commencement exercises on the San Pedro Avenue campus of San Antonio College. He had a long career as an oil well completion engineer and retired to Fort Worth.

[The "Moody Word" for today is "penultimate," adjective: next to the last of a series (of profiles in this case). It was a big word that Dean Moody suggested to this writer ca. 1955, and I have been trying ever since to work it into conversation or writing. There follows in Appendix E the last of the series of profiles or vignettes about the namesakes of some of the buildings at San Antonio College. Moody's profile, therefore, is penultimate in the three-part series in the Appendices.]

and Lillian Moody to you —
Best wishes to you —
W.P.Moody—

Wayland D. Moody

Dean of the College

Best wishes + luck to you —

A.B. – University of Texas
M.A. – Southern Methodist University
D. Ed. – University of Texas

Administrative Assistant
San Antonio Union Junior College District
Instructor in Education & Psychology

El Alamo - 1948

THE SAN ANTONIO JUNIOR COLLEGE

I. O. LOFTIN, President

SAN ANTONIO 5, TEXAS

GREETINGS TO THE STUDENTS OF JUNIOR COLLEGE,

I, too, am a newcomer to the Junior College. However, in the short time I have been here, I have come to appreciate the useful place that the Junior College has in your lives.

It is my most sincere desire and hope that your stay in Junior College will contribute something worthwhile to help you to live a fuller and more useful life. If we as administrators and teachers fail in this responsibility, remember that we too are only human. As you continue to work here and throughout your future, may you carry this thought with you.

"Do what you feel to be right;
Say what you think to be true;
And leave with faith and pa-
tience the consequences to God."

El Alamo - 1948

Wayland P. Moody
Dean

157

APPENDIX E

Vignettes of Namesakes of Major Buildings

Students walking among buildings or spending hours in classrooms and laboratories on the campus of San Antonio College may never wonder--or even care--about the namesakes. The personalities and contributions behind the official names of buildings is outlined for posterity's sake. On the former campus of San Antonio Junior College, vintage buildings did not have formal names. On the San Pedro campus, a building was a building described by its use until it got a person's name and became a "Center." [After the first two or three buildings with prestigious persons names became "Centers," John Igo, professor of English, adroitly chided and admonished the administration, "Please, no more Centers." There had been several buildings labeled "Hall," in traditional collegiate style.]

G. S. McCreless Hall--The first building constructed on the new campus site during 1949-50 was called the Classroom-Administration Building and originally housed in addition to ultra-modern classrooms and faculty offices, the library, small auditorium, and offices of the president, dean, registrar, and business manager. Major additions were made in 1957 at the growing school.

The hall was named for G. Sealie McCreless, one of the seven original trustees elected October 30, 1945, who became the third president of the San Antonio Union Junior College District. He was born prematurely with his twin brother, Sollie, in 1902 in Colorado City. They moved to San Antonio when the twins were 14 years old. In 1918 Sealie started work as a grocery store clerk and became a store manager at the early age of 17. He was a food broker, but in 1936 his career shifted to building houses--some 2,000--and developing McCreless Mall on the Southside. He was a member of Lions International civic club; a founder and past-president of Goodwill Industries, past-president of the Boys' Clubs, and other organizations. He was a Life Deacon at Trinity Baptist Church. His two daughters by his first wife, the former Gladys Armistead, are prominent San

Antonians Grace Ann (Mrs. Robert E. Durr) and Merry Christine (wife of Dr. D. Ford Nielsen, former District trustee and city councilman).

Mr. McCreless died September 22, 1992, age 90. The McCreless name also appears on the McCreless Library, a city branch.

Manuel C. Gonzales Science Hall--The second building constructed at 1300 San Pedro Avenue was connected by a two-level covered arcade to McCreless Hall offering a U-shaped front elevation to passersby on San Pedro Avenue. The view was photographed and used on official publications, namely the catalogs. The two buildings were occupied in the spring 1951, with the classrooms and laboratories for the sciences complementing McCreless facilities.

It was named in honor of M. C. Gonzales, an attorney, who was a trustee and fourth president of the Board; he served a total of 24 years. Born on October 22, 1900 in Hidalgo County, Texas, he said that he experienced discrimination in his early life because he was a Mexican-American. Gonzales was in diplomatic and consular services and the private practice of law. For 20 of the 50 years as a lawyer, he served as an Assistant District Attorney in Bexar County. He was a founder and national president of the League of United Latin American Citizens (LULAC). He was the father of four children: Melissa, Margot, Manuel, Jr. and Michael.

Gonzales was a 32nd degree Mason, and a Scoutmaster. He served several terms as president of the Mexican Chamber of Commerce and as president of the Pan American Optimist Club and Boys Clubs of America.

Bill C. Candler Physical Education Center--The building constructed in 1951 under the first phase of the master campus plan was the Health Education Building in the 1200 block of San Pedro Avenue. It was occupied in February 1952 but officially had no name until November 1998 when the Board--acting on a recommendation from faculty and sanctioned by administrators--formally named the greatly expanded and modernized complex after Bill Candler. The

160

dedication was held on the gymnasium floor April 29, 1999, and attended by many former students that he had taught and coached since employment by Mr. Loftin in September 1949.

Candler was born in October 1926 in Greenville, Texas; reared in Wheeler County in the Panhandle between Briscoe and Mobeetie. He lettered and won honors in basketball for four years--after his freshman year college attendance was interrupted by military service--at North Texas State College. At San Antonio College he coached nearly all intercollegiate sports and served as chairman of the Physical Education Department for 37 years until he retired with emeritus status. Candler and his wife Barbara have been married for over 50 years and divide their time between their home in San Antonio and Hill Country living.

J. O. Loftin Student Center--This building and the fine arts center with the large (1,300 seats at the time) auditorium were constructed with funds from a second bond issue to keep pace with increased enrollment. Built in 1954 and dedicated to President Loftin, who had been at the helm since August 1941, the gala featured a banquet and then a dance to christen "Shangri-la Ballroom" (so named by Mr. Loftin) on December 11, 1954. He was still serving as president until the fateful accident in Kerrville about noon on December 31, 1955, just a year after the Loftin Student Center was dedicated. A widower since 1936, Mr. Loftin and Mrs. Matilda Glidden Fuller, former librarian at the college, had been married only five years. (Refer to Appendix C for Profile.)

W. W. McAllister Fine Arts Center-- Walter W. McAllister, Sr., (at right) a financial and political legend in San Antonio, is the namesake for the building on campus best known to the public because of its year-round activities in the mid-size auditorium that now boasts 1,000 seats. The Center was opened in April 1956 for the teaching of music, art, drama, and radio/television. "Mister Mac," as he was affectionately known, was elected the first president of the

board of trustees of the District on November 5, 1945, and he served faithfully until September 1960 when he accepted an interim appointment as a member of City Council in a vacancy left by the late Ted Pinson. McAllister was a stalwart member of the Good Government League that had sought reform and backed the city manager-council form of government. Later he was elected to five consecutive terms as mayor.

The remaining six trustees selected Walter McAllister, Jr. to take his father's vacated seat on the board. He won re-election to the board in 1962, 1968 and 1974. He continued leading the building committee and personally worked the area neighborhoods of San Antonio College and St. Philip's College, calling on homeowners, letting them know that the District would be willing to purchase their property if they wished to sell in the future. His keen skill in real estate and working with the people helped, piece by piece, to gain sufficient parcels to expand both campuses. Walter "Junior" deserves recognition for his dedicated services for the next 20 years and was ready to continue the work as chairman of the board until he was defeated in the 1980 election, thus ending the 35-year span of McAllister contributions to the welfare of the District. Both were leaders in the savings and loan association business and civic projects.

[People have said the son lived in the shadow of his outgoing father, but "Sono" cut his own swath in life; contributed greatly to the city and the college district. He was a "chip off his own block," this writer happens to believe.]

It is interesting to note that McAllister, Sr. was a pupil at the old German-English School, was graduated from Main Avenue High School and received a degree in engineering from The University of Texas in 1910. He and Leonora Alexander were married in 1913; she died in 1969. Their children are the late Elizabeth M. Solcher, the Rt. Rev. Gerald McAllister (an Episcopalian bishop), and Walter, Jr. Mayor Mac died September 13, 1984 at the age of 95. He had suffered a stroke on August 28th. Walter Junior lived until September 26, 1988. He was 70. Edith McAllister in May 2002 maintains an active civic participation, including support of San Antonio College. She said that her husband never begrudged his father's fame. Their children are Walter William "Bo" McAllister, II, Taddy JoEllen, Reagin Scott and Eloise Edith McAllister.

162

A double display case featuring photos of Walter Sr. and Walter Jr., brief biographical sketches, and quotable quotes from persons who knew their personalities and contributions to the College and the District was unveiled May 10, 2002 in the foyer of the McAllister Fine Arts Center. Members of the McAllister clan and college officials heard remarks from President Vern Loland, Edith Scott McAllister and Bishop McAllister in recognition of the duo, now side-by-side for public appreciation.

***Clyde R. Nail Technical Center*--** Governor John Connally, a friend of public junior colleges, commended the contributions San Antonio College and other two-year colleges were making at the time, but said the people of the State would expect an even wider role in preparation for the future. At the dedication November 10, 1966, the Governor described San Antonio College as the largest and finest among Texas' 33 public junior colleges. [One of the governor's brothers was on the faculty.]

Dr. Clyde R. Nail--who had developed the college's evening division for seven years before becoming Vice-President and Dean in January 1956--was largely responsible for the planning of the three-story building and development of technical programs. He was still an active administrator when the Board honored Nail for his dedication and coordination of efforts between the District, the College, the Texas Education Agency and federal agencies to further technical courses which often led to immediate employment for skilled hands and minds. The cost of NTC was $2.249 million, with the state and federal governments paying a share totaling $922,250. Former SAUJCD board chairman W. W. McAllister, Sr.--now Mayor of San Antonio--was a special platform guest.

Nail was born January 17, 1910; was graduated from Brackenridge High School, Southwest State Teachers College and The University of Texas. He was a principal and superintendent of Cristoval public schools from 1931-41. He served 39 months in the U. S. Navy Reserve as a lieutenant commander; worked in vocational rehabilitation section of the Veterans Administration in San Antonio before becoming director of the night school on the South Alamo campus of San Antonio Junior College in 1949.

He was awarded a Doctor of Laws degree (LL.D.) from Howard Payne College for his many years of service in the technical and academic fields of education and for his work in the community. (He said that he was active in 26 local civic organizations.) He was prominent in Lions International Club and the San Antonio Council of Presidents, among others.

Dr. Nail and Frances Belle Dowdy were married January 23, 1932. Their son, Clyde Gerald (Jerry) Nail, and wife Barbara have four children and 15 grandchildren at this writing.

Trustees in January 1971 wanted to give President Moody a back-up after Moody indicated "two more years" before his retirement. They named Nail President-elect on a two-year contract beginning September 1, 1971. However, in a letter to Dr. Moody dated March 26, 1971, Nail thanked Moody for the past association and opportunity for future lead-

ership but for health reasons asked that he enter retirement effective August 31, 1971 after 22 years employment.

Dr. Nail died on November 27, 1980; his wife survived him until her death on May 19, 1995.

Jesse N. Fletcher Administration Center--This three-story building was named for Jesse N. Fletcher who served as an officer on the board for 27 years after his election on October 30, 1945 at the time the District was approved. The building housed the district officers, registrar, dean, counselors, business manager, print shop, mail room and other ancillary functions. It was completed in April 1972 with the formal dedication taking place at a dinner event held in the *Entre Nous* Room of the Loftin Student Center. The insurance agency manager was lauded as an educator, civic and church leader, and as a family man. He had served as vice-president in the W. W. McAllister era and succeeded him to become the second president of the board on October 4, 1960. The Center took 17 months to construct at a cost of $1.616 million. He died April 10, 1986 at age 82.

Jesse Fletcher was president of the San Antonio Junior Chamber of Commerce in 1936 and was named "Outstanding Young Man of the Year" in San Antonio in 1938. he had been a student at the former San Antonio Junior College. Jesse and Ruby Fletcher had two children: Shirley Fletcher (Mrs. Jimmy Elrod), and Dr. J. C. Fletcher, Baptist minister who served as president of Hardin-Simmons University in Abilene.

***Wayland P. Moody Learning Center*--** The largest and only high-rise--seven floors containing 201,000 square feet of space--building on campus was designed as a learning resources center incorporating print and non-print materials, audio-visual services, 64 modular classrooms and offices for 84 faculty. Coincident with the building occupancy, a dedication of the Library-Classroom-Faculty Office Building was held March 19, 1968.

On May 18, 1973, trustees granted Dr. Moody's request for retirement, effective August 31, 1973, and recognized him as the first President Emeritus upon the conclusion of 50 pioneering years in education. They went a step further in their praise by naming the large functional building in his honor. When the formal dedication of the Moody Learning Center was held, Librarian J. O. Wallace (later called Director of Learning Resources on the new organizational chart) counted 180,000 volumes, but said he could accommodate 750,000. The building was planned for four floors, with three upper levels optional as growth and funds dictated. The architect's model had a lift-off portion for the upper three floors to demonstrate expansion capabilities. Trustees considered going ahead with all seven levels, but not finish-out the upper three. In the end, all seven were furbished--and none too soon for the demand on facilities. Initial cost: $4.25 million for the plant.

Invited speaker Dr. Harry H. Ransom, chancellor of The University of Texas, was unable to attend. Dr. C. C. Colvert of the University--a well-known, junior college professorial advocate--read Ransom's speech. It highlighted the theme that "Libraries are the focal point of the educational system." Moody agreed, among others. (Refer to Appendix D for a Profile featuring Dr. Moody.)

***Truett L. Chance Academic Center*--** After the board had designated several buildings officially honoring the first four board presidents and the first two college chief executives--namesakes most deserving--the faculty recommended through administrative channels all the way to the board that the next one should be named for Dr. Truett L. Chance. The trustees agreed. Chance began as a social science instructor in January 1947, just as veterans like himself were enrolling in colleges; worked his way up the ladder to full professor and chairman of the department of social sciences which included at the time economics, government and history.

In May 1975, Dr. Chance (who earlier had earned his doctorate at The University of Texas) was selected as dean of the college. After District administrative reorganization under Chancellor Byron McClenney the distinguished professor became president of San Antonio College and served until his retirement in June 1982.

Dr. Chance gave 35 good years as teacher and administrator combined--preferred teaching, he admitted--and was instrumental in establishing the Faculty Senate and the San Antonio Chapter of the American Association of University Professors. The dedication and unveiling his portrait in the building that has become the central logo for SAC was held March 13, 1997 with many family members and friends in attendance. Infamous red punch and other refreshments were served at the reception in Loftin Student Center, named for the man who hired Chance and was a colleague for nine, all-too short years...

Dr. Chance, Professor and President Emeritus, and his late wife,

Opal (a career teacher) had one daughter, Trudy Jo (Mrs. Paul Kinnison, Jr.). Grandchildren are Abigail and Chance Kinnison.

———

There are at least a dozen more buildings on campus that provide instructional facilities or support, but none as unique as the **Scobee Planetarium/Observatory** built in 1961 concurrently and as an appendage to the Chemistry-Geology Building (at a total cost of $1.250 million). It is hailed as the only observatory within 200 miles and was dedicated January 17, 1975, featuring NASA Shuttle Program Manager G. B. Whisenhunt as keynote speaker. [Fortunately it was not named "Moody's Igloo," as some students had dubbed it.]

The story has been told that President Moody and Board Chairman W. W. McAllister attended a junior college convention in California in the late 1950s; they toured some two-year college campuses looking for ideas; one had a planetarium. Moody quoted McAllister as saying, "We had to get one of those" for San Antonio College (*The Ranger*, September 14, 1984).

Bryan Snow, for the past 30 years has served as the coordinator of the Planetarium, provided information that the facility was named officially the "Scobee Planetarium" in ceremonies July 9, 1994 in perpetual honor of Colonel Francis Richard (Dick) Scobee, commander of the ill-fated Space Shuttle Challenger when it exploded January 28, 1986. Scobee was born May 19, 1939 in Cle Elum, Washington. he attended evening classes at San Antonio College during the summer of 1960 through spring 1963.

What's in a building's name? Plenty!

APPENDIX F

District Trustees 1945 - 1956

The first seven trustee candidates were unopposed in the October 30, 1945 election which created the San Antonio Union Junior College District of some 154 square miles carved out of school districts in the greater San Antonio area. The slate of candidates was proposed by the San Antonio Junior Chamber of Commerce which had taken the lead in the election campaign again in 1945 after the young men had been thwarted in the earlier attempt to create a junior college district in November 1941. They circulated petitions among qualified voters to support nominations of the handpicked businessmen. Terms of office were staggered for two-, four- and six-year periods to insure continuity of the board.

Bexar County Commissioners' Court certified the election results on Monday morning, November 5. That afternoon trustees were sworn to uphold the oath of public office administered by a faculty member of the current San Antonio Junior College (still under the auspices of the local school board) who was a notary. The original board members consisted of Walter W. McAllister, Sr., elected president in absentia at the organizational meeting on November 5; Jesse N. Fletcher, insurance executive, vice-president; Lee A. Christy, contractor, secretary. Other members were Ernest A. Baetz, banker; E. H. Keator business; G. S. McCreless, builder and realtor; and Leo Brewer, attorney, and former president of the Board of Education.

N. Bernard Gussett and James V. Graves replaced Brewer and Baetz whose terms expired in April 1947. Gussett resigned from the board in August 1949, when he moved to Iowa. Travis B. Moursund was named in Gussett's place in February 1950, served out the unexpired term through 1952 and then was elected for a term expiring in 1958. Graves served until May 1952. Moursund and Graves were practicing attorneys, both members of the Kiwanis Club of San Antonio whose members included McAllister, Fletcher, Baetz, and College President J. O. Loftin. Other trustees would take places on the board, including G. J. Sutton, James M. Goodman, Manuel C. Gonzales (who served for 24 years); in the early 1960s well-known executives John T. Steen, William G. Conway and W. W. McAllister, Jr. (all members of the Alamo Kiwanis Club) took seats on the board and made contributions for many years.

Five former trustees were given citations for community service at a meeting of the board in January 1953. W. W. McAllister, board president, lauded members for their contributions to the organization and operation of the infant college district.

"This is one political entity that has lived within its means." he said, before presenting certificates to E. H. Keator (April 1945 to April 1948); Leo Brewer (Nov. 1945 to April 1947); E. A. Baetz (Nov. 1945 to April 1947); James V. Graves (April 1947 to May 1952); and presented in absentia to N. Bernard Gussett (April 1947 to Feb. 1950) who had moved out of state (*San Antonio Express*, January 24, 1953).

[Later, positions on the board became politically driven for the power and prestige board membership may have brought to an individual or a coalition. There were those other than McAllister, Sr. who ran for city and county offices, some successfully. But at this writing on election day May 4, 2002, a net (some candidates withdrew) of 23 persons are vying for the four seats open in the nine sub-districts of the Alamo Community College District. One incumbent is seeking re-election. From the amount of news coverage and editorials devoted to the junior college trustees' election in the past--and especially in 2002--the board has become more political than ever.]

APPENDIX G

Deans - 1925-1956

The name Naason K. Dupre (sometimes seen as Dupree) stands out as the first person to be titled dean of students at the San Antonio Junior College, also referred to that first academic year 1925-1926 as "The University Junior College." His appointment was announced August 6, 1925 after he was already at work recruiting students a month before the new school was set to open with students in place at 5 o'clock on September 21 at Main Avenue High School. Dupre was a graduate of The University of Texas with B.A. and M.A. degrees. For the previous two years he had been principal of William T. Harris elementary school in San Antonio.

University President Walter M. Splawn, in consultation with School Superintendent Marshall Johnston, appointed Dupre to assist the director of the new college. Splawn explained, as follows:

> The duties of the dean of students require an able man...I believe Mr. Dupre is the man for the job. The duties technically consist of being a good fellow and a real pal to the boys and when they are in trouble he has to get them out...You know how a coach takes care of the athletic side of school? Well, a dean of students has a similar job, only he takes in the entire enrollment (*San Antonio Evening News*, August 6, 1925).

Bertram Harry, M.A. The University of Texas, was a faculty member from 1926 to 1937, and served part of that period as a popular dean of students beginning in 1928. He had joined the College from Southwest Texas State Teachers College where he had been a professor of education. His tenure at SAJC was cut short when he died at age 57 in February 1937, a few weeks after the extraction of abscessed teeth. A portrait of Dean Harry still adorns a wall in the Baskin Rare Books Room of the Library.

Popular instructor Clyde V. Barnes took a turn as dean of students and dean of the college.

Charles S. Gardiner became the dean of students in August 1941

171

and served three years before his title and duties were changed to dean of the entire college. He had been principal at schools in Seguin, San Marcos and Sabinal; taught educational psychology at Baylor University and The University of Texas before he came to SAJC.

Bert W. Musgraves is portrayed as "Dean of Students" in *El Alamo* 1947, but appeared to have worked under President Loftin for the 1946-1947 academic year as dean of the college before leaving for another position in West Texas. He held a B.S. degree from East Texas State Teachers College and a M.S. degree conferred by Texas A&M College. He instructed in sociology and psychology in addition to administrative duties. In March 1952 Musgraves headed the new junior college division of the Texas Education Agency to coordinate all junior college work in Texas. [Later, he served as a representative for a college program established aboard ship which traveled around the world. He made visits to San Antonio College to invite students to "come aboard with classrooms afloat."]

Dr. Wayland P. Moody, former Air Corps major stationed at the San Antonio Aviation Cadet Center and an executive with the Veterans Administration, succeeded Musgraves and was titled "Dean and Administrative Assistant" to President Loftin in September 1947.
Two days after the Loftins died in the automobile accident December 31, 1955, trustees met in an emergency meeting and selected Dean Moody as President of the Colleges: San Antonio and St. Philip's.

Clyde R. Nail was promoted from director of the evening division to vice-president and dean of the college in January 1956 to become the Number 2 administrator in the District. He remained in that capacity until his retirement for stated ill health effective August 31, 1971. He was the board's choice to succeed Moody, if Nail's health had not been a factor.

Wame J. Hallmark, a professor of mathematics who had been on the South Alamo campus since the late 1940s, served as dean of men during the 1950s and 1960s. Likewise for the women, Dr. Lois G. Morrison, professor of English, doubled as dean with some release time from the classroom.

In September 1954, Dr. Lester Beals was employed by Mr. Loftin as the first "Dean, Student Personnel Services" with added teaching duties in education courses. He absorbed Hallmark's former role, while Dr. Morrison continued as dean of women. When Beals left the college in 1957, Hallmark resumed his dean of men title and was a popular figure on campus for at least 10 more years until his retirement.

[In the ensuing years, more "deans" of academic, technical and other divisions came into vogue as result of administrative reorganizations and expansion. In 2002, at least six persons held the title of "Dean" as noted in the catalog.]

APPENDIX H

Registrars - 1925-2002

People used to ask: "What does a registrar do between registrations?" Answer: plenty!

The lower echelon position of Registrar in the administrative college setting can trace its beginning to the Middle Ages when the Dean was a "major beadle" and the "Registrar" was a "minor beadle" or junior assistant. In the "old days" of the modern era, registrars functioned as admissions officers, supervised registration, kept the permanent records of students' grades and issued transcripts of records. They also lettered diplomas and organized commencement exercises for the graduates.

Later, duties and titles of registrars gave way to admissions counselors, directors and deans of admission, director of enrollment management, researchers, recruiters, etc. There are few "Registrars" listed in college catalogs in the 21st Century. During the 14th Century, the minor beadle reminded the major beadle of appointments, class schedules and even carried lunch to the "dean." The minor aspired to be a dean, someday. [That is the way it worked at San Antonio College.]

In larger institutions, students may never have known the name or seen the registrar during registration or anytime during a two- or four-year stay on campus. The name and signature with the impressed seal was affixed to the transcripts. Trustees, presidents and deans usually signed the diplomas and gave handshakes to students as they walked across the stage at graduation.

History of the San Antonio College registrar's office since the beginning has been researched by Phyllis Anderson McCarley who cut her first teeth working as a clerk and in 1978 became registrar to run a modern, full-service office. Much of the chronology and names associated with the development of the office are attributable to her.

At the outset of the "University Junior College" in San Antonio in the fall of 1925, functions of the school were performed under the direction of The University of Texas and its Division of Extension which selected the director and instructors in coordination with the San Antonio Independent School District. Records, too, were kept by The University which later furnished to San Antonio Junior College photostatic copies in white-on-black paper of student records for the first academic year.

Mrs. Clyde E. Barnes, wife of one of the earliest instructors in business courses, served as the first registrar of San Antonio College. Her husband had been a coordinator of the University teaching center before the concept of a junior college materialized. In 1932, Mrs. Barnes set a precedent by attending a state convention of collegiate registrars in Dallas and being reimbursed for her expenses. Mrs. Barnes, a comely lady at age 32, died in an Austin hospital in June 1936 following an illness of only a few days while she was attending the summer session at The University of Texas.

There was a succession of nine registrars, all women, including Mrs. Reynolds (1936); Mrs. London (1937); Doris Yeargan (1940); Miss Charlie Neal Young (1941); Nell Fly (also 1941); Marjorie Warren (1942); Amy Florence Hickerson (1944); Geraldine Long (1945); Betty Lou Dahlberg (also 1945); Kathryn Martin, acting (1947); and Glynda Bess Brown (1947). [And one for whom there is no date, Betty Ruth Gaines.]

In late August 1954, the womens' stereotypical hold on the registrar's position was broken when President J. O. Loftin reached Jerome Weynand in the City Hall press room and asked him to come to the campus after work that day to talk about a job. Miss Brown had given notice to pursue a master's degree. Loftin offered the job to Weynand who accepted with a handshake. Bennye Edgeworth (Frazier), assistant registrar, and Gladys Bemus, clerk, helped Weynand get through the impending first registration period. Another clerk and a transcript clerk were added in 1956. Glenda Scott (Jennison) handled office matters in the evenings.

While Weynand was on modified leave to complete graduate studies from June 1960 to June 1962, Warren P. Kohls from the history department became acting registrar for two years; then he remained on staff as associate registrar from 1962-65.

The first full-time secretary--all previous registrars did their own typing of correspondence and other duties without the help of a secretary--was employed by President Moody to assist the registrar who now had six employees to cope with increasing enrollment. Cynthia Ann Dean (she became Mrs. Robert Guyon in 1963), who had worked as a student assistant in the office and was an honor graduate of the secretarial science program, began in September 1962 after first considering civil service employment. [Mrs. Guyon became administrative secretary to the dean of students, vice-president, and president of the colleges in the next 18 years. In 2002 she is Executive Director of the Baumberger Endowment scholarship program.]

Wilbur Dennis, former instructor in the physical education department, was named associate registrar in 1965 and succeeded to become registrar in 1966 when Weynand became dean of student affairs. Glenn Doolittle then assumed the position in 1970 and Phyllis McCarley was named his associate in September 1972.

Clyde R. Nail became the director of the evening program in 1949 while still on the former campus. One clerk assisted him. Charles U. Breeden became Nail's assistant director in 1954, and another clerk was added; then a third was needed in 1955. [Breeden later became director of guidance and counseling in the day school.]

Edwin Keasler filled Nail's position in January 1956, after Nail was promoted to vice-president and dean of the college, when Moody became president on January 2, 1956 after Mr. Loftin's death. Clarkson Groos was assistant director for the evening division in 1958 and remained for years until his advancement to director of technical education. Byron McClenney assumed the assistant director's job in 1966 and stayed until 1968. [McClenney would return in 1982 as chancellor of the district.]

It appeared a game of musical chairs, when Glenn Doolittle took McClenney's vacated slot and the position was re-named assistant registrar in 1968. Glenn Snyder replaced Doolittle in 1970 with the dual titles of assistant registrar/assistant director evening division.

Dr. Irving J. Benedict, former biology professor, was named associate dean and director of the evening program upon Dr. Keasler's retirement in 1972. Snider returned to the classroom in 1973, and his position was split. Robert Brown was made assistant director in the evening while Patrick Terrell became assistant registrar. Also, a secretary was added in 1973.

After Mrs. McCarley retired with full plaudits and the title of "Director of Admissions and Records Emeritus," Rosemarie Hoopes was promoted from within the staff to succeed McCarley and is still "holding the fort" in May 2002 as the woman in charge.

Records-keeping functions certainly have improved over the past 76 years in the history of the San Antonio College's "registrar's" office. From paper and pencil, to McBee Keysort with its perimeter holes and ice-pick sorters, to the basic three IBM machines, to the computer age of today has been highly progressive. [This writer requested an official transcript of his old record via FAX one morning; the next morning's mail brought the requested document. Overnight service.]

That beats the old technology and service when transcripts of permanent records had to be hand typed, then various facsimile processes from darkroom printing and developing, to dry and wet duplication methods to computer accessible, instant retrieval of records--not forgetting registration by telephone. Indeed, the services provided by the new registrar's offices have come a long way.

Joe Bates and Cleo Flowers register at San Antonio Junior College with Mrs. C. E. Barnes, registrar, in September 1931.
(The Institute of Texan Cultures, No. 1301-F: San Antonio Light Collection.)

APPENDIX I

Student Organizations

Students attending "J.C."--as they were wont to call their college in the early period 1926-1950, when the campus was on South Alamo Street--were joiners. They banded in a variety of clubs, pseudo-Greek-letter fraternities and sororities, and--for qualifiers--national scholastic honor societies in various interest-fields of endeavor. Some of the organizations forged traditions and have remained viable on the present-day campus. Other groups were created, but activities waned according to the rise and fall of students' interests.

All official campus organizations had assigned faculty sponsors who gave of their after-hours time to foster extracurricular activities without monetary remuneration or reduced teaching loads. Many of the earlier faculty sponsored two or three clubs concurrently. Personal satisfaction came in the form of association with students outside class-rooms. The administration of the College believed in the worth of extra-class activities and "urged" faculty participation.

Among (some may have been overlooked) the clubs and other organizations--most "open" but a few boasted "cliquish" memberships--featured in stories and photos appearing in *El Alamo* yearbook and *The Ranger* weekly newspaper are the following examples:

Adda Dabba Pouda Sorority--Formed in 1925, it boasted of being the first social club at SAJC. Designed to create "an enduring and vigorous school spirit," and to form a more perfect union of friendship, the ADPs promoted student activities, held social functions on and off campus: rush tea for pledges, slumber party for girls only, a candy pull, banquet, filling Christmas Cheer baskets, cake sale, and a spring prom. They were best known for cooperatively staging the annual coronation ball with king and queen. Sponsor was Mrs. Clyde E. Barnes, registrar.

Alpha Sigma Kappa--This elite group welcomed as members students interested in all sciences and the growth and prosperity of the West. Membership remained small and there was little social contact beyond having lecturers on campus.

Bar Association--The life of the club which brought together pre-law majors in 1935 was ephemeral. [Not to be confused with O'Con's Bar where some Veterans' Club members assembled on occasion.] Pre-

179

law students joined the Senate and Cowboy Clubs for debate competitions, among other jousts.

Beta Phi Gamma--In 1950, the SAC chapter joined Beta Phi Gamma--national, junior college, honor journalism fraternity--and invited into membership those students who had done outstanding work for the college publications and ranked scholastically in the upper half of the class. One of the functions was the selection of the "First Lady of San Antonio College" who was presented with great fanfare at the annual recognition banquet. Adah Louise Staph (Cooke), first journalism teacher, was the instigator of the honor society.

Business Administration Club--The assemblage of business majors had a rather short run in the 1940s.

Clef Dwellers--Formed by music students and others interested in helping San Antonio Symphony stage concerts, club life was not sustained after the mid-forties.

El Club Cervantes--When the J. C. was established, El Club Cervantes furnished opportunities for "boys and girls to speak the Spanish language." It mainly attracted as members those students who stood highest in their Spanish classes and those who spoke the language. Members enjoyed singing Spanish songs, field trips to the Spanish missions, picnics in Brackenridge Park to honor former club members, visits to San Fernando Cathedral, and socials. Miss Mary McGill was sponsor for many years.

Cowboys--Jeff Nash and Tabor Stone are credited with organizing in 1931 the Cowboy Debating Society under sponsorship of O. H. Hamilton. As the name implied, it was organized to promote debating--a big "sport" on the campus in the 1930s--and was considered one of the "in" clubs. By the mid-1940s, the purpose had shifted more to active participation in varsity and intramural athletics. Senators were the primary challengers and competitors about everything on campus with their archrivals, the Cowboys.

Ye Old Cheshyre Cheese--The "Cheeses" were organized November 16, 1926--reportedly the second oldest club on the new J.C. campus--by 13 girls who wanted a literary club and to have fun. The organization of the club was based on Dr. Samuel Johnson's famous club in London which met at Ye Olde Cheshyre Cheese Inn. While keeping with the study of literature, members also delved into dramatics and other fine arts; their social activities involved teas, poetry readings, and banquets. Dr. Janie Baskin was sponsor for many of the early years. Later, young men were admitted as members of the Club, which at last report was till going on the modern-day campus.

Delta Psi Omega--A national dramatic fraternity, membership was drawn from excelling members of the Speechcrafters. It was founded on campus in March 1948. Popular instructor Carl A. Atkins was a devoted sponsor of the thespians.

Distributors--Participants in the club, organized in Fall 1947, were distributive education students who were employed part-time in on-the-job training as "D.E." students. Distributors had their own classroom-office trailer on the back lot of the old campus.

Jaysee Gates--"Hello, Gates" was the sisterly greeting exchanged by the female members of the Jayseegates (preferred spelling) organized in 1941 and called the "friendliest club on campus"--at least by its members. "J.C. Gates" (a name it also used) had a gate logo. It sponsored the Winter White Parade and held teas for initiates.

G.O.A.L.--"Go On And Learn" was the motto of this club which offered opportunities for married and older women who began studies at SAC in the early 1950s. Dr. Lois G. Morrison, dean of women and professor of English, was their champion and sponsor who encouraged the women to enter and remain in school.

Kampus Kouples Club--In the Fall 1946, many of the ex-GIs entering SAJC to resume or begin college classes were married. Family socials were held and members reinforced each other in "stickability" to full-time course loads leading to degrees and professions. It soon became a tradition for the father of the youngest baby automatically to serve as president of the Kampus Kouples. The member who had been married the shortest time was the vice-president. [E. Howard Jones and Dorothy Schaefer Jones were charter members. Jones served concurrently as president of the KKC and the Veterans' Club. It was learned at the Brackenridge HS Reunion of the Forties held in April 2002 that the Joneses have been married for 58 years and counting...]

Los Paisanos--Fellow countrymen promoted interest in the Spanish language and Latin American cultures. Paisanos Club was the popular successor in the mid-1940s to the original Spanish-interest El Club Cervantes of the 1920s era.

Pan American Collegiate Club--Organized in 1948, it was composed of students with a mutual interest in Spanish literature, lore, and language.

Phi Alpha Tau--A boys' club organized on the South Alamo Street campus for the purpose of producing inter-school dances. It held both open and closed social events among other college and university students.

Phi Chi Delta--The SAJC chapter affiliated with the national Hi-Y fraternity on November 20, 1931. Members met bi-weekly on Fridays at the downtown Young Men's Christian Association (YMCA) building. Charter members included Gus Levy, William R. Sinkin, William Thomas, Herschel Childers, Fred Slimp, Ellison Echterhoff, Leonard Schelper, Earl Odell, Earl Arnett and Ernest Powers.

Pi Gamma Phi--Strictly a girls' social club known mainly for staging the Autumn Nocturne formal dance.

Phi Theta Kappa--One of the oldest student organizations with the longest run--still very active on the SAC campus in 2002--is the Beta Nu Chapter of Phi Theta Kappa, nationally recognized honor fraternity of the American two-year colleges founded in 1918. Beta Nu was established on April 14, 1932 to promote scholarship, develop character, and cultivate friendship among students. Eligibility for membership include good moral character and scholastic rank in the upper 10 per cent (about 3.5 GPA) of the student body.

First officers chosen were Pat Webb, president; Lucille Rock, vice-president; Mary Campbell, secretary; and Margarite Hammonds, treasurer. Director J. E. Nelson, Dean Bertram Harry, and Miss Mary McGill, charter sponsor, helped to organize the chapter. Among other first-year members were Elizabeth Westrup, Bernice Weininger, Nadone Allen, Lewis C. Lee, Margaret Upshulte, William R. Sinkin, Oscar Spitz, Otto Holekamp, Burdette Taylor, and Elizabeth Milam. In May 1933, 22 freshmen were inducted. [In the mid-thirties Jean M. Longwith, later to become a professor in speech and radio/television; and J. O. Wallace, assistant librarian under Mrs. Matilda Fuller and on the San Pedro campus the long-serving Director of Learning Resources, were members of PTK. More future faculty and administrators at the College had been inducted into the chapter during the 1940s through 1960s.]

Pie Club--This "exclusive" club focused on one thing: pie. Organized in 1931, originally named Epsilon Beta Pi, it promoted the interest and enjoyment of "that great American dish, namely pie...and to satisfy the craving of the inner man for pie." Membership at the outset of the club was limited to eight men with the motto of "absolutely no girls allowed."

The handful of men met at noon every Thursday on campus to eat pie usually provided by a different girl who was invited to speak briefly before the club president declared that she was "the most beautiful girl on the campus." Flattery got them pies. It had taken the group only three weeks after inception of the club to change the bylaws allowing for a female honoree to come before the members, pie in hand. Bernice Weininger may be remembered as the first lady chosen; Helen Marrs Ruble was the second honoree. Co-eds were singled out by vote of the members and the announcement of the weekly honoree was always accompanied by a rose given at the assembly of the Students' Association.

Piemen antics were evident for over two decades at the hands of brothers who later had distinguished careers as an Air Force general officer, physician, lawyer, banker, Baptist missionary, business executive, Purple Heart recipient and others--all men of "healthy appetites for pie, good sense of humor, and prankish." The club name changed and was nicknamed "Etta Bita Pie" from the original Epsilon Beta Pi; "Eta Bita Pie" (1936); and "Eta Beta Pi" (1947). But, whatever the name, "Piemen" were bound by their fellowship, unique chanty sung at meetings, and by the inner password or fraternity greeting: "I like your crust." And, by their mutual love of pie.

> Pie, pie, we want our pie,
> Cocoanut or cherry,
> Peach or huckleberry.
> Pie, pie, we want our pie;
> That's the way piemen die.
> –*Junior Ranger*, Nov. 23, 1934

Pre-Law--Students who were preparing for the legal bar formed a Pre-Law Club in December 1945 because the Bar Association of 1935 no longer existed on campus. It offered fellowship among the attorneys-to-be and afforded an opportunity to learn elementary principles of law.

Pre-Med--Of a more serious nature than the Pie Club was the Pre-Med Club organized in 1930 under the fraternity name of "Alpha Sigma Kappa." It also used an assumed name, "Pi Mu Sigma" before settling on the "Pre-Med Club" title. Dr. Ava Josephine McAmis, Ph.D. Yale University and professor of chemistry, was a sponsor in the 1940s.

Rangerettes--The Girls' Athletic Association was formed ca. 1926, when each new member donated a U.S. silver dollar. Later, the name was changed to Gamma Alpha Alpha, and the members were known as the "Rangerettes" as they cheered the boys' athletic teams, supported forensics, and student publications. Members also participated in sports, maintained good grades, were cooperative with other campus groups, attended debate contests and sports awards presentations. They walked in the solemn Pilgrimage to the Alamo each April during Fiesta Week.

Rangerettes appeared in memorial services for Henry M. Hein (Class President in June 1944 who was killed in action in Germany in 1945) held in conjunction with the planting of a tree on the City Hall lawn in the Spring 1945. The girls wore their latest western-motif uniforms of drill and leather jackets with fringes. Several uniform changes were made over the years, but always in the color theme of orange and white.

Readers and Writers Club--Little information was found about the students who met to discuss stories and articles they had read and to talk over their own compositions in the peer group. They also attended movies as a group and discussed the movie plot and screenplay afterward.

Der Schiller Verein--Organized in the Fall 1927, Der Schiller Verein's purposes were three-fold: to increase the interest in the German language, to develop an appreciation of German literature, and to aid other organizations in providing social activities on campus. Stanley H. Schmidt was elected president of Der Schiller Verein and Miss Lena Koch, instructor in German and history, was the sponsor in the 1933-34 period. The original name was replaced by another club with the same objectives, the German Club. Members held picnics on the campus; played hosts to the St. Patrick's Day parties, and helped to stage reunions for former German-English School students.

Senators--The Senate Debating Society claimed to be the oldest boys' club on the campus in 1926-1927. Senators stood for the advancement of forensic activities, the establishment of good fellowship, and the promotion of athletics. Their archrivals in forensics, sports and other competitions were the Cowboys.

Members honored outstanding debaters, participated in the Adda Dabba Pouda Coronation Court and Carnival by providing skits, held dances, picnics, and honored new and ex-members at banquets. William H. Tyre, veteran history and government teacher, served for many years as sponsor. Gale H. Nelson, son of Director J. E. and Lillian Nelson, was a Senator in 1933-1934.

Sigma Phi Alpha Tau--Using four Greek letters, this group of girls had "friendship" as a theme in forming contacts to hold "Tri-Sorority Parties," the only known purpose.

Students of Service--"S.O.S." was not a distress signal, but the acronym or call letters used by students in the club created in 1949 for fellowship and the furthering of community services by students volunteering as social workers in the community.

Speechcrafters--Organized in May 1947, the purpose was to unite students interested in dramatic and forensic activities such as plays, speech and debate contests. Carl A. Atkins was the sponsor and drama teacher for years.

Steinmetz Engineers--A "sleeper" of a club with only a mention in the school newspaper on the old campus.

Students' Association--A composite of the entire student body led by elected executive officers to ensure order and good communication for the every Wednesday assemblies outdoors on the old campus, and for coordinating observances on special days. It dates to 1927 and was still going strong until 1950, at least. The Association operated with limited guidelines from the administration and served as an advisory body on projects and vital school questions. It was an "umbrella" respected by the general student body.

Freshman and sophomore classes formally organized and elected officers, but they were not as active or influential as the Students' Association. The Student Council was a ruling and advisory body, as well, subordinate to the administration and faculty. The Council was composed of the officers of the Students' Association, presidents of the freshman and sophomore classes, presidents of four social clubs, two service clubs, and two academic clubs; also, the editors and business managers of school publications were on the council. It was noted that there was a lot of democratic input from students allowed to manage their own affairs in the early days of SAJC.

Honorary Teachers--As the name suggests, the club attracted students who intended to enter the teaching profession. It was founded in 1928. A desire to teach and a high scholastic rating were the only requirements for membership. Regular programs were held using prominent educators as resources. Most of the members were female students. During the Depression Years they sold two tamales for a nickel on Tuesdays to bolster the treasury of the club. Reportedly, tamales sold better than pies.

Veterans Club--By far the largest interest group on campus during 1946-1949 was the Veterans Club because half of the student body was composed of military ex-GIs. It was organized in September 1945 to give veterans attending J.C. a chance to have an organization of their own and enabling them to keep abreast with news developments affecting the former servicemen. They held parties and dances under their own banner, but members also participated fully in leadership roles of other campus organizations. Truett L. Chance, who began teaching history and government in January 1947, was the long-time sponsor. He was a veteran, too, and had come to the College from a civilian position at Fort Sam Houston.

White Collar Girls--Members of the first-year class in business administration organized in the Fall 1946. They held monthly meetings featuring successful business women as speakers on problems facing career girls on the job.

After the San Antonio College campus was relocated from 419-423 South Alamo Street to 1300 San Pedro Avenue in February 1951, there was a definite trend toward more Greek-letter organizations. By 1963, there were 44 College-sponsored organizations on campus. Also, the French and Latin Clubs were started; the Newman Club, Baptist Student Union, Methodist Student Movement, Church of Christ Center all emerged on the campus perimeter to supplement in the 1950s the wide variety of activities available to urban two-year college students. As stated earlier, these students were joiners. Missing from the all-campus scene would be the decades-old traditional "Farmers' Day" celebrations enjoyed by students and faculty alike on the old campus--but "hayseed tomfoolery" is not politically correct anymore. Absent, too, was Billy Simon's Bowling Lanes--next-door neighbor--always available as a retreat from classes or a good hamburger.

APPENDIX J

Student Publications: *The Ranger*, *El Alamo* and *Fourth Write*

Student publications--by whatever names--have always played active roles on the campus as a means of communication, entertainment, and leaving a trail of history to follow major and minor events. The *Junior Ranger* was established March 25, 1926 six months after the college was started. It was a mimeographed, eight-page newspaper circulated free and without advertising on the Main Avenue High School grounds where the junior college had use after 3 o'clock in the afternoon.

"Hello there, meet the kid, *Junior Ranger*," promising "cutting criticism" from a "clever and remarkably precocious youngster," the editor wrote in the first issue. The second edition appeared on April 6 and from then on--with few interruptions for The Depression and World War II--a junior college campus paper (which made it clear it did not pretend to be a "newspaper") would be written and published by students with advice from faculty sponsors. Later, the Lanier and Brackenridge High School shops printed the paper until some local printing companies started "caviling" (objecting). Price was a nickel, then three pennies, later "free" under the student activity fee.

Noteworthy are the first staff members elected to office, as follows: Thea Goldschmidt, editor-in-chief; Clyde Lightfoot, associate editor; Joe Serna, business manager; Dorothy Owens, feature writer; Catherine Owens, art editor; Juanima Wells, joke editor; Vivian Waters and Monty Hawthorne, reporters; Dick McMahan, circulation editor.

The name of the paper evolved from *Junior Ranger* to *Jaysee Ranger* to *The Ranger*; it was published in many formats, sizes, and number of pages--with and without cigarette ads--but always a publication of merit to win awards.

The Alamo was the name given to the first yearbook published in 1928 and dedicated to the "Lady in Blue," in reference to a passage from Miss Adina de Zavala's *History and Legends of the Alamo*. The legend held that the Lady "is always ready to help the rich and poor, the artist, the artisan, the writer, the children--the whole people of her beloved Texas land." The Foreword of the first edition was printed in Old English typeface and the content makes for compelling reading as follows:

Foreword

A young college we, but a proud one. Gathered by the stern idealism of The University of Texas, mothered by the cosmopolitan culture and the heroic traditions of our City of the Alamo, we glory in our heritage and feel that verily we have a charge to keep. Clothed we may be for the moment in poorest raiment; yet we stand unashamed, dedicated as we are to the 'primacy of the spirit,' to the love of Truth and Beauty and Courage.

Perhaps we even find room for the pride in a very contrast of our surroundings and ideals, scorning as we do a cheap superficiality that sees no deeper than the surface. We have not broken faith with our heritage; we shall not. We go to meet the Future with confidence.

If our book reflects something of the idealism, the same idealism which made eternal those men of the Alamo and is today incarnate in our Mysterious Lady in Blue, then we are well content.

The Staff

The *Fourth Write* emerged as a student publication in the Fall 1967 with Volume 1, Number 1 as a successor--sort of--to *El Alamo* yearbook which had diminished support from students who didn't have their photos taken and would not, or could not, afford to pay the $7 or $8 price for the traditional annual. Joe Fuentes was the editor and discussed the change in concept and format which he noted was used at other two-year colleges.

It was a dilemma, but Fuentes said at the outset "that the problem worked itself all the way through the College board of trustees and, of course, you know what they decided." [He was right in that the process worked through channels testing the pros and cons of the issue. Edith Fox King, experienced former teacher at Fox Tech High School who later became the journalism teacher and sponsor of publications at San Antonio College, and Dean of Students Jerome Weynand had worked with students, faculty and staff for months to resolve the problem. They made the presentation and final recommendation at a meeting with the board which approved the magazine approach as an official campus publication. At least two other student publications in magazine format were short-lived: *Eight Seasons* and *Acequia*.]

A contest was held to give the new magazine a name. Some 248 suggestions were submitted before judges chose Linda Stevens' *Fourth*

Write entry. The name won easily in the vote by a committee of students, faculty, staff, and administrators with consensus the name evoked a solid tie-in with journalism and had a good sound.

Thousands of campus leaders contributed time and talents to the production of the student publications. A few staff members entered professional journalism, but each editor, reporter, business or circulation manager, artist, photographer, and proof-reader gained something personally by getting a little printer's ink on their hands and leaving an individual thumb print at the College. The names of the editors-in-chief or top editors are listed as follows:

Ranger	Year	El Alamo
Thea Goldschmidt	1926	
John Herbert May	1927	
Renwicke E. Cary	1928	Edwin Orville Moffett
Renwicke E. Cary	1929	Emily Schramm
	1930	Elizabeth Grother
LeRoy Cole	1931	Frances Briggs
LeRoy Cole/Richard Smith	1932	Fred Slimp
Richard Smith/Raymond Dowdy	1933	
Raymond Dowdy (combined issue)	1934	Hugh Reveley
Jerry Chapman	1935	Melba Janszen
Mildred Maule	1936	Gloria Shepherd
Bernice Barnett	1937	Maxine Wood
Jack Howard	1938	Betty Mary Mauer
Maxine Murray	1939	Jeanne Alford
Mendez Marks	1940	Sadie Gray Stafford
Colegate Villaret/Annsie Remy	1941	Margaret Blome
John M. Naff, Jr.	1942	Audrey Mills
	1943	
Geraldine Long	1944	
Geraldine Long	1945	Joyce Tucker
Bobbie Willis Armstrong	1946	Betty Lou Noll
John E. Blakey	1947	Patricia Helen Ebeling
Robert Johnson	1948	Dolores Marquez
Dorothy Hartman	1949	Audrey Traugott
George Jackson/Mike Olive	1950	Loyce Jean Martin
Betty Whall	1951	Rose Gold/Bobby Lange
A. L. Staph, instr./Herb Walker	1952	Martha Gerhart
Herbert A. Walker	1953	Jeri Richards

Ben Siegal/Shirley Insall	1954	Howard Yaws/Jane Shelton
John B. Rogers	1955	Jane Shelton
Bill Peck/Pattie Rose	1956	Martha Schulz
Don Cross	1957	Joan Hammett
Jack Allen	1958	Bob LaFontaine
Bill Morris	1959	Rosemary Jersig
Doran Williams	1960	DaLorris Lee
Lupe Gutierrez	1961	Anne Juraschek
Patty Midgett	1962	Teddy Sawyer
Maxine Gorneau	1963	Sharon Pierce
Josephine Briseno	1964	Robert Felling
Martha Sifuentes	1965	Robert Felling
Patricia O'Brien	1966	Martha Atlee/Luis Mercado
Patricia O'Brien	1967	Jeanne Kotowski

APPENDIX K

Athletics

Students at San Antonio Junior College asked for, and got, the start of a music program or, at least, the opportunity to form an orchestra. The school board agreed on October 3, 1927, beginning the second year of operation of the college, to pay a maximum of $250 for the academic year for a part-time director and to buy sheet music. What about athletics?

The first yearbook in 1928 was named *The Alamo*. It depicted many clubs had been established and mentioned football (1927 team photo), track, basketball, tennis and golf activities for "boys" and organized sports in basketball, tennis, baseball and swimming for "girls."

Students also asked for a coach of athletics. The board complied September 17, 1929, and hired Robert Clifton Greenwade, a teacher and coach at Brackenridge High School, on a two-fifths assignment to teach for $600 and coach for $900 for nine months at the junior college.

"Probably the saddest news of the day is the announcement by Mr. J. E. Nelson, Director, that we will have no football team to represent the college this year" (*The Junior Ranger*, September 21, 1931). The action came as a surprise to students and faculty after Mrs. Clyde Barnes, registrar, sold the equipment in order to pay an old debt, the article revealed.

School board Minutes did not reflect further mention of college athletics until the meeting on December 10, 1940, when J. W. Boggus, a teacher at Washington Irving Junior High School, was appointed basketball coach for 1940-41.

After the newly created junior college district assumed full operation of San Antonio Junior College on September 1, 1946, President Loftin tried to revive intramural and intercollegiate athletics by hiring an older student to coordinate programs. He was replaced by another mature student after it was learned that bills had not been paid for uniforms and letter jackets. Loftin called on a friend and veteran public school teacher and coach Jack Tolar to take over activities.

Without facilities, it was difficult to stage sports other than intramurals. However, a varsity basketball team used the gym at the downtown YMCA. Cowboys and Senate rivalries in debate and intramural sports continued. The "SAC Rangers" played in a City Recreation

Department softball league during 1947 and 1948.

In 1948, Candler recounts, a "pick-up" track team composed mostly of ex-servicemen, made national news as the "Hitchhiking Rangers" to enter meets at the Border Olympics in Laredo, Fat Stock Show track meet in Fort Worth, and the Texas Relays in Austin. A football team was formed without official school sanction in 1949 using scrounged equipment from St. Mary's University and the army.

A new era was about to begin with construction plans for a new campus and physical education facilities on the horizon. Also change would come when Bill Candler, recent graduate of North Texas State College, entered the picture. Candler drove to San Antonio on a Sunday evening in September 1949 to be ready for a job interview on Monday. he couldn't find the college campus spanning the 417-419 South Alamo Street, and passed it by traveling south several miles. He was looking for a campus, not an acre!

Candler passed the scrutiny of Loftin who gave the new coach an admonition: "Play like ladies and gentlemen: win graciously and lose gracefully." Candler said he would abide. [Bill Candler was the 20th faculty member employed by San Antonio College. He served as chairman of the department of health and physical education and coached interscholastic teams in major sports for 37 years until he retired in 1986 with emeritus status. He is the namesake of the greatly expanded and modernized complex dedicated April 29, 1999 as the "Bill C. Candler Physical Education Center."]

Returning to that first year in 1949, Candler recalls that the basketball players suited up in old uniforms, they were responsible for laundry and purchase of their shoes. He spent under $700 during 1949-50 on official teams involving men's basketball, track, tennis and golf; and on women's tennis team. Basketball practice was held at night in the St. Philip's College gym at the invitation of Coach Bill Hudgins. Candler used the tracks at Alamo Heights High School, Harlandale High School, Fort Sam Houston, and Northeast ISD stadium.

San Antonio College, still without facilities for athletics, succeeded in becoming a member of the Texas Junior College Athletic Conference and participated fully for many years.

When the new health building was being planned on the new campus, Mr. Loftin really wanted an indoor swimming pool to be included at extra cost. His dream was realized when the board approved the heated pool as part of the facility which was completed in 1952, the third building constructed on the San Pedro Avenue campus. Candler was able to do a little "payback" courtesy by allowing high schools to use the pool.

The period 1952-53 stands out as a good time for basketball at the college. One of the "stars" was Tom Smith who made all-district and won the coveted Hallmark Trophy named after the late Jimmy Hallmark, son of Dean of Men Wame J. and Nell Hallmark. Dean Hallmark often made out-of-town trips with the team, but didn't try to coach although he had the experience.

Some of Smith's teammates (many had careers in education) were Roy Middleton, Carroll Smith, Roger Tatsch, Jerry Cook, Manuel Chacon, Lee Rux, Tom Moseley, Dale Bates, Myrle Schultz, Gerald Nail, Jerry Myers, Ernest Jones, Ed Staffel, Preston Littrell, Al Sadovsky, David Phillips, Tony Vasquez, Bob Shultz, among others.

Tom Smith returned to San Antonio College as an instructor in health and physical education and assumed coaching duties. He guided the basketball team through the period before full integration when some schools didn't want to play a team with Black players. Candler remembers that "Tom handled the situation well." [An ancedote recalled is that when Smith's team played a junior college in near East Texas where the protocol of the restaurant was to admit Blacks only through a rear door, Coach Smith refused to separate--segregate--his team and took all of them through the back door to eat in the kitchen.]

In later years, men's swimming and baseball and women's basketball, volleyball and swimming were added to the sports venue. The programs were successful in winning zone, conference, state and national recognition. [After the 1980s, Candler recalls, all student semi-intercollegiate and intramural sports were transferred to the jurisdiction of the office of Student Affairs.]

Among other programs which brought recognition and even fame to San antonio College were in folk dance and synchronized swimming. Merle Dulin, women's P.E. teacher, produced water shows for five years before her health precluded the activity. Margaret Swan Forbes took over, enlarged the program and brought national acclaim to herself and the college.

Dulin recommended Nelda Drury, who had been teaching at Brownsville Junior College, to Candler's attention for employment as an adjunct instructor with experience in teaching dance curriculum and focused on folk dancing to produce troupes that entertained at functions and participated in international dance festivals coordinated by Drury-- she's still going in 2002, even after "retirement."

25th Anniversary

The San Antonio College Faculty Wives Club celebrated its 25th Anniversary with a luncheon honoring the Founding Members on April 5, 1975, in the Fountain Room of La Louisiane. Each guest received a 35-page "Cookbook" featuring 70 favorite recipes. From the kitchen of the 1974-75 FWC President Dorothy Johnston (Mrs. Doug) came these recipes:

Brown Sugar Cookies

1/2	cup shortening or butter
2 1/2	cups brown sugar
2	well-beaten eggs
2 1/2	cups flour
1/2	teaspoon salt
1/2	teaspoon soda
1	cup pecans (or walnuts)

Slowly cream shortening and sugar; add eggs and beat well. Add sifted dry ingredients, then nuts. Drop from teaspoon 2 inches apart on greased cookie sheet. Bake at 350 degrees for 10-12 min.

Sock-It-To-Me-Cake

1	package Duncan Hines Butter Recipe Golden Cake Mix
1	cup (8 Oz.) dairy sour cream
1/2	cup Crisco oil
1/4	cup sugar
1/4	cup water
4	eggs

Filling: 1 cup ;chopped pecans; 2 tablespoons brown sugar; 2 teaspoons cinnamon.

Pre-heat oven to 375 degrees. In a large bowl blend cake mix, sour cream, oil, sugar, water, and eggs. Beat at high speed for 2 minutes. Pour 2/3 of batter in a greased and floured 10" tube pan. Combine filling ingredients and sprinkle over batter in pan. Spread remaining batter evenly over filling mixture. Bake at 375 degrees for 45-55 minutes, then remove from pan. Glaze: Blend 1 cup confectioner's sugar and 2 tablespoons milk. Drizzle over cake.

APPENDIX L

Faculty Wives Club

Probably the most "delicious" tradition in the wide range of activities and memories of the faculty and staff was the regular Wednesday morning "coffees" that the Faculty Wives Club held for so many years.

Organized in 1949 under the leadership of Mrs. Wayland Moody, Lillian served as the first president of the Club of 12 members who met on the South Alamo Street campus. The 25th Anniversary Yearbook of the Club boasted a membership of 240 in 1973-74.

It was a social club with the primary purpose of providing opportunities throughout the academic year when faculty spouses got together to know one another better. Meetings were held once a month with five wives serving as hostesses, either in a home or other locations, including on campus. At times members would dine out for a luncheon at a restaurant. After the College acquired the Koehler Home, meetings were held in that turn-of-the-century Victorian mansion. Featured speakers were faculty or persons outside the college circle. Parties at Christmastime and Valentine's Day sometimes were held for husbands and wives.

One of the pleasures of the members--as mentioned in the scrapbook--was to serve coffee and "homemade" goodies to the faculty each Wednesday morning in a hallway nook, later the *Entre Nous* lounge in the Loftin Student Center and Fletcher Center. Volunteers of the club took turns as hostesses at the coffees. By necessity--as the faculty and staff grew--those "homebaked" coffee cakes and rolls were brought in from the college cafeteria.

There was an Active Wives Group and an Associate Group for the working wives who usually met twice a year. In 1975-76, interest groups were formed in crafts, bridge, sewing, etc. The Club published a newsletter. By 1980-81, dues of $5.00 a year were paid by members. Wives took shopping trips to the local Mercado in San Antonio and ventured to Laredo. Tours of San Antonio's special places included the Missions, Los Patios, Artisans' Alley, Scrivener's, the Bright Shawl for lunch and style show; wives even rode the double-decker bus when it was introduced to San Antonio transit riders. They held their own style shows and held bake sales.

Not all of the activities were centered around fun things or eating!

Wives helped out on campus in the library and during registration and welcomed visitors to campus. For a time the Faculty Wives offered a scholarship for a deserving student. The Club remained a viable organization into the 1980s, having served San Antonio College so well since 1949. While space doesn't allow the listing of all of the wives, here is a list of the names of the Presidents: Mesdames

Wayland P. Moody	Lillian	1949-50
Wame J. Hallmark	Nell	1950-51
Vernon LaBauve	Ann	1951-52
Clyde R. Nail	Frances	1952-53
Henry B. Webb	Zelma Lou	1953-54
J. O. Loftin	Matilda	1954-55
(Mother of Ada L. Staph)	Alice Staph	1955-56
Wayland P. Moody	Lillian	1956-57
Jerome F. Weynand	Adrienne	1957-58
Julian P. Cook	Adah Louise (Staph)	1958-59
Elmer Jones	Janie	1959-60
Vernon Helmke	Jackie	1960-61
Perry Gragg	Marilyn	1961-62
James O. Wallace	Lillie Ruth	1962-63
Tom Smith	Theresa	1963-64
John D. Brantley		1964-65
Harvey Summers	Genie Sue	1965-66
Lon Rowlett		Fall 1966
Charles Lewis	Nita	Spring 1967
James Lincoln	Thelma	1967-68
Thomas Frazier	Bennye	1968-69
Joe Harber	Jo Ann	1969-70
Jack Shaw	Laura	1970-71
Ron Bramble	Kathy	1971-72
Robert Brown	Mary Ann	1972-73
John Fardal	Pat	Fall 1973
Richard Davis	Hazel	Spring 1974
Doug Johnston	Dorothy	1974-75
Allan Nowotny	Maureen	1975-76
James Dye	Barbara	1976-78
George Katz	Linda	1977-78
		1978-79
Ron Culpepper	Betty	1979-80
Jerome F. Weynand	Adrienne	1980-81

In the Spring of 2001, the SAC Faculty Wives Club still boasts a membership of 26 retirees' wives and widows. The group still holds scheduled monthly meetings--usually with luncheons--centered around fellowship and care for one another.

From Adrienne's Kitchen

Included in the Faculty Wives Club "Cookbook" were two recipes by College First Lady Adrienne Weynand, as follows:

Scotch Teas

1   cup butter or margarine
2   cups brown sugar
2   teaspoons baking powder
1/2 teaspoon salt
4   cups oatmeal (quick cooking)

In saucepan combine butter and sugar. Cook and stir until butter melts. Stir in baking powder and salt. Add oats and mix well. Pour into greased 13x9x2 - inches pan and bake at 350 degrees for 20 or 25 minutes. Cut into bars or diamonds. Makes: 4 dozen or more.

Date Pecan Balls

1   cup soft butter   2   cups ground pecans
1/2 cup sugar   1   cup whole dates finely cut
2   teaspoons vanilla
2   cups sifted flour

Cream butter and sugar. Add vanilla and mix. Add flour and mix. Blend pecans and dates. Roll teaspoonsfuls of dough into balls. Refrigerate for 1 - 2 hours. Bake at 350 degrees on greased cookie sheet for approximately 20 minutes. Remove from pan and roll balls in powdered sugar. After cooled, again sprinkle with powdered sugar.

Commencement Exercises Program May 1944

Commencement Exercises

of the

Graduating Class

of the

San Antonio Junior College

HORACE MANN JUNIOR HIGH SCHOOL

Friday Evening, May 26, 1944

8 O'clock

PROGRAM

PROCESSIONAL, "Triumphal March" .... Grieg
San Antonio Vocational and Technical School Orchestra
Directed by R. A. Dhossache

INVOCATION .... Rev. William Parrish

VOCAL SOLO, "The Maids of Cadez" .... Delibes
Ruth Harp, Accompanied by Evelyn Heye

OVERTURE, "Light Cavalry" .... Suppe
San Antonio Vocational and Technical School Orchestra
Directed by R. A. Dhossache

VOCAL SOLO, "Aloha Oe" .... Hawaiian Farewell Song
Emil Martinez, Accompanied by Evelyn Heye

ADDRESS .... Judge Charles Anderson

PRESENTATION OF CLASS .... Mrs. M. G. Fuller
Dean of Women

CONFERRING OF DEGREES .... J. O. Loftin
President of the College

PRESENTATION OF DEGREES AND DIPLOMAS .... Randall Taylor

ANNOUNCEMENT OF SCHOLARSHIP AWARDS .... C. E. Barnes
San Antonio Junior College

BENEDICTION .... Rev. William Parrish

RECESSIONAL, "Pomp and Circumstance" .... Elgar
San Antonio Vocational and Technical School Orchestra
Directed by R. A. Dhossache

CANDIDATES FOR THE DEGREE OF
ASSOCIATE OF ARTS

Anderson, Barbara Charlotte

Biskamp, Alice Thekla

Bonner, Martha

Cohen, Sylvia

Duke, Elizabeth Louise

Evans, Mary Katherine

Flake, Evelyn

Ford, Charles William, Jr.

Gaines, Betty Ruth

Hildebrandt, Lucille Lydia

Layer, Lorraine

Mason, Patricia Frances

Nye, Dorothy Louise

Owens, Emily Kathryn

Waldeck, Joyce Sheridan

Williamson, Sara

CANDIDATES FOR THE DEGREE OF
ASSOCIATE OF SCIENCE

Dietz, Clifton E.

Hendricks, Virginia Lee

Hein, Henry M.

Hickerson, Martha Sue

Horan, Shevaun Irene

Lundeen, Vernon Plarr

Morse, Dick Gould

Wulfe, Jesse Edmond

Zalim, Albert Ned

CANDIDATES FOR GRADUATION WITH
JUNIOR COLLEGE CERTIFICATE

Bass, Lornadelle

Herblin, Anita Jo

Kahn, Rosa Lee

Dedicated to the San Antonio Junior College boys serving in the armed forces of the United States:

Beware
of entrance to a quarrel; but, being in
Bear't, that th' opposed may beware of thee.

. . . . Shakespeare

Lt. Adams, George
Pfc. Adams, Paul
Lt. Allen, R. C.
Arnold, James M.
Barrow, Jesse Lee
Blake, Guy Roy
Blundell, Bernard
Lt. Bogle, Muller
Lt. Brauback, John
Lt. Breit, Eugene
Brooks, Neywood
A/C Brown, Billy
Brunkhorst, Harold
Brunkhorst, Robert
A/C Bryant, Frank
Camacho, Jesse
Campbell, F., Jr.
Cimmerman, Fred
A/C Cowan, Tommy
Cullwell, Thomas
Cunningham, Sam
Lt. Davis, Pleas
Denny, Herbert
Lt. Dickey, J. C.
Diebel, Edwin A.
Lt. Dunham, John
Lt. Dunham, Walter
Col. Dunn, Frank
Pvt. Farris, G. T.
Fitzpatrick, Billy
Fitzpatrick, Jack
Capt. Fitzhenry, O. C.
A/S Flowers, Herbert
A/S Flowers, Paul A.
A/C Fontaine, Lawrence
Cpl. Fontain, Henry
Forbrich, Earl
Forbrich, Ernest
Cpl. Galvin, Robert
Garcia, Joe H.

Garza, Ray
***Lt. Gonzales, Omar
Grunwald, E. J.
Harrison, Paul
Lt. Henderson, Dan
Hetherington, Charles
Higginbotham, John
A/C Hill, Edwyn
Hirsch, Marvin Del
Lt. Hodges, Cecil
**Ens. Howard, Jack
Pvt. Hudspeth, Edward
A/S Huebner, Alfred
A/S Huebner, Harry J.
Lt. Hurst, Frank
Japhet, Richard C.
A/C Johnson, Louis
*Lt. Johnson, Wirt A.
Jones, Robert John
Pfc. Kilman, Victor
Kittinger, Elbert
Pvt. Kuehn, Richard
Kumler, Dick
A/S Lahourcade, John
Lamm, Edwin, Jr.
A/C Law, James G.
Lt. Lindberg, Robert
Lt. Loftin, James K.
Pvt. Long, Frank
Capt. McAnneny, Adrian
Lt. McCaleb, Garnett
*Lt. McCall, Ben J.
McGovern, Terry
McKinney, William F.
Lt. Marshall, George
Martinez, Anthony
Merking, Bryan
Ens. Maurer, Linn
A/S Merl, Lawrence
Pvt. Metz, A. R.

Morgan, James
A/C Navarro, R. A.
*Lt. Negley, Richard
Lt. Neuham, Harold
A/C Orr, Merritt
**Ott, Roderich
Pizzini, Herman
*Lt. Purdon, W. I.
Lt. Risinger, Fred
Roark, Hal King
Roberts, Edwin W.
Rodriguez, Abel
Pvt. Roland, Floyd
Pvt. Rushton, Jack
Schelper, Lenord
Salik, Charles Eliot
Lt. Salas, Gregory
A/C Scruggs, Bill
*Lt. Sellers, William
Ens. Seriff, Jack
A/C Shaw, Albert
St. Simpson, Louis
Sivley, Ray
A/C Slaughter, William
A/S Smiley, Logan
Pvt. Spiro, Herbert
Capt. Stuart, Harold
Capt. Strieber, E. M.
Ens. Stuve, Fred
Stuve, Leroy
Pvt. Sullivan, Tommy
Taylor, John
Lt. Tollett, Robert
Villaret, Colgate
2/S Wallace, C. L.
Lt. Williams, W. A.
Ins. Wilson, Aubrey
Wilson, Chester
Woodard, Bruce
Yeager, Cois

*Killed in Action   **Missing in action   ***Prisoner of War

There are probably many others of whom we have no record.

Campus Dedication and Open House Program May 1951

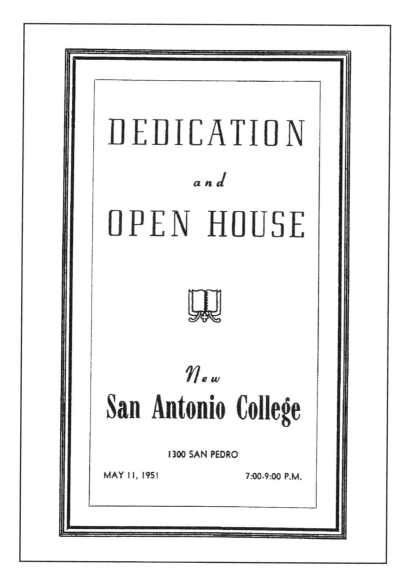

DEDICATION
and
OPEN HOUSE

New
San Antonio College

1300 SAN PEDRO

MAY 11, 1951   7:00-9:00 P.M.

Program.....

Band Concert
> Edison High School, Jean Sarli, Director

DEDICATION EXERCISES
Presentation of Guests
> J. O. Loftin, President

San Antonio College Chorus
> James Gambino, Director

Greetings from Junior College Consultant
> Dr. C. C. Colvert, University of Texas

Address
> Honorable Clyde E. Barnes

Response
> W. W. McAllister, Representing Board of Trustees,
> Faculty and Students

Response
> Jerome Weynand, Representing The Alumni Association

Benediction
> Reverend Chess Lovern

Alumni Meeting............... - ....Little Theater

Open House Visitation

OUR COMMUNITY HAS PROVIDED AN EXCELLENT COLLEGE TO S E R V E, PRACTICALLY FREE OF TUITION, THE EDUCATIONAL NEEDS OF THE YOUTH AND ADULTS IN THE GREATER SAN ANTONIO AREA. YOUR PRESENCE IS APPRECIATED, AND YOU ARE URGED TO VISIT ALL DEPARTMENTS.

Platform Guests

Board of Trustees

Public School Administrators

Representatives of Local Colleges

Representatives of Civic Clubs

City, County and State Officials

Representatives of I. and E. Centers of Armed Services

Architects and Builders

Alumni Association Officials

Out of City Guests

How lovely is Thy dwelling-place

By JOHANNES BRAHMS

How lovely is Thy dwelling-place, O Lord

of Hosts! For my soul, it longeth, yea,

fainteth for the courts of the Lord.

My soul and body crieth out, yea, for the

living God. Blest are they that dwell

within Thy house. They praise Thy name

evermore! How lovely is Thy dwelling-place!

APPENDIX O

Commencement Exercises Program May 1951

S.A.C.

Class of 1951

Commencement Exercises

of the

Graduating Class

of the

San Antonio College

★

1300 San Pedro Ave.

Wednesday Evening, May 30, 1951

Eight O'clock

Program:

PROCESSIONAL, "Fest March" from Tannhauser.............................Wagner

INVOCATION...Rev. Erwin A. Juraschek

CHOIR, "The Music of Life"...Noble Cain
San Antonio College Choir
James J. Gambino, Director

INTRODUCTION OF SPEAKER..President J. O. Loftin

ADDRESS...Mr. W. W. McAllister
President, Board of Trustees
San Antonio College

PRESENTATION OF CLASS...Dr. W. P. Moody
Dean of the College

CONFERRING OF DIPLOMAS..President J. O. Loftin

PRESENTATION OF DIPLOMAS...Mr. Jesse Fletcher
Vice-President, Board of Trustees
San Antonio College

ANNOUNCEMENT OF SCHOLARSHIPS AND AWARDS....Mrs. Lois G. Morrison

RECESSIONAL, "Prelude to Act III": Lohengrin................................Wagner

Candidates for Diploma of Associate of Arts

Ambrus, Sandor Jr.
Batla, Grace Alice
Beatty, Barbara
Brown, Glendora
*Carnes, Marie
Caruthers, Kenneth B.
Chesney, Bascom N. Jr.
Coleman, Peggy Sue
Cooper, Robert Lee
*Crane, Billy
Cuellar, Conception
Davis, Dorothy
Dugat, Joyce Marie
Ebsenberger, Clarence
Farr, Cleburne Loyd
Fierro, Lupe
Flores, Yvonne Joy
*Fresenius, Roberta
Garza, Sergio
Gayle, Willie May
Gayoso, Mary Nell
Gibson, Mary V.
*Gill, John C.
Gold, Rose Sylvia
Harber, Ernest Joe

Harvey, Carol Jean
Holland, James W.
Hord, Mary Elinor
Jackson, Goy Lee
*Jasso, Chris
*Johnson, Bobbye Del
Jones, Marion E.
Kern, Charles W.
Klinkerman, Robert Dale
Lacey, Larry Lee
Lange, Bobby
Laughlin, Thomas Jr.
Linder, Orville
Lombardino, Frank J.
Magnon, Bernard A.
Matthews, Richard Alan
Monk, Galloway
Moody, Wayland Pierce
*Moreno, Victor Manuel
Murphee, W. T.
Mussey, Edna A.
Newman, George Thomas
*Orona, A. Socorro
Patino, Josephine Marie
Peace, Robert C.

Candidates for Diploma of Associate of Arts

(Continued)

Peck, Charles
Pfanstiel, Do Ann
Rabago, Jesus
Rahn, John E.
Rick, Barbara Hope
Roach, Betty Irene
Rodriquez, Robert B.
Rouse, Clarice Evelyn
Scarborough, Betty K.
Schuetze, Barbara Jean
Smith, Barbara J.
Spitta, Adolph F.
Stemm, Jordan Ann

*Sylvest, Ruth
*Taylor, Mary F.
Tatum, Richard A.
Trevino, John V.
Trevino, Viola Mae
Valdez, Adolfo J.
Walbridge, Nyra
Wall, George B.
Whall, Betty C.
White, Delcye Anne
Woo, Mary
Wright, William A.
Wulfe, Carl E.

Candidates for Certificate of Completion

Amann, Olga
Berger, Theodore John
Broughton, Bernard
Casas, Rudolph A.
Jackson, Lester B.

Markey, Paul Robert
Murray, Robert Wiseman
Reed, Thomas Edwin
Wehman, Louis C.

*Completed requirements for graduation January, 1951.

Junior Chamber of Commerce Brochure
for 1945 Junior College Election

A NEW

JUNIOR

COLLEGE

FOR SAN ANTONIO
and BEXAR COUNTY

★ ★ ★

Endorsed by

The San Antonio Board of Education
The County Board of Education
The State Board of Education
The San Antonio and Bexar County
Planning Board

★ ★ ★

A Post War Project

Sponsored by

THE SAN ANTONIO

JUNIOR CHAMBER OF COMMERCE

Election October 30

SCIENCE BUILDING

The
New Junior College

THE PRESENT JUNIOR COLLEGE

San Antonio has benefited from the excellent program of its Junior College for the past twenty years. During this period thousands of students have been permitted to remain at home and receive a high quality of instruction in small classes where individual attention has been given by sympathetic instructors. As a result of this thorough grounding in their first two college years, their efforts in senior colleges have been more successful, and their work more enjoyable. Many of these Junior College graduates have entered successfully into the business and industrial life of this community.

The Junior College buildings, however have failed to attract a majority of the high school graduates, who have left their homes and city to enter other colleges with beautiful campuses and buildings. They have spent much money in travel, board, room, tuition, and fees. This money should have been spent in San Antonio, and not drained from the business interests that support this community.

ADMINISTRAT

The Modern Idea

Junior Colleges have gradually discovered the particular work for which they are best suited. The courses of study have become more technical, vocational, and practical. The students with limited time, or limited means, or the students who work part time, have requested intensive courses designed to fit them into a business or profession in the shortest possible time.

New Plans

The San Antonio Board of Education had these purposes in mind when it voted to project plans whereby a Union Junior College District could be formed and whereby a small tax of eight cents on county valuations, and bonds for a new college plant could be authorized.

The San Antonio and Bexar County Planning Board have endorsed the new Junior College and financed the preliminary plans and estimates. Also the petitions have been signed, the approvals of the County Board of Education and the State Board of Education

ION BUILDING

secured, according to the state law. The new Junior College now awaits the approval of the property voting citizens within the eleven school districts comprising the proposed Union Junior College District.

New Buildings

The Administration Building has been planned to dominate the cluster of four Spanish type buildings for the San Antonio Junior College. It will house the administrative offices, the library, the auditorium, the business administration room, the F. M. Broadcasting Studio, and fourteen classrooms. This building will be the first to be erected, and the others will be built according to the post war needs for employment and conditions favorable to labor and material markets.

The Science Building will house the science laboratories on the upper floor. Because of the practical nature of the natural sciences, the shops will be located in the same building. The application of the college sciences to industrial problems will be possibly by the interchange of scientific principles with practical problems in shop laboratories.

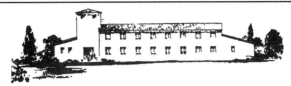

ARTS BUILDING

The Arts Building will house not only the music, art, drawing, and kindred subjects, but also the student activities center. One wing will contain the student recreation room, where a luncheonette, dining room, and student activities in general may have attractive facilities.

Individual sound proof practice rooms and teaching studios provide the best teaching facilities. The band, orchestra, and chorus room will provide the essential equipment for mass music instruction.

The Health Education Building has been planned to build better bodies for the Junior College students. Remedial exercises, hot and cold baths, swimming, and play courts will be provided for improving the health and physiques of all students. A large gymnasium will house fifteen hundred spectators, and may be available for all public schools engaging in interschool contests.

Buildings for St. Philip's Junior College

The St. Philip's Branch will have a combination Health Education and Auditorium Building and two laboratory shop buildings. These three buildings when added to the very good administration building now on their campus will provide ample space and facilities to meet the needs for a Junior College of the first class.

215

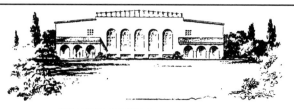

HEALTH EDUCATION BUILDING

Location

The governing board for the new college must be chosen at large from the Union Junior College District. This board will have the authority to locate the site and contract for the buildings. Certain standards have been set for a college location. Among these are: Sufficient size (probably six city blocks); accessibility to bus lines and converging streets; freedom from excessive noises; refined and cultural surroundings. Any site chosen should meet each of these standards.

Sponsoring Agency

Realizing the great service a Class A Junior College can render San Antonio, the Junior Chamber of Commerce of San Antonio has accepted the sponsorship of the new Junior College. They believe the Junior College should receive a prime consideration among all the post war projects that may be submitted to the people. Whether judged by the financial income to the city, or the college opportunities afforded so many youths and adults, or the ideal of San Antonio becoming a cultural and educational center, the Junior Chamber of Commerce urges every public citizen to join them in making possible the San Antonio Union Junior College.

Questions About The

1. Why separate the Junior College from the city schools?

The Public School Board desired that the new district encompass all of San Antonio and suburbs, since students from all the Greater San Antonio High School Districts attend the Junior College.

2. Why does the proposed district have the broken outside limits?

The law requires all of a school district to be included if any part is included in a Union Junior College District. The districts included are those adjacent to San Antonio.

3. How will the new college be financed?

The student will pay from sixty to seventy-five dollars, the state will pay sixty to one hundred dollars on each student, and the county tax rate of eight cents will pay for the buildings and partial support. (The annual tuition now is $120.00 per year.) The rates for the new college will be about $60.00 per year.

4. Will non-residents pay the same tuition as resident students?

No. They will have to pay about twenty-five dollars more than the resident students, because they will not furnish any tax revenue.

5. Who will govern the new college districts?

A new board of seven men to be chosen from the entire district. The sponsoring agency will choose the men from among the successful business and professional men of Bexar County.

New Junior College

6. Will the school have dormitories?

No. A Junior College is exclusively for regular day students and evening students. The local youth are to be served with courses fitted to their needs.

★ ★ ★

7. Can the Junior College courses be transferred to Senior colleges?

Two years of standard academic and pre-professional courses will be offered in the new college. These credits may be transferred to senior colleges. Students desiring a Bachelors Degree will have only two additional years away from home.

★ ★ ★

8. Will vocations be taught in the new college?

Yes. College courses on the technical and scientific level, especially for foremen and technicians. National statistics reveal that seven technicians are required for each engineer.

★ ★ ★

9. What are some of the "Terminal Courses"?

Stenography; typewriting; engineering and architectural drafting; medical technology; dental assistant; nursing; pre-law; business English; accounting; conversational Spanish, French, and German; hotel service; institutional cooking; technical vocations; airport occupations; and numerous other courses of the terminal nature.

★ ★ ★

10. Will regular college activities be promoted?

Yes. There will be bands, orchestras, choirs, athletics, forensics, plays, clubs, and various other student activities. Junior College students usually enjoy the social life and club life of their school more than the senior college students. The Junior College students also make lasting friendship among the people with whom they will live.

APPENDIX Q
Some Outstanding Former Students

San Antonio College began in 1982 to honor some "Outstanding Former Students" with an award and placed their names on a plaque displayed in the Fletcher Administration Center Lobby showcase; also, the names of honorees have been listed in the College *Catalog*. The names and dates of the award are as follows:

Congressman Henry B. Gonzalez	1982
Judge Blair Reeves	1983
Congressman Albert Bustamante	1984
Dr. William Kirby (Former State Comm. of Education)	1985
Capt. Larry Pearson (Navy pilot, Blue Angels C.O.)	1986-87
Lisa Brown (archaeologist)	1987-88
Judge Edward Prado (U.S. District Court)	1987-88
Dr. Jerome F. Weynand (Educator; Baumberger Endowment)	1987-88
James R. Vasquez (Former Edgewood ISD Supt.)	1988-89
Judge Sarah Garrahan (Bexar County court-at-law)	1988-89
Frank Gonzalez (Oceanographer)	1989-90
Nancy Klepper (Educator)	1989-90
Diana Gonzales (Journalist)	1990-91
Bill Hayden (Founder/CEO CompuAdd)	1990-91
Jesse Trevino (Artist)	1991-92
Patsy Torres (Entertainer)	1992-93
Dr. Felix D. Almaraz (Columnist, Historian)	1993-94
William R. Sinkin (Banker)	1993-94
Dr. Judith Ann Loredo (Educator)	1994-95
Steven C. Hilbig (Bexar County District Attorney)	1994-95
Dr. Robert L. Jimenez (Psychiatrist)	1995-96
Dr. Leo Sayavedra (Educator)	1995-96
Francis R. Scobee (Challenger Astronaut)	1995-96
Tino Duran (Publisher)	1996-97
Al A. Philippus (San Antonio Chief of Police)	1996-97
Dr. Cynthia Gambell Broderick (Educator)	1997-98
Dr. Jesse T. Zapata (Educator)	1997-98
Dr. James V. McLean (Veterinarian)	1998-99
Marinell Garcia-Murillo (Community Relations)	1998-99
Congressman Ciro D. Rodriguez	1999-00

Dr. Martin Basaldua (Physician)	1999-00
Oscar Hernandez (Educator)	2000-01
Rodolpho Sandoval (Educator)	2000-01
Judge Sara Kleban Radin (Los Angeles courts)	2001-02

Source: San Antonio College Public Relations Office

Honored Alumni of San Antonio College

These 75 alumni were chosen by the San Antonio College Alumni Association as outstanding alumni and honored at the Fourth Scholarship Gala held October 7, 2000 as a highlight of the 75th Anniversary year-long celebration. Each received a trophy presented by President Vern Loland.

Mr. Moses Aguilar, '84
  Banker
Dr. Felix D. Almaraz, '56
  Historian
Judge Alfonso E. Alonzo, Jr., '57
Dr. Francisco Barrera, '78
  Physician
Dr. Martin Basaldua, '70
  Physician
Dr. Cynthia Broderick, '66
  Educator
Mr. Ernest Bromley, '71
  Advertising Executive
Dr. Lisa Brown, '72
  Archaeologist
Hon. Albert Bustamente, '56
  U.S. Congressman
Mr. Val S. Calvert, '90
  Educator
Constable Charlie Campos, Jr., '65
  Justice Precinct #1
Dr. Lou Ann Cook, '69
  Nurse Educator
Mr. Tim Daniels, '83
  Business Executive
Mr. Tino Duran, '58
  Publisher
Dr. David Espino, '75
  Physician/Educator

Mr. Ruben Escobedo, '56
  C.P.A.
Mr. John Flood, '78
  Nurse
Ms. Teresa Garces, '60
  Health Educator
Mrs. Marinella Garcia-Murillo, '86
  Comm. Relations Spec.
Judge Sarah Garrahan, '61
Col. Viviano Gomez, Jr., '46
  U.S. Army, Retired
Dr. Cecilia Gonzales, '59
  College Administrator
Ms. Diana Gonzales, '66
  Journalist
Mr. Frank Gonzalez, '61
  Oceanographer
Dr. Hector Gonzalez, '59
  Nurse Educator
Hon. Henry B. Gonzalez, '35
  U.S. Congressman
Ms. Kathryn (Kaki) Gueldner, '37
  Administrative Secretary
Dr. Douglas L. Hall, '65
  Educator
Mr. Bill Hayden, '65
  Businessman
Mr. Steven C. Hilbig, '70
  Former District Attorney

Ms. Mary Alice Hoover, '64
High School Principal
Dr. Robert Jimenez, '58
Physician
Dr. William Kirby, '85
Fmr. Texas Comm. Education
Ms. Nancy Klepper, '89
Science Educator
Mr. Daniel (Cappy) Lawton, '65
Restauranteur
Ms. Florence Lieb, '34
Educator
Dr. Judith A. Loredo, '64
College Administrator
Mr. Pete Martinez, '71
Business Executive
Mr. Michael McKay, '62
Statistician/Project Mgr.
Dr. James McLean, '98
Veterinarian
Mr. Joseph (Sonny) Melendrez, '64
Radio/Television Host
Ms. Sharon Midgett, '86
High School Educator
Mr. Frank P. Olvera, '79
Probation Officer
Mr. Hector E. Pacheco, '72
Pharmacist
Capt. Larry Pearson, '62
U.S. Navy, Retired
Hon. Bobby Perez, '84
S.A. City Councilman
Chief Al Philippus, '74
Fmr. S.A. Police Chief
Judge Edward Prado, '67
U.S. District Court
Mr. John Quinones, '72
News Correspondent
Mr. Bernard Rapoport, '35
CEO/Insurance
Judge Blair Reeves, '48
Bexar Co./4th Ct. C. Appeals
Dr. Juan Reyna, '66
Physician
Ms. Linda Robinson, '70
Attorney

Hon. Ciro Rodriguez, '66
U.S. Congressman
Ms. Norma S. Rodriguez, '88
S.A. City Clerk
Ms. Elizabeth Ruiz, '79
News Anchor/Talk Show Host
Dr. Leo Sayavedra, '56
Texas A&M System Provost
Col. Francis R. Scobee, '63
USAF, Challenger Astronaut
Ms. Sharon Jones Schweitzer, '71
Public Relations Executive
Dr. Cynthia Shade, '68
Educator
Mr. Nelson E. Scheler, '60
Mortuary Executive
Dr. Adelina Silva, '72
College Administrator
Mr. William R. Sinkin, '32
Banker/Solar Energy
Mr. Hugo Sosa, '68
Social Worker
Dr. Herbert Spiro, '44
U.S. Ambassador
Ms. Patsy Torres, '75
Entertainer
Mr. Jesse Trevino, '69
Artist
Mr. Henry Troell, '55
Federal Govt. Executive
Dr. Thomas Uribe, '59
Dentist
Mr. James Vazquez, '51
School Superintendent
Dr. Jerome F. Weynand, '48
Educator
Dr. Earl Wright, '60
Educator
Ms. Esperanza Ytuarte, '83
SAPD Crisis Officer
Dr. Jesse Zapata, '66
University Administrator
Dr. Robert Zeigler, '59
College Administrator

Source: Official Program of San Antonio
College 75th Anniversary Scholarship
Gala, October 7, 2000.

APPENDIX R

Typical San Antonio Junior College Diploma
for Associate of Arts Degree May 1948

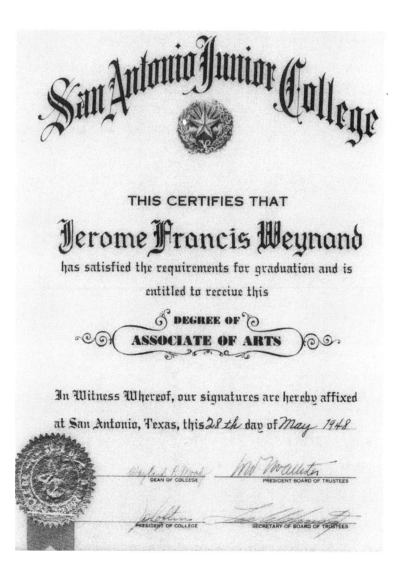

APPENDIX S

San Antonio College Associate of Arts Degree May 1951
Typical of First Class to Graduate on San Pedro Campus

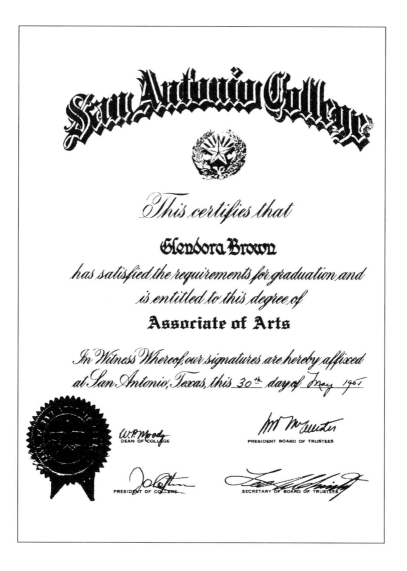

225

APPENDIX T

San Antonio College Associate in Arts Degree January 1964
Typical of Diplomas With New College Seal

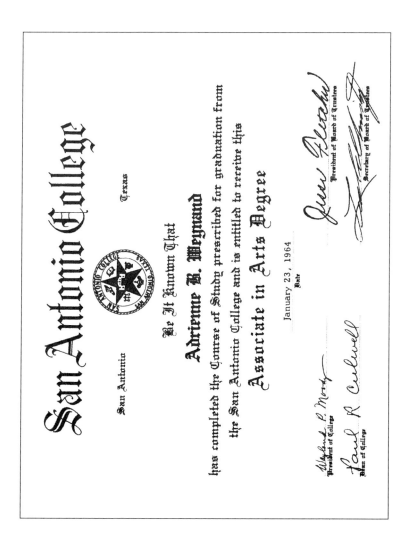

227